Using *Sams' Teach Yourself in 24 Hours* Series

Welcome to *Sams' Teach Yourself in 24 Hours* series! You're probably thinking, "What, they want me to stay up all night and learn this stuff?" Well, no, not exactly. This series introduces a new way to teach you about exciting new products: 24 one-hour lessons, designed to keep your interest and keep you learning. Because the learning process is broken into small units, you will not be overwhelmed by the complexity of some of the new technologies that are emerging in today's market. Each hourly lesson has a number of special items, some old, some new, to help you along.

Minutes

The first 10 minutes of each hour lists the topics and skills that you will learn about by the time you finish the hour. You will know exactly what the hour will bring with no surprises.

Minutes

Twenty minutes into the lesson, you will have been introduced to many of the newest features of the software application. In the constantly evolving computer arena, knowing everything a program can do will aid you enormously now and in the future.

Minutes

Before 30 minutes have passed, you will have learned at least one useful task. Many of these tasks take advantage of the newest features of the application. These tasks use a hands-on approach, telling you exactly which menus and commands you need to use to accomplish the goal. This approach is found in each lesson of the *24 Hours* series.

1
2
3
4
5
6
7
8
9
10
11
12
13
14
15
16
17
1
21
22
23
24
25
26
27
28
29
30
31

40 Minutes

You will see after 40 minutes that many of the tools you have come to expect from *Sams' Teach Yourself* series are found in the *24 Hours* series as well. Notes and Tips offer special tricks of the trade to make your work faster and more productive. Warnings help you avoid those nasty time-consuming errors.

50 Minutes

By the time you're 50 minutes in, you'll probably run across terms you haven't seen before. Never before has technology thrown so many new words and acronyms into the language, and the New Terms elements found in this series will carefully explain each and every one of them.

60 Minutes

At the end of the hour, you may still have questions that need answered. You know the kind—questions on skills or tasks that come up every day for you, but that weren't directly addressed during the lesson. That's where the Q&A section can help. By answering the most frequently asked questions about the topics discussed in the hour, Q&A not only answers your specific question, it provides a succinct review of all that you have learned in the hour.

Sams'
Teach Yourself
PHOTOSHOP® 4
in 24 Hours

Sams'
Teach Yourself

PHOTOSHOP® 4

in 24 Hours

Carla Rose

Hayden
Books

201 West 103rd Street
Indianapolis, Indiana 46290

Sams' Teach Yourself Photoshop® 4 in 24 Hours ©1997 Hayden Books

Library of Congress Catalog Number: 97-73667
ISBN: 1-56830-425-0

Printed in the United States of America 2 3 4 5 6 7 8 9 0

Warning and Disclaimer

Trademark Acknowledgments

President   Richard K. Swadley
Associate Publisher   John Pierce
Managing Editor   Lisa Wilson
Director of Marketing   Kelli S. Spencer
Product Marketing Manager   Kim Margolius

Acquisitions Editor
Rachel Byers

Development Editor
Robyn Holtzman

Production Editor
Kevin Laseau

Copy Editors
Terrie Deemer
Kevin Laseau

Tech Editor Coordinator
Lorraine E. Schaffer

Technical Editor
Bill Vernon

Publishing Coordinator
Karen Williams

Cover Designer
Tim Amrhein

Book Designer
Gary Adair

Manufacturing Coordinator
Brook Farling

Production Team Supervisor
Brad Chinn

Production Team
Michael Dietsch
Polly Lavrick
Paula Lowell
Mary Ellen Stephenson

Indexer
Chris Barrick

Contents at a Glance

Contents

About the Author

Carla Rose started her photography career at the age of eight with a Brownie Hawkeye. A graduate of the School of the Museum of Fine Arts in Boston, she has been a TV news photographer and film editor, as well as advertising copywriter and graphic artist, before discovering the Macintosh. Carla has written all or part of more than 20 computer books, including *Maclopedia, Sams' Teach Yourself Digital Photography in 14 Days, Sams' Teach Yourself Photoshop in 14 Days*, the *Whole Mac, Managing the Windows NT Server, PageMaker 6.5 Complete, Mac Online, It's a Mad, Mad, Mad, Mad Mac, Turbocharge Your Mac*, and *Everything You Ever Wanted to Know About the Mac*. Carla lives near Boston with her husband, audio guru Jay Rose, sons Joshua and Daniel (both presently in college), and a fluctuating number of cats. She welcomes email sent to momcat@pinkcat.com.

Dedication

This book's for Ernie, who would have *loved* Photoshop.

Acknowledgments

No project this big could ever get started, much less completed, without help from a lot of wonderful people. I'd like to thank the folks at Hayden, especially Robyn Holtzman, Rachel Byers, Terrie Deemer, and Kevin Laseau. Special thanks to Bront Davis and Steve Mulder for their contributions. Thanks to my friends in the ABC's for their moral support as I worked 20-hour days to meet the deadlines.

Finally, hugs and eternal gratitude to Josh and Dan who still managed to smile after the hundredth picture, and to Reebok and Hacker, the cats who grace these pages and enrich our lives. And the biggest hug and deepest gratitude of all (and Happy 25th Anniversary!) to my wonderful husband, Jay, who does what needs to be done.

Hour 1

The Basics

Photoshop is a powerful graphics program, primarily used for photo-retouching and image manipulation. You can also use it to create original art, either from scratch or based on a photograph. It's fun to use and not as complicated as you might think.

Finding Your Way Around

When you first open Photoshop, you'll see the Toolbox on the left side of the screen, menu headings at the top of the screen, and four windows on the right. (You'll also see your desktop, or whatever else is open at the time.)

You won't see a work area because Photoshop, unlike most graphics programs, doesn't automatically open a new page for you. This makes sense because most of your work in Photoshop will be done on pictures that you have brought in from some other source. Maybe you'll be using digital images from your digital camera or scanner. Possibly you will work on files you have downloaded from the Internet, or on photos from a CD-ROM. In the second hour, you will learn all about opening these pictures. Right now, let's open a blank page so that you can try out some of Photoshop's tools.

Starting a New Page

File➡New is the first item on the first Photoshop menu. When you select it, you open the New file dialog box, shown in Figure 1.1. You may enter a title for your new file at the top of the dialog box, such as My New Page, or leave it untitled for now. The following sections will give you a brief overview to get you started on setting up a new file.

Figure 1.1

Use the New file dialog box to define the size of your work surface.

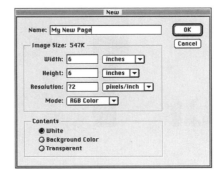

Image Size

In the Image Size dialog box, you specify the size of your image—width and height—in pixels, inches, centimeters, points, picas, or columns. These are available in drop-down menus that you can access by clicking the small arrow next to the unit of measurement. For now, choose inches. Make your page big enough to work on comfortably. The page in Figure 1.1 is 6 inches square, which is a good size to display full size on the screen.

Resolution

Resolution refers to the number of dots of ink per inch (if you're printing) or pixels per inch (if you're looking at the computer screen). It's important because the resolution of the image determines the quality. Higher resolution gives you a better quality image, but uses more memory. Most images that you see in print are close to a resolution of 300 dpi—or dots per inch.

Your computer's monitor, on the other hand, has a resolution of 72 dpi, which is substantially lower. Therefore, you always set the resolution depending on what your output will be. For now, keep the resolution at 72 dpi because we're just looking at the screen. Set the Contents button to white to give you a white canvas. (We'll cover the background and transparent options later on.)

1

TIME SAVER

If you intend to publish your images on the web, then anything over 72 dpi is a waste. Computers can't display pictures at higher resolutions. If, on the other hand, you are printing to a high-quality laser printer, set the resolution to 200 dpi. You would only use 300 dpi if you are looking to create professional color prints.

After you click OK in the New file dialog box, you'll see a new window. This is the active window, and the canvas is the large white square within it. Figure 1.2 shows the canvas. You can have more than one window open within Photoshop at a time, but only one can be the active window. If the window is active, there will be a strip of color across the top; inactive windows are gray. The canvas is where you will create and edit images.

Figure 1.2

This is your "canvas."

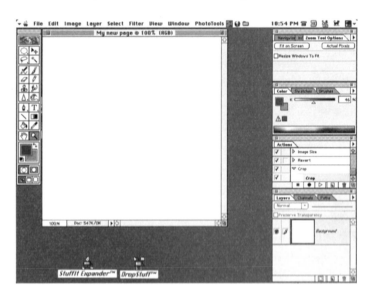

Set your mouse cursor at the lower-right corner of the window, and then click and drag. The window expands, but notice that the canvas size stays the same. After you have created a new file, you can only change the size of the canvas by selecting Image➡Canvas Size. This command enables you to specify a new height and width for the canvas. The anchor section in the dialog box enables you to specify the base area from which the canvas will expand or shrink (see Figure 1.3).

Figure 1.3

Click a white square to locate your current canvas in that part of the new canvas.

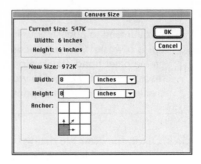

The Toolbox

The Toolbox, like an artist's worktable or paint box, holds all of the tools you'll use to draw, paint, erase, and otherwise work on your picture. There are four types of tools in the box:

- ☐ Selection tools
- ☐ Painting tools
- ☐ Viewing tools
- ☐ Specialized tools for working with type, gradients, and so on

Let's take a quick look at these tools. (We'll talk about them in detail later on.) Figure 1.4 shows the Toolbox, with the tools labeled.

Figure 1.4

In the Photoshop Toolbox, the tools are grouped by type.

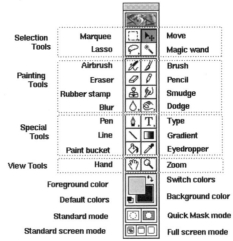

JUST A MINUTE

Notice that some of the tool icons have a tiny black triangle in the lower-right corner of their icon. This means that there are more tools of the same general kind available on a pop-out menu. Point to any tool that has a triangle and hold down the mouse button to see what other tools are available.

Selection Tools

At the top of the Toolbox are a group of tools called selection tools. They are used to select all or part of a picture. There are three: the Marquee, the Lasso, and the Magic Wand. A selected area is indicated on the screen by a blinking selection border, called a marquee, like the movie theater marquee lights that flash on and off. The Marquee and Lasso tools work by dragging the tool over the part of the image that you want to select. Figure 1.5 shows the pop-out menu for the marquee selection tools.

Figure 1.5
The marquee selection tools.

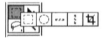

The fourth tool in this set is the Move tool. Use it after you have made a selection to move the selected area elsewhere on the page.

Painting Tools

Within the set of painting tools, there is an Airbrush, Paintbrush, Pencil, and Rubber Stamp. These all apply "paint" to the screen in one way or another. There's also an Eraser which, as you might expect, takes away part of the picture. Finally, there are tools that move, blur, and change the color of the image. These are the Smudge, Blur, Sharpen, Dodge, Burn, and Sponge tools. The latter two are found on pop-out menus. These tools will be covered in detail in Hours 7–9.

Viewing Tools

There are two Viewing tools: the Hand tool and the Zoom tool. (The Zoom tool is represented in the Toolbox by a magnifying glass.) The Zoom tool lets you zoom in by clicking the image to see a magnified view or zoom out again by pressing (Option)[Alt] as you click the image. You can also click and drag to enlarge just a specific section of the image. When you zoom in, the picture is usually too big to see all at once. The Hand moves the image within the window and is useful after you use the Zoom tool to enlarge the picture. Use the Hand, as shown in Figure 1.6, to slide the part of the picture you want to see or work on into a convenient spot.

Figure 1.6
*The Hand moves
an image within its
window.*

Special Tools

These tools aren't as easy to classify as the painting tools or the selection tools. They do different, useful, things. The letter T represents the Type tool, which puts type on your picture. You'll learn all about type in Hour 17. The Pen tool draws paths, which are a means of drawing a curved line or shape. Paths can be used as a selection tool or as a drawing tool. (See what I mean about being hard to classify?) In Hour 13, you'll learn how to work with paths.

The Line tool draws straight lines, just as if you had a pencil and ruler. The Gradient tool lets you create backgrounds that shade from one color to another, or even all the way through the rainbow. The Paint Bucket (which really belongs with the painting tools) pours paint into any area you select. The Eyedropper tool picks up a sample of any color you click and makes it the "active" color so that you can paint with it.

TIME SAVER

> To draw a line at exactly 45 degrees, or one that's precisely horizontal or vertical, press the Shift key as you draw the line. Photoshop will constrain it to the exact angle.

Tool Shortcuts

Every one of these tools can be selected by clicking its icon in the Toolbox. Photoshop, however, gives you another, even easier way to access the tools. Instead of clicking the tools you want to use, you can type a single letter shortcut to select each tool. To toggle through the available tools where there are pop-out menus, type the letter again until you reach the tool you want. Table 1.1 lists the tools with their shortcuts. Dog-ear this page so you can refer to the table until you have memorized the shortcuts.

1

Table 1.1. Tool Shortcuts

Tool	Shortcut	Tool	Shortcut
Marquee	M	Move	V
Lasso	L	Magic Wand	W
Airbrush	A	Brush	B
Eraser	E	Pencil	Y
Rubber Stamp	S	Smudge	U
Blur	R	Dodge	O
Pen	P	Type	T
Line	N	Gradient	G
Paint Bucket	K	Eyedropper	I
Hand	H	Zoom	Z
Crop	C	Switch background/ foreground colors	X

Try out some of these tools. Go ahead. Click the Paintbrush and draw some squiggles and lines. Click the Eraser and erase part of them. Try dragging the Smudge tool across one of the lines. Select a piece of line with one of the selection tools and move it to another part of the page. Explore. You're not going to break anything.

What's on the Menus?

The menus across the top of the screen contain the commands that enable you to open and manipulate files. They are accessed by simply clicking and holding the mouse button and dragging down to the desired command. Whenever you see an arrow or an ellipsis off to the right of a menu command, that indicates that there is either a subcommand, in the case of the arrow, or a dialog box, in the case of the ellipsis.

File and Edit Menus

The first two menus are File and Edit. Photoshop's File and Edit menus hold no surprises for anyone who has used any other Macintosh or Windows program. The File menu lets you work with files: opening, closing, saving, exporting, and printing them, and of course, quitting the program. The Edit menu includes all of the editing commands you're familiar with from other applications: cut, copy, paste, clear, and the most important one—undo.

CAUTION

Unlike some graphics programs that enable you to back gracefully out of your mistakes with multiple undo commands, Photoshop only undoes the *last* thing you did, whatever it may have been. Always save your work before you make any major changes, and use the File➡Revert command to go back to the last saved version if you can't undo.

The following six menus that are unique to Photoshop:

☐ Image

☐ Layer

☐ Select

☐ Filter

☐ View

☐ Window

The Image Menu

The Image menu, which is shown in Figure 1.7, has several submenus. The first of these, Mode, is shown in the figure. As you can see, it enables you to select a color mode in which to work. Most of the time, you will be working in RGB mode because that's what your monitor displays. Color modes are discussed in detail in Hour 5.

Figure 1.7

The Image➡Mode submenus.

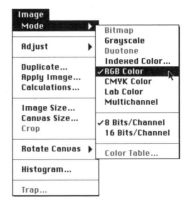

The Image menu also has the tools to adjust the colors and the lightness and brightness of your picture. You will learn how to use the tools on the Image➡Adjust menu in Hour 6.

When you want to make a picture smaller, or turn all or part of it sideways, you'll use the Image➡Crop or Image➡Rotate Canvas menu. In Hour 4, you'll learn how, and when, to use these tools.

1

The Layer Menu

Arguably the most powerful feature of Photoshop is the layering capability. This enables you to combine images and create collages by working on one part of an image at a time. Think of it as working on sheets of transparent plastic. Each layer is totally separate from the others. You can paint on a layer, change its opacity, or do whatever you want with it, without disturbing the background or other parts of the image on separate layers.

The Layer menu opens dialog boxes to create new layers, and also has commands to merge them and to work with them. Figure 1.8 shows what's on the Layer menu. Hour 6 and Hour 11 will teach you about working with layers.

Figure 1.8

The Layer menu.

The Select Menu

You have selection tools, so why do you need a selection menu? In Hour 3, you'll learn all the tricks for selecting parts of a picture. The Select menu works with the tools to let you modify areas you have selected. You can grow or shrink the selected area by as many pixels as you want, or feather its edges so that the selection appears to fade into a background you paste it on.

The Filter Menu

Filters are the tools that make Photoshop fun. The Filter menu lists a dozen different categories of filters: Some blur or sharpen the picture, some distort it, and some turn it into imitation paintings, colored pencil drawings, or neon light sculpture. There's so much for you to do with filters that we'll spend Hours 14–17 applying them to your pictures.

Photoshop filters are called plug-ins, and many work with other graphics programs as well. If you install any third-party filters or plug-ins, such as Alien Skin's Eye Candy series or MetaTools KPT, they'll appear at the bottom of the Filter menu.

The View Menu

Like the Magnifying glass, the View menu has commands that let you zoom in and out on the picture. As you can see in Figure 1.9, it also has the ruler, grid, and guides commands that enable you to measure and locate objects precisely within the work area.

Figure 1.9

The View menu.

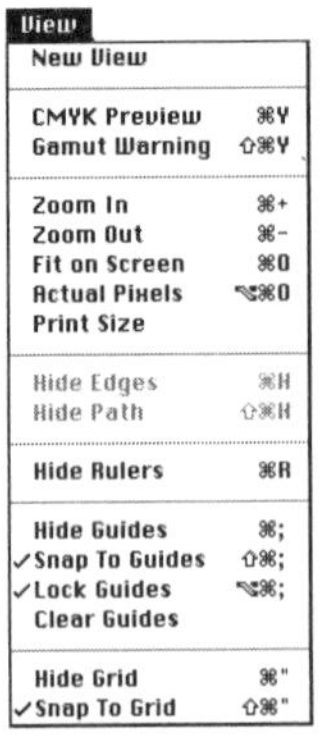

```
View
New View

CMYK Preview        ⌘Y
Gamut Warning      ⇧⌘Y

Zoom In             ⌘+
Zoom Out            ⌘-
Fit on Screen       ⌘0
Actual Pixels      ⌥⌘0
Print Size

Hide Edges          ⌘H
Hide Path          ⇧⌘H

Hide Rulers         ⌘R

Hide Guides         ⌘;
✓Snap To Guides    ⇧⌘;
✓Lock Guides       ⌥⌘;
Clear Guides

Hide Grid           ⌘"
✓Snap To Grid      ⇧⌘"
```

The ruler can be set to measure in pixels, inches, centimeters, points, or picas. Choose the measurement you're most familiar with. The setting is done in a Preferences dialog box: File➡Preferences➡Units&Rulers.

Guide lines are lines that you place over your picture, to position type or some other element that you're going to add to the picture. To place guide lines, follow these steps:

1. Select View➡Show Rulers. This makes the rulers visible at the edges of the canvas.

2. Select View➡Show Guides, or use the keyboard shortcut (Command-;)[Control-;].

If you haven't encountered keyboard shortcuts in other programs, they may seem confusing at first. It simply means that pressing a combination of two keys brings about the same action that selecting the command from a menu does. In this case, you would press and hold the Command key (the one with the apple and cloverleaf symbols on it) if you have a Mac,

1

1

or the Control key if yours is a Windows machine, and at the same time press the semicolon key. It's easier if you press Control with your left hand and semicolon with your right. You'll find keyboard commands for many actions, and they can save a lot of time.

3. To place a horizontal guide line, put the mouse pointer on the ruler at the top of the screen and drag downward. You'll see a line scrolling down the canvas as you drag. The left ruler shows you the position of the line.

4. To place a vertical guide line, put the mouse pointer on the ruler at the left of the screen and drag across. You'll see a line scrolling across the canvas as you drag. The top ruler shows you the position of the line. See Figure 1.10 for an example.

Figure 1.10

Guides let you place type right where you want it.

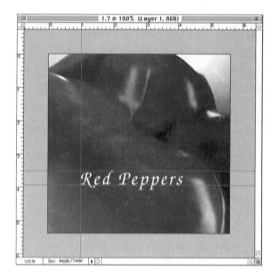

After you have placed a guideline, you can't move it. You can hide it by choosing View➡Hide Guides, or using the keyboard shortcut in Step 2 to toggle back and forth. To get rid of the guidelines, choose View➡Clear Guides.

The Show Grid command, which is also found on the View menu, places an entire grid of guidelines over your image, rather like a layer of transparent graph paper. The Snap to commands make it easier to position an element, such as a block of type. In effect, they make the guideline or gridline "magnetic" so that when you place the element near it, the line pulls the element right up against it.

The Windows Menu

Most of Photoshop's commands can be accessed in several different ways. The windows at the right of the Photoshop screen give you information about your picture, options for many of the tools in the Toolbox, a choice of brush sizes and shapes, colors, and access to Layers, Paths, and Channels. The Windows menu shows and hides these windows. If there are some, such as Actions, that you're not ready to use, close them to keep your screen uncluttered.

Setting Preferences

As you become more familiar with Photoshop, you may want to change the ways it handles certain tasks. You may want to use the System Color Picker instead of the Photoshop version. You might decide to measure in inches for one project and centimeters for another. You might need to change the color of the guide lines because they're too close to the background in your photo. All of these changes, and many more are made in the File➡Preferences➡General dialog boxes. The General Preferences dialog box is shown in Figure 1.11.

Figure 1.11

Set preferences here.

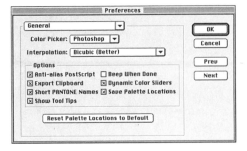

Use the Next button to scroll through the Preferences dialog boxes. You may encounter some preferences that you don't understand. For now, leave the default settings. As you learn more about the program, you can come back and change Preferences as necessary.

Summary

You are starting to learn your way around the Photoshop screen. You learned how to open a new canvas. You've looked at the Toolbox and Photoshop's menus, and learned about grids and rulers. Finally, you learned about setting preferences.

Q&A

Q What are foreground and background colors?

A The foreground color is the uppermost of the two colored squares in the Toolbox. It's the color the brush applies. The background color is the lower square. It's the color you see when you erase the canvas.

Q How do I change the size of a canvas?

A Use the Image➡Image size dialog box. Enter new numbers in the Print size windows. (If you change one number, the other(s) will change in proportion.)

Hour **2**

Opening and Saving

Before you can do anything exciting with Photoshop, you need to learn how to open and view files. Photoshop can open a wide variety of file formats, so you can work on pictures from many different sources. If you have a scanner or a digital camera, you can bring in pictures that you've taken. You can also use photos from CD-ROM collections or images that you have downloaded from some online or Internet source.

This chapter also will cover methods of saving your work, because if you don't save, all the changes you make will be lost.

Working with Files

Photoshop can open and save images in many different file formats. Formats are ways of saving the information in a file so that it can be used by other applications, printed, or put into a web page for use on the Internet.

In the Windows world, file formats are defined by the three letter extensions to filenames, such as .doc for a word processing document, or .bmp for a bit-mapped graphic. Mac users are lucky because they don't need to deal with file format extensions. Macintosh files have what is called a *resource fork* and a *data fork*. The data fork contains the file's data and the resource fork contains the file's information—whether it is a graphic file, a word processing document, or even a sound. Don't let this worry you, Windows users. Filenames are kind of a nuisance, but they aren't that difficult.

The most common file format in Photoshop is .psd, which is the native Photoshop file format (Photoshop document). The drawback to .psd is that, because it is native to Photoshop, other applications may have trouble opening this format. To move files between applications, to print, or to publish on the World Wide Web, you must save your files in a compatible format.

Here are some common formats with brief definitions of their uses:

- **Bitmap (.bmp).** This is a standard file format for Windows.
- **GIF (.gif).** GIF stands for Graphical Interchange Format. It is one of the three formats you can use for web publishing. Because it is a compressed format, it takes less time to send by modem.
- **JPEG (.jpg).** JPEG stands for Joint Photographic Experts Group. JPEG is another popular format for web publishing.
- **PNG (.png).** Stands for Portable Network Graphic, or PNG's Not GIF, depending on who you ask. It's the newest, and arguably best, format for web graphics. It has good compression, like GIF, and unlimited color, like JPEG. (We'll discuss these formats and how to use them for web publishing in the final hour.)
- **TIFF (.tif).** TIFF stands for Tagged-Image File Format. These files can be saved for use on either Macs or Windows machines. This is often the preferred format for desktop publishing applications, such as PageMaker and Quark XPress because of its high resolution and image quality.
- **PICT (.pct).** This is mainly a Macintosh format. It, too, is widely used in desktop publishing.
- **Raw (.RAW).** This format saves image information in the most flexible format for transferring files between applications and computer platforms.

These file formats are available in the Save dialog boxes—File➡Save, File➡Save As, and File➡Save a Copy. Just look for the drop-down menu. Figure 2.1 shows the Save dialog box with the formats available.

2

Figure 2.1

Photoshop can save your work in any of these formats.

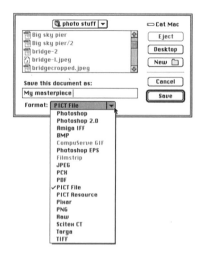

Opening Files

Opening a file in Photoshop is as easy as opening it in any other application. You can open as many images as you want, or as many as your RAM can hold. If a file is of the proper type (a file format that Photoshop recognizes), all you will have to do is double-click it with your mouse to not only open it, but to open Photoshop as well. If Photoshop is already open, you can either double-click a file, or use the File➡Open command.

When you open the Open dialog box, Photoshop will display all of the files in formats it can open. Figure 2.2 shows the Photoshop dialog box. As you can see, Photoshop will display *thumbnails* of any image that has one, and can even create a thumbnail for any useable image that doesn't have one. To see a thumbnail, click the Create button.

 Thumbnail or thumbnail sketch is an artist's term for a small version of a picture, so called because they were often no bigger than one's thumbnail.

To open a file, follow these steps:

1. Choose File➡Open or use the key command (Command-O)[Control-O] to open the Open dialog box.
2. Use the dialog box to locate the file you want to work on.
3. Select it and double-click, or click Open.

Figure 2.2

*Any file that's shown can
be opened in Photoshop.*

Importing a File

The Import command (File➤Import) lets you open files that have been saved in formats that use plug-in import modules. Typically, these would include files saved with the Twain interface, Scitex files, anti-aliased PICT files and PICT resources (Macintosh), and files imported directly from any digital camera that has a Photoshop plug-in import filter.

Importing from Digital Cameras

The Agfa e307 is one of several digital cameras that can import pictures directly into Photoshop. The plug-in filter comes with the camera. To import a picture, you simply plug the camera cable into the computer's modem (Mac) or Com1 (Windows) port, and choose File➤Import➤Agfa e307. Figure 2.3 shows the Agfa import window. Pictures in the camera are displayed as if they were slides on a sorting table.

Figure 2.3

*Other cameras use a
similar system.*

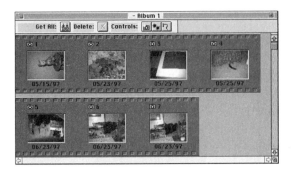

Importing Files from a Scanner

Scanners are much like photocopying machines. They work by making a bit-by-bit image of any document, photograph, or piece of artwork you feed into them. You can import a scanned document into Photoshop and work on it just as you would a digital photo. How you bring the image into Photoshop is determined by your scanning software and the format in which it saves the picture.

2

Importing Files with the Twain Interface

The Twain Acquire and Twain Select commands found under the File➡Import submenu don't actually import images. Instead, they enable you to open the appropriate scanner software to be used from within Photoshop and to use it to import the scanned images. Photoshop supports TWAIN, TWAIN32, and TWAIN_32 standards for scanning. Consult the scanner manual for more information.

Importing Quick Edit Files

Quick Edit is an option for editing large TIFF files. Instead of having to open the entire file, which could take quite a long time, you can open a portion of the file via the dialog box shown in Figure 2.4.

Figure 2.4

Choose the part of the picture you want to work on.

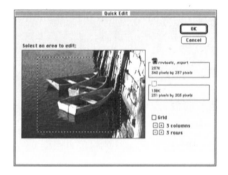

QuickEdit only works on TIFF, Photoshop 2.0, and Scitex files.

CAUTION

Opening only the piece of the picture you want to use can save time in opening, saving, and applying filters to the file. To import a TIFF file using QuickEdit, follow these steps:

1. Select File➡Import➡QuickEdit.
2. Navigate to the file that you want to open.
3. Open the file.
4. You will see the dialog box as shown in Figure 2.4.
5. Drag the crosshairs to select a portion of the image and click OK.

To save your changes, select File➡Export➡Quick Edit Save. This will update the entire file with your changes included.

Saving Your Work

There's one important thing to know about saving your work: Do it often! Computers are prone to unexpected shutdowns and errors. Saving takes only a couple of seconds, and it can make the difference between having to do your work all over again or just reopening it if the computer shuts down.

Because Photoshop has only one level of Undo (you can only undo the last thing you did), saving before you try a new filter or other operation is a good idea. That way, you can use File➡Revert to go back to the most recently saved version of the picture.

The first time you save a picture, you'll see the Save as... dialog box, just as in Figure 2.5. Give the file a name, and select an appropriate format to save it in, from the pull down menu. After this, choose File➡Save, or just press (Command-S)[Control-S] to save the file.

Figure 2.5

Saving a file in Photoshop.

CAUTION

For Macintosh Users Only: If you have to work cross-platform, that is, on both Macintosh and PC, you should choose to include file extensions with your files. This option is found under File➡General Preferences➡Saving Files➡Append File Extensions.

In addition to the familiar Save and Save As commands, Photoshop has a third command; Save a Copy. This command, like Save As, lets you save the file with a new name and in a new location. The difference is that after you use Save As, you're working in the new file. If you use Save a Copy, you'll have saved a copy of the file as it was at that moment, but you'll still be working on the original file, not the copy. Save a Copy is especially useful for making a backup copy before you try a drastic change, or for saving the file in a different format.

Suppose you create a logo for your business and want to use it in print and on the web. You'd save it as a TIFF or EPS file to print, and you'd save a copy as a JPEG or PNG file for your web page. On the Mac, the word "copy" is automatically added to the file name. Windows users can add it.

Reducing File Size

As you start to work with different Photoshop files, you'll notice that your hard drive is starting to fill up. Photoshop files can get very large, very quickly. You can make your files smaller in several ways:

- ☐ Reduce the resolution
- ☐ Reduce the number of colors in the image palette
- ☐ Use a format that compresses the file
- ☐ Use compression after the file is saved

Reducing the resolution is not a good idea if you're going to print the image. If the picture is only going to be viewed on your computer screen, or on the web, reduce the resolution to 72 dpi (Mac) or whatever resolution (72–120 dpi) your PC monitor uses.

Reducing the number of colors means reducing the bit depth. This can make your colors look blotchy, on the screen and in print. If you are working in grayscale (no color in the picture), reduce the bit depth to 8 bits. This gives you 256 shades of gray, which is more than a printer can print.

Using a compressed format means choosing a file format such as TIFF with LZW compression, which automatically shrinks the file down as small as possible when it saves. It does this by a means called "lossless" compression, so there's no image degradation or blotchy color. LZW compression (named for its inventors; Lempel, Ziv, and Welch) is also used by GIF, PDF, and PostScript formats.

There are also formats, such as JPEG, which use "lossy" compression. This means, as you might guess from the name, that some of the data that makes up the image is lost in the compression process. Instead of 20 shades of blue in the sky in a TIFF file, the same image in a JPEG file might have only five shades of blue. And yes, you *can* see the difference. Unfortunately, compression is necessary when you are putting images on the web or into a multimedia presentation, or in some other situation where upload time or storage space are limited. JPEG saves files in the smallest possible form.

When you have files that you want to save for future reference, you can save them in the normal way as .psds (Photoshop documents), or in whatever format you prefer to work in, and then compress the files with a utility like StuffIt (Mac) or Pkzip (PC). Both of these file compression utilities use lossless compression algorithms and will shrink your image files by anywhere from 20–50 percent.

Figure 2.6 is a typical digital photograph, which I saved in a number of different file types. The following chart shows the more common file types and the sizes of the files that this picture required.

Figure 2.6

If storage space isn't a problem, don't compress the picture.

Table 2.1. File Format/File Size Comparison

Format	File Size
.bmp	759 K
.eps	1.1 MB
.jpg (high quality)	99 K

Format	File Size
.pcx	759 K
.pdf	132 K
.PICT	710 K
.png (interlaced)	429 K
.png (not interlaced)	495 K
.psd	710 K
.tif	776 K
.tif (compressed)	396 K

Choosing a Format

With so many possible formats, how can you decide which one to use? It's really not so difficult. As long as you are working on a picture, keep saving it as a Photoshop document (.psd). This makes sense, especially after you learn to work in layers, because Photoshop's native format can save the layers, whereas other formats require that you merge the layers into one.

When you have finished working on the picture and are ready to place it into another document for printing, save a copy as an .eps file, if it's going to a PostScript compatible printer, or as a .tif. If you're going to place your picture into a web page, choose .gif if the picture is line art (a drawing, with limited color). Choose .jpeg or .png if the picture is a photograph or continuous tone art (lots of colors). If you want to import the picture into some other graphics program for additional work, choose .PICT if you are working on a Macintosh or .bmp if you use Windows. These two are the most generally compatible graphic formats.

COFFEE BREAK

Saving Macintosh Startup Screens

Mac users, here's one just for you. You can replace that silly "Welcome to Macintosh" message that pops on when you start your computer with a more interesting picture or message. Macs use a type of file called a PICT resource to create "splash screens" that you see when you start the Mac or when you start an application. Since Photoshop can save in the PICT resource format, you can make any Photoshop picture into a Startup Screen. Follow these steps:

1. Start with any image you like. (If it's not as big as your screen, that's okay. It will appear with a gray border.)
2. Choose File➡Save As. The Save As dialog box appears.

3. Choose PICT Resource from the format pop-up menu and click
    Save.

4. The PICT Resource dialog box opens, as shown in figure 2.6.

5. Name the file StartupScreen, as shown in the figure. (You must
    type it exactly that way, with both Ss capitalized, and no space
    between the words.)

6. Choose None from Compression options. Choose a bit depth: 16
    bits if your monitor displays thousands of colors, 32 bits if it is a
    high-resolution monitor and displays millions of colors.

7. Click OK to save the file.

8. Drag the file to your System folder and restart. The picture will
    appear when you start the computer.

Figure 2.6

*Be sure to type
StartupScreen as shown.*

Summary

Photoshop can work with many different types of graphics files from many sources. Those
that it doesn't open directly, either by double-clicking, or by using the File➡Open dialog
box, can be imported through plug-in filters. If you have a digital camera or scanner, it may
have a Photoshop plug-in that enables you to open the image from within Photoshop. Check
your owner's manual.

Logically enough, Photoshop can also save documents in all of the formats it can open.
Different formats have different purposes and different file sizes. Some are specifically
intended for web use, others for printing. Choose a format based on the intended use of the
image. Always pay attention to the size of the files you are saving, and take steps to reduce
them wherever possible.

Q&A

Q **When should I use Save a Copy instead of Save As?**

A Use Save a Copy when you want to make a copy of the picture you are working on, and then continue to work on the original, instead of the copy. Suppose I have a picture called "Roses," which I have done some work on and saved. If I save a copy as "Roses copy," and then keep working, I will still be working on the original "Roses" and I will also have a copy of the picture in a closed file as it was before I did the additional work.

2

Hour **3**

Selection Modes

Now you're making progress. You have learned how to bring images into and out of Photoshop. The next step is to learn to work with them and edit them. To do this, you have to select the part of the picture to work on. Selections are just what they seem to be—portions of the image that you have selected.

The Selection Tools

There are several ways to select a piece of the picture. You can use any of the selection tools: Marquee tools, Lasso tools, or the Magic Wand. You have different types of selection tools because you sometimes need to make selections in a particular way, such as punching a shape out of an image, or selecting all of the similarly colored sky. Photoshop's selection tools give you the power to select the whole picture or as little as a single row or column of pixels. Just to refresh your memory, Figure 3.1 shows the selection tools.

Figure 3.1

*The selection tools are at
the top of the toolbox.*

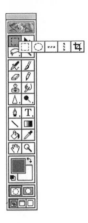

Rectangle and Elliptical Marquees

The Marquee tools, both rectangular and elliptical, are found in the upper-left corner of the Toolbox. To select the rectangular Marquee, just click it, or type the letter M. To select the elliptical Marquee, click and hold the rectangular Marquee in the Toolbox. When the rollout menu appears, select the elliptical Marquee.

Assuming that the rectangular Marquee is the currently selected tool, you can also type "M" to switch back and forth between the two. The elliptical Marquee tool works the same way that the rectangular Marquee tool does.

To experiment with its many uses, first create a new file (go back to the first hour if you can't remember how). Again, give yourself some room to work. Set the dimensions at five inches square.

1. Click the Marquee tool in the Toolbox.
2. Move the tool over the canvas—the cursor will appear as a crosshair.
3. While over the canvas, click and hold the mouse button.
4. Drag out a marquee. Experiment with dragging out an elliptical marquee. Try to get a sense for how they appear. Try dragging from different directions.

If you hold down the Shift key while you're using the Marquee tool, you can make additional selections. Where the selected areas overlap, they'll merge to form one larger selected shape. In Figure 3.2, I've selected several areas with the rectangular Marquee tool and the oval Marquee tool to make larger shapes.

To select an area inside another area, press the (Option)[Alt] key as you drag the inner shape. If, for instance, you have a circle selected and drag another smaller circle inside it while pressing the (Option)[Alt] key, the selected shape will be a donut.

3

Figure 3.2

You can also combine square and round selections.

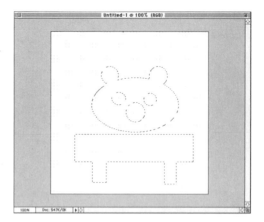

It is important to remember that when you are dealing with selections, for good or bad, only the area within the confines of the marquee may be edited. It is, in a sense, the only active area of the canvas. Thus, after a selection is made, you can perform whatever action you desire, but before you move on, the selection must be turned off, or deselected, by clicking outside the selected area with one of the Marquee tools, or by holding down (Command-D)[Control-D]. Until you do so, you can only edit within the selection's boundaries.

Just a Minute

If you have copied or pasted something into your canvas and then try to select a different part of the picture, you may find that the Marquee tool "doesn't work" or you get a message that says "Could not complete your request because the selected area is empty." This is because you've added a new layer to the picture. For a full explanation of layers, see Hour 11, "Layers."

The Lasso Tool

As useful as the Marquee tools and their modifier keys are, there will come times when you will have to select irregular shapes. Perhaps you might need to select a person out of a crowd, or as in this example, a flower, with all of its irregularly shaped petals.

Using the Lasso tool to select an object in this way requires a steady hand and good hand/eye coordination (see Figure 3.3). As with the marquee tools, you can add to your lassoed selection by holding the Shift key and selecting additional parts of the object.

Figure 3.3

Selecting an object with the Lasso.

TIME SAVER

I've found that when I am trying to make a careful selection with the Lasso tool, and when I am using Photoshop in general, it helps to slow down my mouse. You can adjust this in the mouse section of your machine's Control Panels. Set the slider to just a little above the slowest setting to start with. Experiment to see what works best.

To make a selection with the Lasso tool, follow these steps:

1. Select the Lasso tool from the Toolbox, or type L.

2. Click and carefully drag the Lasso tool around the piece of the image that you want to select. You will see a blinking line, as in the marquees above. Be careful not to release the mouse. If you do, you will lose the marquee (it will automatically close the selection).

3. When you're close to completely enclosing the selection, you can release the mouse button. The two ends of the selection marquee that you have drawn around the shape will automatically join together, completing the selection marquee.

The Polygon Lasso Tool

The polygon Lasso tool behaves in much the same way as the regular Lasso tool. The difference is, as its name implies, it makes irregular *geometric* selections. It's actually easier to use when you need to make detailed selections, because it can be controlled more easily. Instead of simply dragging a marquee line, as you do with the regular lasso, you click the polygon Lasso to place points, and Photoshop inserts a straight line marquee between the points (see Figure 3.4). You can place as many points as you need, as close together or far apart as necessary.

Figure 3.4

The polygon Lasso tool.

To use the polygon Lasso tool, follow these steps:

1. Click the Lasso tool and hold until you see the rollout menu (or type L).

2. Select the polygon Lasso tool.

3. Click once in the canvas. Now drag your mouse. Notice that a line follows your polygon Lasso wherever you move it.

4. Click again. This draws the first line and sets another point from which you may drag. Drag another line and click again.

5. Now, with two lines set, you have an option. You can either continue to select the image or you can double-click. This automatically finishes the selection for you.

6. When you near your starting point, notice that a small circle becomes appended to your cursor. This signals that if you click the selection will be complete.

7. Click to complete your selection.

TIME SAVER

Many of Photoshop's tools, including the selection tools, have additional options for their use. These are found on the Tool Options palette, which is a window that you can open either from the Window menu or simply by double-clicking on the tool. Whenever you select a new tool, double-click it to open its palette.

The Magic Wand

The software designers at Adobe Systems must not have been able to come up with a more descriptive name for this fantastic tool, choosing instead to let it speak for itself—the Magic Wand (see Figure 3.5). Maybe it's better that way.

Figure 3.5
The Magic Wand.

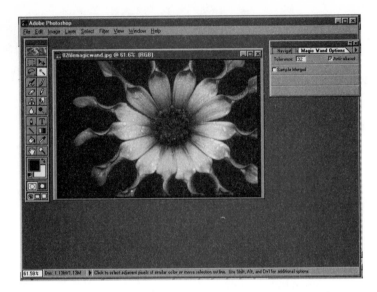

The Magic Wand is a different type of selection tool. So far we've looked at tools that select pixels based on their placement in the bitmap (the picture). The Magic Wand selects pixels somewhat differently; it selects them based on values. This enables you to cut out foreground objects, such as the flower you see in Figure 3.6.

Figure 3.6
Wild rose, selected with the Magic Wand.

Like the previously mentioned tools, the Magic Wand can make and merge selections if you press the Shift key as you click on the areas to select.

The Magic Wand selects adjacent pixels based on color similarities. Its *tolerance* can be set in the Magic Wand Options palette. To open the Magic Wand Options palette shown in

3

Figure 3.7, either double-click the Magic Wand in the Toolbox or select it and then choose Window➡Show Options.

 Tolerance, in this instance, refers to the Magic Wand's sensitivity to color differences.

Figure 3.7
The Magic Wand
Options palette.

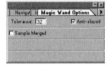

The rule is easy to remember: the lower the Tolerance, the less tolerance the Magic Wand has for color differences. Thus if you set the Tolerance higher (and it ranges from 0 to 255), for example, it will select all varieties of the color upon which you initially select.

The Magic Wand is best used for selecting objects that are primarily one color, such as the flower shown earlier. It's ideal when you need to select the sky in a landscape. In a few minutes, you'll see exactly how to do this, but first there are some other selection tricks to learn.

The Selection Menu

You may have noticed that, in addition to the selection tools you have just learned about, there's also a selection menu. It's shown in Figure 3.8. Probably the most useful commands on the menu are the top three. Select All simply draws a selection marquee around the entire picture. Deselect removes the selection marquee from the image. Inverse lets you select everything *but* an object, by selecting the object and then inverting. In the case of the preceding rose picture, we could select the rose, and then choose Select➡Invert or press and hold (Shift-Command-I)[Shift-Control-I] to select the background.

Figure 3.8
The Select menu.

Feather

Feather lets you make selections with fuzzy, feathered edges rather than hard ones. It's helpful when you want to select an object from one picture and paste it into another because it adds a slight blur, which helps the object to blend in. You can use the Feather dialog box shown in Figure 3.9 to determine how many pixel widths of feathering to apply. Experiment with feathering selections to find out what works best.

Figure 3.9

The Feather dialog box.

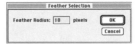

To make a feathered selection, follow these steps:

1. Choose an appropriate selection tool, and use it to select a piece of the picture or an object within the picture.
2. Choose Select➡Feather to open the dialog box.
3. Enter an amount in the window. Start with 5 and increase or decrease as needed, until you achieve an effect that you want. Paste or do whatever you intended to the selection.

Modifying Selections

The Select➡Modify submenu gives you some other options for working with your selections. Border changes the selected area so that instead of the whole object, you have only selected a border around it. You can set the width of the border in its dialog box. Smooth is helpful when you have made a lasso selection with a shaky hand. It smoothes out bumps in the marquee line by as many pixels as you specify. Expand and Contract work, as their names suggest, to make your selection grow or shrink as necessary by as many pixels as you designate in the dialog box.

Tutorial: Selecting the Sky

It's often necessary to select a large part of the picture, like the sky, so that you can darken its color or otherwise change it without changing the rest of the picture. Figure 3.10 shows a picture with a lot of sky, and a very complicated object sticking up into it. There are also some distant mountains, which are almost the same color as the sky itself. Selecting the sky in this case will require careful clicking with the Magic Wand.

To select the sky in this picture, we'll follow these steps:

1. Choose the Magic Wand tool and double-click to open its Options palette.
2. Set the tolerance, in the Options palette, to 20, as shown in Figure 3.11. This will enable us to select only similar shades of blue.
3. Click the Magic Wand on a typical piece of blue (see Figure 3.12).
4. Hold down the Shift key and select additional pieces of sky until you have gotten it all.

3

Figure 3.10

Selecting just the sky will be difficult.

3

Figure 3.11

You can set the tolerance anywhere from 0–255.

5. Choose Select➡Feather and set the feather amount to about 3 pixels, just enough to even out the selection. Figure 3.13 shows the result.

6. Now you can proceed to change the color of the sky, remove it, or do whatever else you intended.

Figure 3.12

You may need to make several selections to include all of the sky.

Figure 3.13

The entire sky is selected.

Find a picture with a lot of sky and practice this yourself. It's not difficult. Remember, if you select more sky (or whatever) than you intended, Undo will deselect the last portion selected, leaving the rest of the selection active.

Cutting and Copying

If you have cut and pasted or copied in any other application, you will find it easy to do in Photoshop. The commands are identical and so are the results. You'll find the Cut, Copy, and Paste commands on the Edit menu.

Cutting and pasting enable us to "borrow" from one picture to add to another. In the examples that follow, I'll take a rose from the photo I used earlier, and add it to another picture. In Figure 3.14, I've selected the rose, and set the feather amount to 3 pixels. Next, I'll use the Copy command (Edit➡Copy) or (Command-C)[Control-C] to copy the flower to the Clipboard.

Figure 3.14

Before you can copy the flower, you have to select it.

Now I'll open the new picture (see Figure 3.15) and paste the flower. Figure 3.16 shows the final result.

Figure 3.15

The new picture, without the added flower.

Figure 3.16

The picture is more balanced with two flowers.

Cropping

Cropping is the artists' term for trimming away unwanted parts of a picture. You could think of it as a specialized kind of selection, which is probably why the people who created Photoshop put the Crop tool in with the selection marquees. The Crop tool is shown in Figure 3.17.

Figure 3.17

The Crop tool.

To crop a picture, follow these steps:

1. Select the Crop tool from the Toolbox. (It pops out from the selection marquee when you hold the mouse button.)

2. Drag it across the picture, holding the mouse button down.

3. Use the handles on the Cropping window to fine-tune the selection. You can even twist the cropping window, by clicking on the dotted line and dragging when the double-headed bent arrow appears. Figure 3.18 shows the cropping window in use.

4. After you have the cropping window placed where you want it, double-click inside it to delete the area outside the window.

Open any picture and practice cropping it. If you crop too much of the picture, you can Undo. If it's too late to Undo, because you have already done something else, just go back

3

to the File menu and choose Revert, to go back to the last saved version of your picture. As long as you don't save, you can keep cropping and undoing as much as you want.

Figure 3.18

The Cropping window in use.

Summary

Some of the most powerful tools in Photoshop are the selection tools. They enable you to edit selectively as well as create interesting effects with the Transformation tools.

Try to develop a feel for when you can use selections. They can save you a great deal of time when you need to fill a space with color or image, when you need to manipulate just a piece of an image, or when you need to extract a piece of an image from a larger work.

We will refer to selections throughout the remainder of the book, so if you need to, dog-ear a page. See you next hour.

Q&A

Q Can I combine selections made with different selection tools?

A Yes. Make a selection with one of the tools. Switch tools, and then press the Shift key before you make your next selection. As long as you hold down the Shift key (making a tiny plus sign visible next to the tool), you can add to your selection as many times as you wish.

Q How can I deselect *part* of a selection?

A The easiest way to do this is to hold down the (Option)[Alt] with the selection tool active. You will see a small minus symbol next to the selection tool. Select the part of the selection to deselect, and it will be removed from the selection and added back to the picture.

Hour 4

Transformations

It's extremely rare, if not impossible, that your pictures will always be the right size and shape for your purposes. You might need to make an object bigger or smaller as you copy it from one picture to another. You may need to straighten a tilted horizon, or even stand the leaning tower of Pisa upright. Or perhaps you simply need to make someone face left instead of right, or turn an object upside down. You can do all this and more with just a few mouse clicks or simple commands. Let's start by looking at making the whole picture bigger or smaller.

Resizing

Photoshop makes it easy to change the size of the picture or of anything in it. You have two resizing options: resizing the image makes the picture bigger or smaller. Resizing the canvas makes the picture *area* bigger while leaving the image floating within it. You'd do this if you needed more space around an object without shrinking the actual image.

Image

To resize an image, open the Image➡Image size dialog box, shown in Figure 4.1. You can see the pixel dimensions in pixels (logically) or percent and the image print size in pixels, inches, centimeters, points, columns, or percent by using the pop-up menus.

When you first open the box, if you set the pixel dimensions to percent, you see 100%. To enlarge or reduce the image, the easiest way is to make sure that Constrain Proportions is checked at the bottom of the dialog box, and then enter new percentages in one of the boxes and click OK. As if by magic, the other numbers change to give you the correct percentage of enlargement or reduction.

If you know what size, in inches, centimeters, points, picas, and so on, you want the image to be, just enter the numbers in the Print size windows, and select the appropriate measurement system from the pop-up menu.

Figure 4.1

The Image Size dialog box.

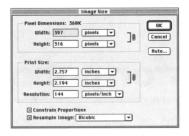

To see how changing the image size affects the file size and dimensions of the print image, reopen the dialog box. The file size is also displayed at the bottom of the image window.

Canvas

Making the canvas larger gives you extra work space around the image, although the image remains the same. Resizing it smaller is another way of cropping the picture by decreasing the canvas area. It's not recommended, since you could accidentally lose part of the picture and not be able to recover it.

To resize the canvas, choose Image➡Canvas Size to open the Canvas Size dialog box and specify the height and width you want the canvas to be (see Figure 4.2). You can specify any of the measurement systems you prefer on the pop-up menu, as you saw in the earlier Image size dialog box. Photoshop calculates and displays the new file size as soon as you enter the numbers. Added canvas always appears in the background color.

Use the anchor to determine where the image is placed within the canvas. Click the middle to center the image on the enlarged canvas, or in any of the other boxes to place it relative to the increased canvas area. Figure 4.3 shows the result of anchoring an image in the upper-left corner of the canvas. The image size hasn't changed, but we've made the canvas bigger.

4

Figure 4.2

The Canvas Size dialog box.

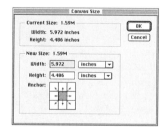

Figure 4.3

Before, on the left; after, on the right.

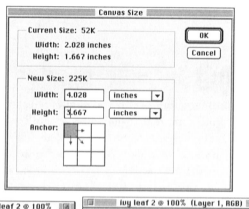

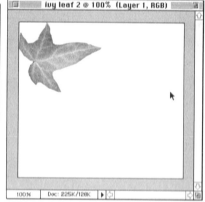

Selection

You can also resize a selected area. To do so, first select the object, or piece of an image to be resized. Use whichever selection tool is most convenient. With the selection marquee active, choose Layer➥Transform➥Scale. This places a window that looks like the cropping window around your selected object (see Figure 4.4). Drag any of the corner "handles" on the box to change the size of the image while keeping its proportions. If you drag on the side handles of the box, you stretch the selection's height or width accordingly.

Figure 4.4
Resizing a selection.

Rotating

There are many reasons why you might rotate an image. If you have a scanned picture or a digital camera image that should be vertical but opens as a horizontally oriented picture, rotating it 90 degrees corrects the problem. This is a common occurrence when you use a scanner because it's usually quicker to scan with the picture horizontal, regardless of its normal orientation (see Figure 4.5). This is, in case you wondered, because the scanner has less distance to travel.

Figure 4.5
Scanned image rotated 90 degrees clockwise.

Picture in flatbed scanner   Picture rotated 90° on computer screen

90 L, 90 R, 180

To rotate the entire image, use one of the Image➡Rotate Canvas submenus shown in Figure 4.6. Choose 90 degrees clockwise or counterclockwise to straighten up a sideways image, or 180 if you somehow brought in a picture upside down.

Figure 4.6

The Rotate Canvas submenu.

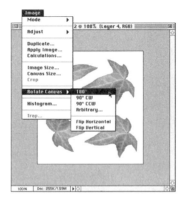

By Degrees

To rotate the canvas by something other than a right angle, choose Image➡Rotate Canvas➡Arbitrary to open the dialog box shown in Figure 4.7. Enter the number of degrees to rotate. If you're not sure, guess. You can always Undo, reopen the box and rotate more, or change the direction. Select the clockwise or counterclockwise button to indicate the rotation direction. Then, click OK to perform the rotation. If you rotate the image a second time, changing the number of degrees in the arbitrary setting rotates the canvas that additional amount. If, for instance, you rotate the canvas 5 degrees, and then decide that 15 degrees would be better, enter 10 in the box, not 15.

Figure 4.7

Choosing Image➡Rotate Canvas➡Arbitrary opens this dialog box.

Tutorial: Straightening the Horizon

Choosing Arbitrary from the Rotate Canvas submenu is one easy way to fix up a picture that needs to be straightened. The picture in Figure 4.8 was apparently taken while the photographer was standing in a hole. Tilted horizons are an easy problem for Photoshop as well.

We can tell just by looking at the picture that it needs to rotate clockwise several degrees. To straighten the horizon, follow these steps:

1. Choose Image➡Rotate Canvas➡Arbitrary to open the Rotate Canvas dialog box. Enter the number of degrees by which you think the horizon is "off."

2. Click the °CW (Clockwise) button to lower the right side, or the °CCW (counter-clockwise) button to lower the left side. In Figure 4.9, we rotated the canvas by 3

degrees clockwise. Now the horizon is level, but the picture is twisted (see Figure 4.9). Cropping squares up the corners again and improves the composition at the same time.

Figure 4.8

Oops, the horizon's not supposed to slant uphill.

Figure 4.9

You can see the background color filling in the corners of the canvas.

3. Select the Crop tool from the tool box or press C. Drag the Crop tool across the picture to position the cropping window. Use the handles to fine-tune your cropping. Figure 4.10 shows the cropping window in position.

4

Figure 4.10

Drag the cropping box until you get rid of the twisted corners of the image.

4. If the horizon isn't completely straight, click the dashed line of the cropping window. When you see a double-pointed bent arrow, you can drag the cropping window at an angle until the horizon looks right.

5. Double-click inside the cropping window when the picture looks the way you want it. Figure 4.11 shows our corrected horizon.

Figure 4.11

The horizon is level, and the composition's better, too.

Rotating Selections

To rotate a selected object, first select it with whatever tool works best for you. Choose Layer➡Transform➡Rotate to place a box around the selection. Rotate the object by dragging the box, as shown in Figure 4.12.

Figure 4.12

The selection marquee is still active inside the box.

Flipping

Flipping sounds like something you'd do with a pancake, rather than a picture, but the general effect is the same. When you flip the pancake, you reverse it so the other side cooks. When you flip the image, you reverse it so you see a mirror image. You can flip horizontally or vertically. Figure 4.13 shows both. For comparison purposes, Figure 4.14 shows the effects of rotation.

Figure 4.13

The top pair of words has been flipped horizontally, and the bottom pair flipped vertically.

4

Figure 4.14
*Rotation 90° CCW and
CW, and 180°.*

Flipping is different from rotating because it changes the up/down or left/right orientation of the image. Of course, sometimes you may need to do both, in order to get the image or selected object oriented the way you want it.

JUST A MINUTE

You can flip almost any object without anyone knowing, as long as there's nothing in it that would give the viewer a clue. You can't flip a picture that has type in it, obviously. You also need to be careful about flipping pictures of people who may be wearing shirts with a pocket on one side, a wristwatch, wedding ring, single earring, or other telltale item. In many cases, it won't matter, but you might find it helpful to edit out the jewelry, shirt pocket, and so on. (You'll learn how to do this in a later chapter.)

Selection Transformations

Resizing and re-orienting, as you've seen, can be applied either to the whole canvas, or to any selected area. The transformation methods that follow can only be applied to selections, not to the whole image (unless you start by selecting the entire image).

Skewing Selections

Skew, according to my trusty Webster's, means "to place at an angle." When you skew an object in Photoshop, you can do more than just slant it. You can twist, stretch, and distort it as if the object were on a sheet of rubber instead of a computer screen. The Skew command found under Layer➡Transform➡Skew enables you to twist your selection in all possible directions. Just click the control boxes and drag the selection. Click the Toolbox or press (Return)[Enter] to apply the setting.

Skew may not seem like a very useful command at first glance, but if you look at the following examples, you'll see how useful it can be. In the original picture (see Figure 4.15), the books on the shelf are straight in the middle but angled outward at the sides of the picture.

Figure 4.15

A messy book shelf. Can we skew the books straight?

We'll start by selecting the whole picture. To skew the entire image, follow these steps:

1. Use Select All; (Command-A)[Control-A] to select the entire picture. (It's faster than dragging a marquee around the image.)
2. Choose Layer➡Transform➡Skew to place the skew window around the image, as in Figure 4.16.
3. Drag the top corners of the window inward until the edges of the books look vertical. You'll see the background color behind the image.
4. Click the Toolbox to apply the transformation.
5. Crop the picture to remove the background. Figure 4.17 shows the result.

4

Figure 4.16
Skewing a selection.

Figure 4.17
The bookshelf looks neater.

Distorting Selections

All the transformation tools operate very similarly. They possess subtle differences in how they can move the selection. The Distort command (Layer➡Transform➡Distort) moves something like the Scale command and Skew command, but instead of changing the size of the image, it crushes or stretches the image. Figure 4.18 shows an image before and during distortion.

Select an object from one of your pictures and practice with skewing and distorting it. Remember that these commands are only available to you when the marquee is blinking, indicating that there's an active selection,

Figure 4.18

The original is on the left. On the right, we've distorted it.

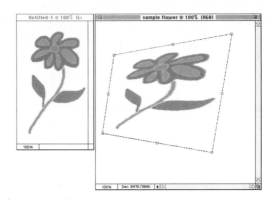

Changing the Perspective of a Selection

Changing the perspective of an image is one of the most useful tools in the Photoshop arsenal. When you want to create an image that appears to diminish in the distance, the perspective command can't be beat. Its movement is completely intuitive. The opposite corner of the one you drag becomes a mirror image—when you pull away, it moves away. When you move in, it follows suit. In Figure 4.19, I'm applying it to a fence that I want to superimpose on another picture. I've arranged the screen so I can see both. By dragging the corners of the perspective box, I can adjust the rose covered fence so it matches the angle of the bare one.

Figure 4.19

Replacing a drab fence with a prettier one.

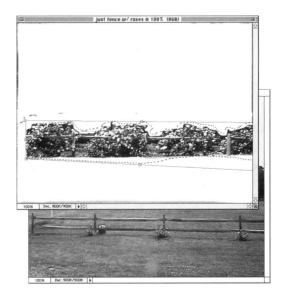

4

Numeric Transformations

This is probably the least intuitive of all the transformation tools because instead of handles appearing on your selection, which you can then drag, this transformation offers a dialog box in which you can enter numeric values for the position, scale, skew, and rotation. Use the pop-up menu to set the unit of measurement to inches, centimeters, points, picas, pixels, or percent for scaling. Unfortunately, there's no way to preview these changes until you apply them. But, there's always Undo.

The Numeric Transformations dialog box is a great option for those of you lucky enough to be able to see numbers in your mind's eye (see Figure 4.20). For the rest of us, we'll have to muddle along with the other tools, grateful once again that Adobe hasn't left anyone out.

Figure 4.20

*The Numeric Transfor-
mations dialog box.*

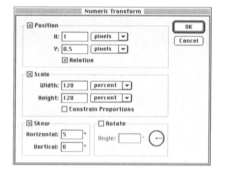

Summary

Transformations are an important function in Photoshop, especially when you're combining elements from different pictures. It's often necessary to shrink or enlarge an object or the entire image. Use the Image Size and Canvas Size dialog boxes to adjust the size of the image or work area. Photoshop also lets you transform selected objects by stretching or distorting them or applying perspective to them. You can do any of these by simply applying a menu command to place a box around the object and then dragging the sides or corners of the box.

Spend some time practicing the transformations. They'll be very useful later on.

Q&A

**Q How do you know when to skew, when to distort, and when to use perspec-
tive? They all seem to do similar things.**

A When you know that a transformation is needed but you aren't sure what kind, choose Layer➡Free Transform. You can also access it by typing (Command-T)[Control-T]. This command places a similar box around the object to be transformed but lets you drag it in any direction, rotate it, distort it, or do whatever seems necessary.

Hour 5

Color Models and Modes

Color is all around us, a blessing few of us take time to think about or recognize. It is as common as the air we breathe, but when you become aware of its presence, you become aware of the minute variations that exist in every color. Notice the shades of green on the tree outside your window. Notice how those greens differ from the green of the grass. Watch the play of light and shadow. It becomes fascinating.

In this hour, we are going to investigate the different properties of color—both in Photoshop and in real life. Some of the information at the beginning might seem a little esoteric, but in the long run, it's useful to know. After all, the more you know about color and how Photoshop addresses it, the better off you are. But don't worry, I'll try to be as brief and painless as possible.

Before we begin, it must be said that the best way of learning this stuff is to have Photoshop up and running on your machine. You glean a certain amount of information from merely reading, but the real learning won't start until you start working in Photoshop. This is so for two reasons:

☐ As we all know, you remember things better when you are doing it yourself.

☐ Photoshop's treatment of color makes it very intuitive. Keep the Color palette open at all times (Window➡Show Color) and keep an eye on the sliders. Notice how they change from mode to mode, as well as the differences and similarities.

Photoshop addresses color in terms of models and modes. The models are methods of defining color. Modes are methods of working with color based on the models.

Color models describe the different ways that color can be represented on paper and on the computer screen. The color models are as follows:

☐ RGB (Red, Green, Blue)

☐ CMYK (Cyan, Magenta, Yellow, Black)

☐ CIE Lab

☐ HSB (Hue, Saturation, and Brightness)

We will examine these models for displaying and *describing* color and then turn our attention to the Photoshop *modes,* which are the ways Photoshop provides for you to work with color.

Color Models

Figure 5.1 shows the Photoshop Color Picker. You can reach it by clicking either of the large blocks of color at the bottom of the Toolbox. The Color Picker has a graduated block of color, which you can click to select a particular shade, and windows that display the numbers for any chosen color in each of the four color models. In addition, Photoshop gives you a color palette, which is also shown in Figure 5.1. Open it by choosing Window➡Show Color. The palette has a strip along the bottom that covers the full color spectrum. Clicking anywhere on it will set the color picker to that range of colors.

Figure 5.1

The Photoshop Color Picker

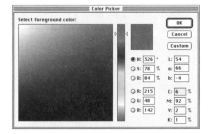

5

CAUTION

> If your Color Picker doesn't look like this one, open File➡Preferences➡ General and set the Color picker to Photoshop.

RGB Model

The RGB model, which computer monitors and TV screens use for display, assigns *values* on a scale of 0-255 for each of the three (RGB) primaries. As an example, pure green (as you can see in the previous figure) has a Red value of 0, Blue Value of 0, and a Green value of 255. Pure white places the values of all three (RGB) primaries at 255. Pure black places the values of the RGB primaries at 0.

NEW TERM Value, in this usage, means the relative strength of the color. Because the RGB model mixes colors of light to achieve white light, the full strength is 255. When you combine all three primaries at a value of 137 (half of 255), you get gray.

CMYK Model

The CMYK model, used for printing, defines colors according to their percentages of cyan magenta, yellow, and black, which are the four colors of printing inks, both in your home inkjet printer and in the fancy, high-resolution color laser printers and printing presses that service bureaus and commercial printers use.

What's Color?

Back a thousand years ago when I went to grade school, every child was given a box of crayons at the start of the school year. The size of the crayon box was determined by the grade you were in. Kindergarten and first grade got flat boxes with eight big thick crayons per box: the primaries, the secondaries, and brown and black. That was how we learned colors, even back then. The primaries were yellow, red, and blue. The secondaries were what you got when you mixed any two primaries: orange, from yellow and red; green, from yellow and blue; and purple, from, red and blue. Brown was the mix of all three primaries, and black was...well, black was black.

That's how we knew them, until high school. By then, we'd outgrown crayons, of course. We filed into our physics class and threw the previous nine years of learning out the window. The primary colors, according to the physics teacher were red, green, and blue. And if you mixed them you got, not brown or even the mysterious black, but...white!

Those of us still taking art classes listened to the physics lecture skeptically, and went down to the art room to try mixing red, green, and blue paint. We got a sort

THIS WILL BE REMOVED

of muddy brown, not the promised white. We asked the art teacher about this, and were sent upstairs to the drama department for a demonstration. The stage lights had filters in red, green, and blue. When all of the lights were on, the result was, sure enough, white light. Why? When you're dealing with light, the drama teacher explained, colors are subtractive. They cancel each other out. When you're dealing with paint, the colors add to each other, giving that muddy brown mess. Aha! We were enlightened.

When you bought your computer system, you had to deal with this issue, whether or not you knew it at the time. Your monitor uses light to produce color. That's why it's called an RGB (red, green and blue) monitor. Your printer uses ink to produce color. Not red ink, green ink, and blue ink, but a set of colors called cyan, magenta, and yellow, along with our old standby black. This color system is known by its initials, CMYK. Why K for black? Black is *still* mysterious.

HSB Model

When artists talk about color, they generally define it using a set of parameters called HSB. Photoshop also includes this color model. H stands for Hue, which is the basic color from the color wheel; red, blue, or yellow, for example. It's expressed in degrees (0–360°), which correspond to the positions on the color wheel of the various colors.

S is saturation or the strength of the color, and it's a percentage of the color minus the amount of gray in it. Pure color pigment with no gray in it is said to be 100% saturated. Neutral gray, with no color, is 0% saturated. Saturated colors are found at the edge of the color wheel and saturation decreases as you approach the center of the wheel. If you look at the Apple Color Picker in Figure 5.2, it's a little easier to understand this.

Figure 5.2

The Apple Color picker uses a standard color wheel.

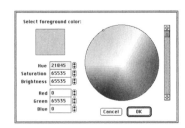

Brightness, the relative tone or lightness of the color, is also measured as a percentage, from 0% (black) to 100% white. Brightness is equivalent to the value used by the RGB model.

CIE Lab Model

The most encompassing of these color models is CIE Lab. It defines a color gamut that is broader than any of the other models. Photoshop uses the CIE model to convert from model to model because its gamut is so broad. Lab color is designed to be device independent, meaning that colors defined in this model appear and print the same regardless of whether you are seeing them on paper or on the video screen. This is probably not a model you will use frequently, however. Let's focus our attention on what works and what you need to know to get up and running.

TIME SAVER

> I suggest that you work in either RGB or CMYK, depending on whether your final image will be printed or viewed onscreen, as a picture on the World Wide Web, for instance. Use CMYK for color print and RGB for video.

Photoshop Modes of Color

First, forget about Lab color. It's exists, but you needn't concern yourself with it. The other three models, RGB, CMYK, and HSB will have much greater impact on your work in Photoshop. The difference between the modes and the models is simple. HSB is the only model without a directly corresponding mode. Otherwise, the other color models, CMYK and RGB, have corresponding modes in Photoshop. There are also modes for black and white, grayscale, and limited color work.

The Photoshop modes available under Image➤Modes are as follows:

- Bitmap
- Grayscale
- Duotone
- Indexed Color
- RGB Color
- CMYK Color
- Lab Color
- Multichannel

Bitmap and Grayscale

We'll start out here with the most basic of the color modes available within Photoshop—Bitmap and Grayscale.

5

The Bitmap mode uses only two color values to display images—black and white, whereas the Grayscale mode offers 256 shades of gray that range from white to black (see Figures 5.3 and 5.4 for examples).

Figure 5.3

The same image in the Bitmap mode.

Figure 5.4

An image in the Grayscale mode.

Notice the vast difference in quality. The grayscale image is clear and crisp, whereas the bitmap image is not. There are, however, a number of ways to convert to Bitmap mode, which we'll discuss later today.

There are really only four color modes that you'll use often. We've already touched on them—Grayscale, RGB, CMYK, and Indexed Color. Now, let's take a closer look at what they do and how you can apply them.

Whenever a picture will be printed in black and white or grayscale, for instance, as part of a newsletter or brochure, it makes sense for you to work on it in Grayscale mode. Doing the conversion yourself rather than sending a color photo to the printer gives you the opportunity to make sure that the picture prints properly. You can tell by looking at it whether the darks need to be lightened or the light grays intensified to bring out more detail.

To convert a color photo to grayscale, choose Image➥Mode➥Grayscale. You are asked for permission to discard the color information. Click OK, and the picture is converted to grays.

RGB

RGB is the color mode for working on pictures that will be viewed on a computer screen. If you are preparing pictures in Photoshop that will eventually become part of a desktop presentation, a video, or a web page, stick with RGB for the best color rendition. If your work is only going on the web, I still recommend doing the color adjustments in RGB and then converting the picture to Indexed Color when you save it in its final form.

Indexed Color

Indexed Color, when it can work for you, is a wonderful thing. It is a palette, or rather, a collection of palettes—256 to be exact. With this mode you know exactly what you are getting, and if you don't like any of the palettes Photoshop supplies, you can build your own.

Indexed Color is perfect for the World Wide Web. Web browsers can only accurately display 216 colors and the Indexed Color mode includes a specific web palette. Indexed Color doesn't really limit you to 216 colors, though. *Dithering* takes place in Indexed Color images. Choose Image➥Mode➥Indexed Color to take a look at the Indexed Color dialog box (see Figure 5.5).

 Dithering means that certain colors are *combined*, that is, adjacent pixels are blended onscreen to create a third color.

Figure 5.5
The Indexed Color dialog box.

You are given a number of palette choices when you work with Indexed Color. They are as follows:

- ☐ **Exact**—This option takes the colors in the RGB version of the image for its palette. This only works if there are less than 216 colors in the original image.
- ☐ **System (Macintosh)**—This option uses the Macintosh system palette.
- ☐ **System (Windows)**—This option uses the Windows system palette.
- ☐ **Web**—This palette uses the colors most often used by web browsers. If you are planning to publish your work on the World Wide Web, this is the palette in which you should do most of your work. Otherwise, you might have problems with incompatible colors dropping out when viewed with a web browser.
- ☐ **Uniform**—The Uniform option bases the colors in the palette on a strict sampling of colors across the color spectrum.
- ☐ **Adaptive**—This is your best bet for most work in the Indexed Color mode. During conversion, this option samples the most frequently used colors from the original. Adaptive will usually provide you with the closest match to the original image.
- ☐ **Custom**—If none of the other options suit you, you can always build your own palette. See the Photoshop manual for instructions.

CMYK

As you saw above, CMYK mode should be used when your image will be printed. By working in CMYK (and being aware of gamut warnings), you can make sure your nice yellow banana or flower doesn't end up a muddy brown, or your bright blue sky doesn't print as purple.

Converting between Modes

All you have to do to convert an image, at least mechanically (this is not taking into account image degradation or changes), is choose Image➡Mode and then choose your poison.

Although Photoshop uses the model (Lab) with the broadest gamut of color to change color modes (as if all of the other modes are circles that will fit with Lab color), this is no guarantee that your colors are going to turn out the same in another mode as they did in the original mode.

The rule of thumb is this, and I can't stress it enough: Don't work in RGB if you are going to output your images to print. Instead, work in CMYK. If you are going to publish your images on the web, use Indexed Color (or use RGB and then convert). Knowing this will save you many hours of wondering why that web page that looked great on the office Mac looks funky on the Windows machine you use at home, or why the yellow in your printed piece looks brownish.

5

But what if the color mode you want happens not to be available in the Image➡Mode submenu? Nothing to worry about. It is true that sometimes the mode you want will not be available, but you can always get to it by first converting to Lab Color and then to the color you want. When you have created or imported an image that is in Indexed Color, for example, the CMYK option is grayed out, or not available. You actually have two choices here. Convert to Lab or RGB and then take the image over into CMYK. But beware: Make sure that color is the one you want.

Tutorial: Getting Started with Color

Just for fun, why don't we dive in with some hands-on before we go any further? Working through this exercise gives you a better idea of the concepts and ideas that we have been talking about because the pictures in this book are in black and white. Let's look at a colorful image and examine how the modes affect the way the color appears.

1. First, find a colorful picture, and open it. If yours doesn't have the letters RGB in parentheses after the title, choose Image➡Mode➡RGB Color. This is our starting point. If your monitor is correctly adjusted, you should see very good color (see Figure 5.6).

Figure 5.6

Rowboats, Wychmere Harbor.

2. Select Image➡Mode➡Grayscale. A dialog box appears asking you if you want to discard the image's color information. Click OK. Photoshop then proceeds to examine your image and assign all the colors to 256 shades of gray that range between white and black, inclusive.

   Notice in the status bar at the bottom of the picture how the size of your file diminishes. This is because color is difficult for a machine to reproduce. The amount of information or data in a color image is much greater than that required to display a grayscale image (see Figure 5.7).

Figure 5.7

Changed to grayscale. All of the color values were assigned a value of gray between 1 and 256—1 being white and 256 being black.

3. Before we move on, we need to return the image to its original RGB state. Select File➡Revert. When Photoshop asks if you want to return to the last saved version of your file, click OK.

   This time, let's change our RGB image to CMYK. This process becomes enormously important for anyone taking his or her images to print. There are a number of colors that RGB can display that CMYK, by the nature of its four inks, cannot reproduce. The inks, for instance, can only approximate neon colors.

   Before we make the mode change, let's take a closer look at some of the colors in our RGB image to see if they can be reproduced in CMYK.

4. Click the Eyedropper tool in the Toolbox.

5. Next, open the Colors palette by selecting Window➡Show Colors.

6. Use the Eyedropper to select (click) a color in the image. Try clicking a very bright one (see Figure 5.8).

Figure 5.8

The triangle symbol means gamut warning.

5

7. Look in the Color palette. Is there an out of gamut warning there? This little triangle indicates that the selected color cannot be reproduced precisely by the process colors of CMYK.

   To get an idea how far out of gamut your colors are, select View➡Gamut Warning. This gives you an indication of the colors that will be lost or modified during the translation of RGB mode to CMYK. Figure 5.9 shows what the gamut warning looks like for this picture. Click the warning triangle to select the nearest color that can be achieved with CMYK colors.

Figure 5.9

The black patches are out of gamut.

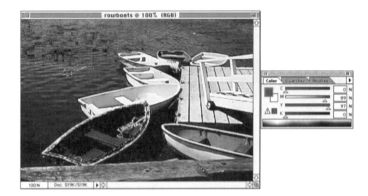

8. To change the mode from RGB to CMYK, select Image➡Mode➡CMYK.

9. After you've seen and perhaps printed the picture in CMYK mode, feel free to experiment with the other modes, too.

JUST A MINUTE

To change the color used in the display of the Gamut Warning, select File➡Preferences➡Transparency & Gamut. Click the color swatch at the bottom of the dialog box and choose a color. I use red because it is the easiest to see.

If you have a color printer, you might want to print your picture and compare it to what you see onscreen. Does it look OK? If so, you're in luck. Your monitor is accurately calibrated. If not, you need to calibrate your monitor so that the images onscreen accurately display the colors as they will print. We discuss calibration in a sidebar later on when we talk about printing.

Color Recognition

The human eye is extremely sensitive to even the slightest variation in color. Think for a moment about something familiar: a can of Coca-Cola. I'll bet that if you were shown two swatches of red that you could, without much hesitation, select the Coke red and differentiate it from, say, the red used on the cover of Time magazine. If you saw cans of Coke displayed with a slightly off-color red, you'd probably think they were either out-dated, or perhaps counterfeit. Most people are very much aware of even slight color changes. That is why color becomes so important in the branding of products through advertising.

Summary

Color is fun to play with, but it's also rather complicated to understand. The world in general, and Photoshop in particular, uses color models as a way of describing colors. The four color models are HSB, RGB, CMYK, and Lab color. There are also color modes that enable you to work with color.

In this chapter, we discussed the color modes and the specific color models in Photoshop. We also looked at a few of the more salient issues regarding converting between modes. Try, if it is at all possible, to work in the mode in which you output your final product.

Next hour, you delve deeper into the world of color by learning how to make tonal adjustments and general adjustments.

Q&A

Q What's a duotone, and how can I use it?

A Duotones, and their cousins monotones, tritones and quadtones, are quite simply grayscale images printed in various numbers of colored inks. The colors blend to reproduce tinted grays. There's a good reason for using duotones, rather than black ink, when you want really good reproduction of a grayscale image. The bottom line is quality. A grayscale image can have as many as 254 shades of gray, plus pure black and white. The best a printing press can do is to reproduce only about 50 levels of gray per ink. If you print in black (or any monotone color), your pictures automatically get compressed, each five steps of gray becoming one. So the image comes out looking a lot coarser than it would if two inks are used. When you convert the grayscale to a duotone, you add another fifty levels of gray, and immediately your image looks better, less compressed.

Duotones can be printed with a black ink and a gray ink, but more commonly black plus a color is used, giving a slight tint to the midtones and highlights. You can also make a duotone with two contrasting colors for a more unusual and colorful effect. To create a duotone, start by converting the image to grayscale, then open the Image➡Mode➡Duotone dialog box and choose color(s) for the duotone. Photoshop will translate the image into duotone.

5

Hour **6**

Adjusting Color

Are you one of those people who likes to play with the color adjustments on the television set? If you are, you're going to be absolutely astounded by Photoshop's color adjustment capabilities. If you haven't a clue as to what we mean by adjusting color, that's okay, too. By the end of this chapter, you'll be able to turn red roses blue, change a sky from midday to sunset and back again, bring out the detail in shadows, and manage every imaginable aspect of color manipulation.

Photoshop includes a full set of tools for making color adjustments. You can find them all by choosing Image➡Adjust (see Figure 6.1). Some of these terms, such as Brightness/Contrast, may be familiar to you; others may not. Don't worry. You'll learn about them all in this chapter.

Figure 6.1

The Adjust submenu gives you all the tools you need.

Before you adjust color, you need to evaluate what kind of color is in the picture and how you'll use the image. You learned about color models and color modes last hour, so you know that RGB color is the color displayed on computer screens and CMYK color is the kind that is printed. If you're going to adjust the color in a picture, it makes sense to adjust it according to the way it will be displayed. If your picture is going on a web page, you should work in RGB mode. If it's going to be printed in color, make your adjustments in CMYK mode. If it's going to end up in grayscale, forget about trying to make the sky a perfect blue. Change the mode to Grayscale and make the contrast perfect instead.

Adjusting with Variations

The most obvious way to make a color adjustment is to compare a "before and after" view of the image. In Photoshop, the tool for doing this is called Variations. It's the last item on the Image➡Adjust submenu. Variations combines several image adjustment tools into one easy-to-use system that shows you thumbnail variations of the original image. You simply click the one that looks best to you. You can choose variations of hue and brightness and then see the result (called Current Pick) compared to the original.

JUST A MINUTE

If Variations doesn't appear on the Adjust submenu, it's because the Variations plug-in may not have been installed. Consult the Photoshop manual for information about using Plug-in modules.

Figure 6.2 shows the Variations dialog box. When you first open it, the Current Pick is the same as the Original image because you haven't yet made changes. You can set the slider to the left (Fine) or right (Coarse) to determine how much effect each variation applies to the original image. Moving it one tick mark in either direction doubles or halves the amount. The finest setting makes changes so slight as to be almost undetectable. The coarse setting should be used only if you're going for special effects and want to turn the entire picture to a single color. The default (middle) setting is the most practical for "normal" adjustments.

Figure 6.2

The six, left-hand thumbnails adjust hue, whereas the right-hand set of three adjusts brightness.

When you use Variations to adjust a color image, you also have the option of individually adjusting shadows, midtones, highlights, or overall color saturation. Shadows, midtones, and highlights are Photoshop's terms for the dark, middle, and light tones in the picture, or what would be black, gray, and white in grayscale. Overall saturation adjusts all of them at once. When you select Shadows, Midtones, or Highlights, you adjust the hue and brightness of only that part of the picture. The advantage here is that you can adjust the midtones one way and the highlights or shadows another way, if you choose. Each setting is independent of the others, and you can, for example, set the midtones to be more blue, thus brightening the sky, yet still set the shadows to be more yellow, offsetting the blueness they inherently possess.

JUST A MINUTE

Hue refers to the color of an object or selection. *Brightness* is a measurement of how much white or black is added to the color. *Saturation* refers to the percentage of color compared to the percentage of gray.

6

Selecting Saturation changes the strength of the color in the image, giving you a choice of less or more. In Figure 6.3, I'm adjusting the saturation of this photo. Remember that you can apply the same correction more than once. If, for instance, "less" saturation still leaves more color in the image than you want, apply it again to get even less.

Figure 6.3

Less Saturation gives you a lighter image. More Saturation gives you a darker one.

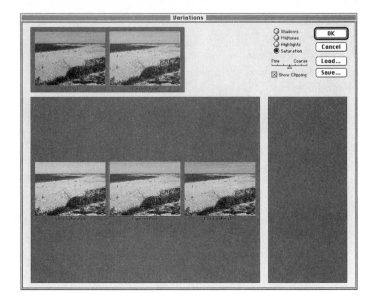

To adjust an image using the Variations command, use the following steps:

1. Open a color image. Choose Image➡Adjust➡Variations.

2. Set the radio buttons according to what you want to adjust: shadow, midtone, highlight, or saturation.

3. Use the Fine/Coarse slider to determine how much adjustment to apply.

4. To add color, click the appropriate color thumbnail.

5. To reduce a color, click its color wheel opposite. To reduce magenta, for example, click green.

6. To adjust the brightness, click the thumbnails for a lighter or darker image.

7. If you're not sure what to do, click the image that looks most "right" to you.

8. If you think you may have overdone your corrections and want to go back to the original image, press (Option)[Alt] to change the Cancel button to Reset. This restores the settings to zero and reverts to the image saved prior to changes. (Note: This works with all Adjustment windows.)

9. Click OK when done or Cancel to undo all your adjustments.

Making Other Adjustments

As you've seen, Variations is the quick way to adjust color, but sometimes it doesn't give you enough control. Other times you just want to experiment. Maybe you have a picture that's mediocre. But if you play with the colors in it and increase the contrast, you can make something out of it. This is when you want to work with individual adjustment settings. Let's start with Levels and Curves.

COFFEE BREAK

Adjusting with Histograms

There's a menu item under the Image menu called Histogram. It doesn't actually *do* anything, but if you learn how to use it, you can save a lot of time.

If you took a course in statistics, you already know that a histogram is a kind of graph. In Photoshop, it's a graph of the image reduced to grayscale, with lines to indicate the number of pixels at each step in the grayscale from 0–255.

You might wonder why this is important. The main reason is that you can tell by looking at the histogram whether there's enough detail in the image so that you can apply corrections successfully. If you have an apparently bad photo or a bad scan, studying the histogram tells you whether it's worth working on or whether you should throw away the image and start over. If all the lines are bunched up at one end of the graph, you probably can't save the picture by adjusting it. If, on the other hand, you have a reasonably well-spread-out histogram, there's a wide enough range of values to suggest that the picture can be saved.

The histogram also gives you a sense of the tonal range, or the *key type*, of the image. An image is said to be either low key, average key, or high key depending on whether it has a preponderance of dark, middle, or light tones. A picture that is all middle gray would have only one line in its histogram that falls in the middle.

All you need to know is that when you look at the histogram you should see a fairly even distribution across the graph if the image is intended to be an average key picture. If the picture is high key, most of the lines in the histogram will be concentrated on the right side, with a few on the left. If it is low key, most of the values will be to the left, and a few to the right.

6

Levels and Curves

Levels and Curves are two methods of adjusting the brightness of an image. They accomplish essentially the same purpose, the difference being that Curves does it with more subtlety. Let's start by looking at the Levels window (see Figure 6.4). As you can see, it has a histogram, along with some controls that you can use to adjust the values.

Adjusting with Levels

The Levels window is a tool for adjusting the brightness of an image based on the information in the histogram. Setting the black point (absolutely saturated black) to match the concentration of darkest levels in the image and the white point (completely unsaturated white) to match the concentration of the lightest levels in the image forces the rest of the levels to reassign themselves more equitably.

Figure 6.4

Be sure to click the Preview box so you can see the effect of your changes.

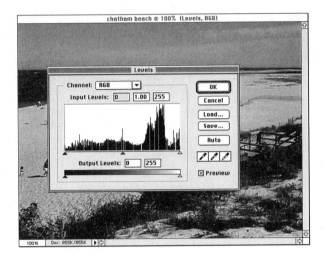

To adjust the brightness using levels, follow these steps:

1. Choose Image➡Adjust➡Levels or press (Command-L)[Control-L].

2. Click the Preview box to see your changes in the image window. If you leave this box unchecked, everything on the desktop changes as you move the sliders.

3. In a color image, you can adjust the composite RGB or CMYK color image, or individual colors, by using the Channels pop-up menu. For now, stay with the composite. (You learn more about channels later in this chapter.)

4. To set the black point in the image, move the slider at the left side of the histogram to the point at which the dark lines begin to cluster.

5. Set the white point by moving the right-hand slider to the point where the light pixels begin to rise.

6. Adjust the midrange by watching the picture while you move the middle slider left or right. Figure 6.5 shows the settings for this picture.

7. To adjust the contrast in the image, use the sliders on the Output Levels bar. The black slider controls the dark tones. Moving it toward the center darkens the image. The white slider controls the light tones. Moving it toward the center lightens the image. The gray slider controls the midtones. Moving it left darkens (or right lightens) the mid-range.

8. Click OK when you're done.

Figure 6.5

Adjusting the darks helps bring out shadow detail.

You can also use the eyedroppers to adjust the levels. Click the white eyedropper and click the lightest part of your image. Then click the dark-tipped eyedropper to select it and click the darkest point on the image. If you have an area in the image that seems to be right in the middle, click it with the midrange eyedropper.

TIME SAVER

If you click Auto in the Levels window or choose Image➡Adjust➡Auto Levels, Photoshop adjusts the levels based on its evaluation of the tonal range. This is usually not satisfactory, however. Try it, but be prepared to Undo.

Adjusting with Curves

Adjusting curves is much like adjusting levels. You can use the Curves window instead of the Levels window to adjust the brightness. The big difference is that instead of adjusting at only three points (black, middle, and white), you can adjust at any point (see Figure 6.6). When you open the Curves window, you don't see a curve. You don't see the histogram, either. Instead, you see a different kind of graph—one with a grid and a diagonal line. The horizontal axis of the grid represents the original values (input levels) of the image or selection, whereas the vertical axis represents the new values (output levels). When you first open the box, the graph appears as a diagonal because no new values have been mapped. All pixels have identical input and output values.

Figure 6.6

On this kind of a graph, the zero point is in the middle.

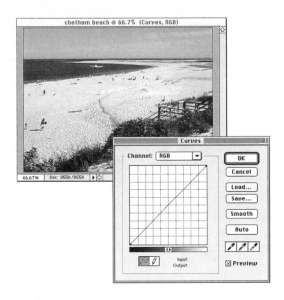

As always, be sure to check the Preview box so you can see the effects of your changes.

As with the Levels window, you can click Auto or use the eyedroppers to adjust the values. But, because the Curves window gives you so much more control, you may as well take full advantage of it.

Hold down the mouse button and drag the cursor over a piece of the image that needs adjusting. You'll see a circle on the graph at the point representing the pixel where the cursor is. If there are points on the curve you don't want to change, click them to lock them down. If, for instance, you want to adjust the midtones while leaving the darks and lights relatively untouched, click points on the curve to mark the points at which you want to stop making changes; then drag the middle of the curve until the image looks right to you. Dragging up lightens tones, whereas dragging down darkens them. Figure 6.7 shows what this looks like. To get rid of a point that you have placed, drag it off the grid.

Figure 6.7

You can add up to 15 points on the curve.

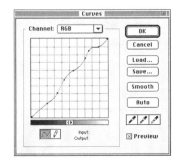

6

To see the Curves displayed with a finer grid, press (Option)[Alt] and click the grid.

Balance

In order to really understand color balance, you have to look at the color wheel. In case you don't remember the order of the color wheel, there's a reference in Figure 6.8.

Figure 6.8

It's difficult to reproduce this in gray. Use your imagination.

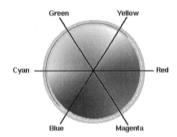

Every color on the wheel has an opposite. If you draw a line from one color through the center of the wheel, you reach its opposite. Cyan is opposite to red; green is opposite to magenta; and yellow is opposite to blue. When you use the Color Balance window to adjust colors in a picture, you're adding more of the color opposite the one you want to reduce. Increasing the cyan reduces red. Increasing red reduces cyan and so on, around the wheel.

Figure 6.9 shows the Color Balance window. The Color Balance feature is intended to be used for general color correction rather than correcting specific parts of an image, although you can use it that way by selecting only the part to correct. It's especially helpful if you have a scanned image that is off-color, such as an old, yellowed photograph. It's very simple to apply the Color Balance tools to remove the yellow without altering the rest of the picture.

Figure 6.9

Check Preserve Luminosity to avoid changing the brightness of the image.

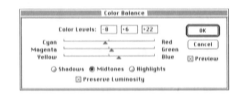

To apply Color Balance, use the following steps:

1. Select the image or portion of the image to correct. Open the Color Balance window by choosing Image➡Adjust➡Color Balance or pressing (Command-B)[Control-B].

2. Choose Shadows, Midtones, or Highlights. Generally it's advisable to start with midtones if you are correcting the whole picture because they comprise 90% of it.

3. Check Preserve Luminosity so you don't change the brightness of the image as you shift colors. If maintaining the brightness isn't important, don't check the checkbox. Be sure to select Preview so you can see how your changes affect the image.

4. Move the sliders to adjust the colors. The numbers in the boxes change to indicate how much of a change you are making. The numbers range from 0 to +100 (toward red, green, and blue) and from 0 to -100 (toward cyan, magenta, and yellow).

5. Adjust the shadows and the highlights; then repeat the corrections until the image looks right to you.

6. Click OK to apply the changes.

If the Color Balance feature doesn't seem to do what you want, undo it.

Hue/Saturation

The Hue/Saturation window is a very powerful tool with a slightly misleading name. Sure, it lets you adjust the hue (colors in the image) and the saturation (the intensity of the colors), but it also gives you control over the brightness.

First, let's look at the controls in the Hue/Saturation window (see Figure 6.10.) On the left side of the box, you see radio buttons and blocks of color. The top button, labeled Master, adjusts all the colors in the image, or selection, at once. If you only want to adjust one color range at a time, click the button for that color.

Figure 6.10

The color swatches indicate the range of colors in that family, not specific colors.

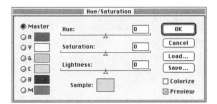

The Hue slider moves around the color wheel. With Master selected, you can move all the way from red (in the middle of the slider), left through purple to blue or blue-green, or right through orange to yellow to green.

The *Saturation* slider takes you from zero, in the center, to 100% saturated (pure color, with no gray) on the right, or 100% unsaturated (no color) on the left.

The *Lightness* slider lets you increase or decrease the brightness of the image, from 100 through zero in the center, to plus 100 on the right.

Lightness is technically the same as brightness. The Hue, Saturation, and Brightness (HSB) color model uses these terms to define a color, as opposed to the RGB and CMYK models that define lightness as percentages of the component primaries, which, of course, are either red, green and blue for RGB or cyan, magenta, and so on for the CMYK model.

The sample swatch, by default, shows the foreground color selected. Click any color in the image to place it into the sample swatch. Then you can more easily see the effect that your slider adjustments have on that particular color.

To adjust an image using the Hue/Saturation window, do the following:

1. Open the window by choosing it from the Image➡Adjust menu or by typing (Command-U)[Control-U]. Click Preview to see your changes as you make them.

2. Choose Master to adjust all the colors or click the button next to the color you want to adjust.

3. Drag the Hue slider left or right until the colors look the way you want them to. The numbers displayed in the hue text box refer to the degree of rotation around the color wheel from the selected color's original color.

4. Drag the Saturation slider left to decrease the saturation of the colors and right to increase it.

5. Drag the Lightness slider to increase or decrease the lightness of the image.

6. Click OK when done.

Brightness/Contrast

If you need to make a simple adjustment to the tonal range of an image—if you have a picture that scanned too dark, for example—the Brightness/Contrast window (Image➡Adjust➡ Brightness/Contrast) is an easy way to adjust everything at once (see Figure 6.11). Instead of separately correcting the dark, middle, and light values, it applies the same correction to all tones in the image. Although this doesn't give you the same control that you'd have if you made the adjustments using levels or curves, or even the Variations window, it's quick and easy. Sometimes it's all you need. Many images are improved by just raising the brightness and contrast by a couple points. As always, be sure to check the Preview box so you can see the effect your changes have on the image.

Figure 6.11

Use the sliders to adjust the brightness and contrast.

Dragging the sliders to the right increases brightness and contrast. Dragging them to the left decreases them. If you're not happy with the results you get with this tool, undo your changes and use the Variations window, or levels or curves, to adjust the brightness and contrast.

Using Adjustment Layers

An important point to remember about color correction is that you can apply it to the whole picture, selectively to a single area, or to all but a selected area. When you apply a correction to the whole picture, it may improve some parts and make others worse, so you really need to look carefully at the end result and decide whether the good outweighs the bad.

Fortunately, there's an easy way to apply a correction and then change your mind. One of the best features of Photoshop is the ability to work in layers. You could think of layers as sheets of cellophane that you place over your image and paint on or paste on. If you like what you do, you can merge the layers so that the additions become part of the image. If not, you can throw them away and try again. In addition to the layers that you paint on, Photoshop lets you apply *adjustment layers*. These work like normal layers except that instead of holding paint or pasted pictures, they hold the color adjustments that you make to the image.

To open an adjustment layer:

1. Choose Layer➡New➡Adjustment layer. A dialog box opens (see Figure 6.12).
2. Select the particular kind of adjustment that you want to make from the pop-up menu. Click OK to open the appropriate adjustment dialog box.

Figure 6.12

The New Adjustment Layer box.

Summary

In this hour, you learned to work with color. You learned how to use variations to make simple, "by eye" adjustments, and how to read and use histograms and curves to apply adjustments more scientifically. You learned how to make the sky a perfect blue and the grass a greener green. Now you know that adjusting levels lets you set limits for dark, middle, and light tones in an image. You have learned about the Color Balance feature and how to apply changes to hue and saturation. You have seen how to change the brightness and contrast ratio of an image.

Color adjustment is one of Photoshop's most used features, and one that you'll rely on whenever you need to touch up a photo or a scanned image. Practice with it as much as you can, using your own favorite images.

Q&A

Q **I have a sepia tinted photo (brown tones) that I have scanned into the computer, but the scan came out yellow. Is there a way to get rid of the yellow cast without losing the sepia?**

A The easy way is to convert it to grayscale so that you get rid of *all* the color. Then convert it back to RGB. Open the Image➡Adjust➡Curves dialog box. Instead of RGB on the Channels pop-up menu, select red and drag the curve up until you have added an appropriate amount of red. Then set the pop-up menu to green, and drag the curve down until you have added enough of that color. Finally, set the pop-up menu to blue and drag down until you have removed the blue and achieved a reasonable sepia. Experiment until you get the color you want, then click OK.

Hour 7

Paintbrushes and Art Tools

You are already a quarter of the way through, and now it's time to have some fun. Photoshop, as I'm sure you're coming to realize, is mainly an image editor. It was created for that purpose, and it accomplishes its purpose very elegantly. Yet, there is more to Photoshop than just editing. You can also create artwork from scratch, just as in any good graphics program. Photoshop's art tools include the following (see Figure 7.1):

- Airbrush
- Paint Brush
- Eraser
- Pencil
- Line
- Gradient
- Paint Bucket
- Eyedropper

Figure 7.1

Tools for painting and drawing.

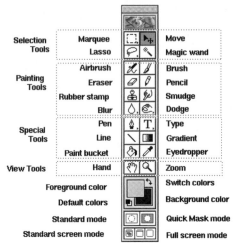

In this chapter, we'll concentrate on the tools for actually applying and removing paint, specifically the brushes, Pencil, Line, and Eraser tools. We'll cover the Paint Bucket and Eyedropper tools in the next hour and the Gradient tool in Hour 20, "Compositing."

Each tool has many options. You can adjust such settings as diameter, hardness, roundness, angle, opacity, and so on. It's easy, too.

The Brushes Palette

Before we discuss specific brushes, let's take a brief look at the Brushes palette (see Figure 7.2), which is available by choosing Window➥Show Brushes. Although each tool has its own set of options (available through choosing Window➥Show Options or by double-clicking the tool in question), the Brushes palette works with all the art tools, from the Airbrush down to the Dodge tool. The Brushes palette gives you the ability to select any of Photoshop's preset brush shapes, or to create your own.

Figure 7.2

The Brushes palette.

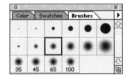

Click to select one of the preset brush shapes. The size and shape you see in the box is the size and shape of the brush. The only exceptions are the brushes with numbers beneath, which indicate the diameter of the brush in pixels. A brush can be up to 999 pixels wide, which translates to almost 14 inches. Remember, this doesn't select a tool. You have to do that in

7

the Toolbox, or by typing a letter shortcut. The brushes palette just influences the shape of the tool you select.

Brush Options Dialog Box

Double-click a brush, and the Brush Options dialog box appears (see Figure 7.3). Here you can select the diameter, hardness, spacing, angle, and roundness of the brushes.

Figure 7.3

The Brush Options dialog box lets you design custom brushes.

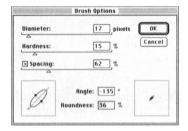

The harder a brush is (near 100%), the more defined the edges of paint will be. A brush with a setting of around 20% will give you softer-looking, slightly transparent edges.

Spacing is the next option. If left unselected, the speed of your mouse movements determines the spacing of discrete drops of paint. If you move more slowly, paint appears in a continuous line. If you move the mouse more speedily, circles of paint appear with spaces between them.

By selecting the Spacing checkbox, however, you are able to set a standard spacing of paint, no matter what the rate of the mouse movement is. Anything around 25% should give you a very smooth line of paint. As you move the percentage up (either by dragging the slider or entering a number into the box), the spaces increase (see Figure 7.4).

Figure 7.4

Spacing set at 50%, 100%, and 200%, respectively.

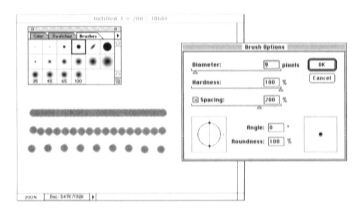

7

Finally, you also can set the Angle and Roundness of your brushes. Play around with this setting some. With a little experimenting, you can end up with a brush that behaves just as a real brush does—painting thicker and thinner depending upon the angle of your stroke.

To make adjustments, you can enter values into the boxes provided, or you can click and manipulate the graphic (on the lower-left of the Brush Options dialog box) with your mouse.

When you find a brush that you are comfortable with, save it with the Save Brushes command found in the Brushes palette menu (the arrow in the upper-right corner). Give the grouping a name, and it will be there and available to you from then on (see Figure 7.5).

Figure 7.5

The Brushes palette menu.

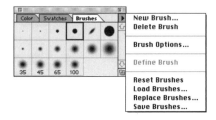

To open a set of your customized brushes, choose either Load Brushes to append brushes to the current set, or Replace Brushes to replace the current set. You'll find several sets of special brushes in Photoshop's Goodies folder.

Tool Options Palette

Photoshop also includes a tool options palette, which you can open by choosing Window➡Show Options or by double-clicking a tool. The tool options change according to the tool you're using at the time. Figure 7.6 shows the options for the Paintbrush tool.

Figure 7.6

The Paintbrush Options palette.

The first thing to notice in the options palette is the Opacity slider. A low setting applies a thin layer of paint—nearly transparent. The closer you come to 100%, the more concentrated the color is.

Wet Edges creates a sort of watercolor effect when you paint. Figure 7.7 shows an example of the same brush and paint with Wet Edges on and off. Paint builds up at the edges of your brush, and as long as you are holding the mouse down and painting, the paint stays "wet." That is, you can paint over your previous strokes. If, however, you release the mouse button and begin to paint again, you will be adding a new layer of paint, and this creates an entirely new effect.

Fade, when used with a brush full of paint, makes the paint run out after a set number of steps. It's just as if you were painting and used up all the paint in the brush. Figure 7.8 shows this effect. You can set the fade amount from 1–9,999 steps. I find that a fade setting of about 24 gives me a nice, easy to control brush stroke. Experiment to see what works best for you.

7

Figure 7.7

The Wet Edges effect darkens the edge of a stroke and lightens the middle.

Figure 7.8

From the top down; fades of 12, 25, and 50 steps.

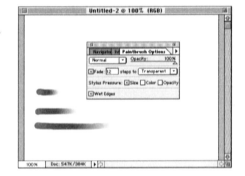

The stylus pressure options affect the way that Photoshop responds to a pressure-sensitive digitizing tablet, such as the Wacom. If you don't have one of these devices, ignore it.

Blending modes affect the way a layer of paint interacts with whatever is under it. You learn about them in the next hour. For now, just leave the blending mode set to normal.

Brushes

Now let's turn our attention to the painting tools themselves. For the rest of this hour, we'll be working with the Airbrush, Paintbrush, Eraser, and Pencil tools.

Before you go any further, why not stop and try out some of these tools? Follow these steps:

1. Open a new page, making it big enough so you have some elbow room. About 6–8 inches square is fine.

2. Open the Brushes palette (Window➡Show Brushes). On the same set of palettes as brushes, you'll see a tab for Swatches.

7

3. Click Swatches to open an electronic paint box. Click any color you want.

4. Type B to select the Paintbrush from the Toolbox.

5. Click the Brushes tab to go back to brushes to choose a brush shape.

6. Press and hold the mouse button as you move the brush over the canvas to paint.

7. Try the Airbrush and Eraser tools, too. Type A for Airbrush and E for Eraser. See what changing the options does for each tool.

The Airbrush Tool

This tool, as its name suggests, sprays paint (or pixels) on the canvas. It's like an artist's airbrush that uses compressed air to spray paint through an adjustable nozzle. The Airbrush tool applies paint with diffused edges, and you can control how fast the paint is applied. You can adjust it to spray a constant stream or one that fades after a specified period. Also, the longer you hold the Airbrush tool in a single spot, the darker and more saturated a color becomes. Type A to activate the Airbrush or click it in the Toolbox. Figure 7.9 shows a drawing done with just the airbrush. The spotty effect comes from using a blending mode called Dissolve. (You'll learn about blending modes in the next hour.)

Figure 7.9

Varying the pressure and changing brush sizes gives the picture some variety.

The Paintbrush Tool

The Paintbrush tool is the workhorse of all the painting tools in Photoshop. Type B to use the Paintbrush, and double-click it to open the Paintbrush Options palette, if it's not already open. The Paintbrush behaves very much like the Airbrush, but paint is applied more evenly. That is to say, that if you hold the mouse clicked in one area, paint does not continue to flow onto the canvas.

7

JUST A MINUTE

Although you can hit Caps Lock to get a precision painting cursor, there is an even better option. Instead, select File➧Preferences➧Display & Cursors. Look in the Painting Cursors section of the dialog box that appears. Here you can select from the following choices: Standard, Precise, and Brush Size. Choose Brush Size because this changes your painting cursor from a paintbrush or a crosshair to a circle that is the actual size of your brush.

If you need to paint a straight line, constrained either vertically or horizontally, hold down the Shift key as you drag the brush. To draw a straight line between two points, click the canvas to set the first point, then Shift-click to mark the end point. A line is drawn between the two points. Figure 7.10 shows some work with the Photoshop paintbrushes.

Figure 7.10

These flowers were drawn with a combination of small and large paintbrushes.

The Eraser Tool

The next tool in the Toolbox that we'll investigate is one that most of us, unfortunately, have to use far too often—the Eraser tool. The one nice thing about the Eraser is that it too can be undone, so if you happen to rid the canvas of an essential element that you wanted to keep, just choose Edit➧Undo.

7

The Eraser tool is unique in that it can replicate the characteristics of the other tools. It can erase with soft edges as if it were a paint brush painting with bleach. It can erase a single line of pixels, as if it were a pencil, or it can erase some of the density of the image, as if it were an airbrush. Of course, it can also act as an ordinary block eraser, removing whatever is there. The first three options are controlled via the Brushes palette—size, hardness, and so on. These characteristics are set on the Eraser Options palette shown in Figure 7.11.

Figure 7.11

The Eraser tool and its options.

The Opacity slider controls how much is erased. This is useful for blending parts of images, and it also can create a nice watercolor effect.

The Fade option works just as the Fade option for the Airbrush tool. After a certain amount of steps, which you specify, the Eraser no longer erases. This is useful to create feathering around irregularly shaped images. Set the opacity to around 75% and the Fade to about 8 steps and then drag away from the image you want to feather.

The Erase Image button is a great option for when you totally mess up and need to start over. Press it and then when Photoshop prompts you to make sure that you want to erase the image, select OK or press Enter. You'll end up with a clean, empty canvas again, ready for a fresh start.

The Pencil Tool

The Pencil tool, in large measure, works like the Paintbrush tool, except that it can only create hard-edged lines—that is to say lines that don't fade at the edges as paint brush lines can. Click the Pencil tool in the Toolbox. Double-click it to bring up the Pencil Options palette (see Figure 7.12).

7

Figure 7.12

The Pencil Options palette.

You can set the diameter of your Pencil in the Brushes Option palette (Window➡Show Brushes), but remember, hardness is not an option. You *can*, however, set all the other options just as we have with all the other tools up to now—I won't bore you with a recap.

The Pencil tool does have one option, though, that you haven't seen before. In the lower-left corner of the Pencil Options palette, there is a checkbox for Auto Erase. When you turn on Auto Erase, any time you start to draw on a part of the canvas that already has a pencil line on it, the Pencil tool becomes an eraser and will erase until you release the mouse button.

Tutorial: Painting and Erasing

Let's do some more practice with the Airbrush, Paintbrush, and Eraser. Follow along with these steps:

1. Start by opening a new page. Make it at least 6 inches square, so you have room to work.

2. Double-click the Paintbrush from the Toolbox to select it and to open the Paintbrush Options palette. Set your opacity to 100%, choose a medium size, hard edge brush, and draw a star.

3. Click the Wet Edges checkbox and draw another star.

4. Choose a soft-edged brush and draw another star.

5. Now, turn off Wet Edges and draw another star with the soft-edged brush. Your result should look something like Figure 7.13. It's not great art, but you have four distinctly different brush looks.

6. Type E to activate the Eraser. Click Erase Image on the Eraser Options palette and then click OK in the dialog box to clear the page.

7. Type A to activate the Airbrush. Set the pressure to 100% and draw a star.

8. Set the pressure to 50%, by typing the number 5, and draw another star. (You can change Paintbrush opacity settings by typing a number, too.)

9. Change brushes. If you have been using a soft-edged brush with the Airbrush, try a hard one, or vice versa. Draw more stars with different brushes and pressure settings.

7

Figure 7.13

Four kinds of brush strokes.

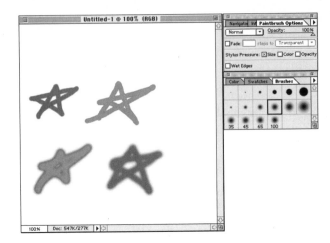

10. Type E to bring up the Eraser. Set the Eraser mode to Paintbrush and the opacity to 50% (Type a number 5.) Try to erase one of your stars. Don't click the mouse more than once while you're erasing.

11. Change the opacity to 100% and erase another star.

12. Experiment with different settings until you are comfortable with these tools.

Summary

Photoshop's painting tools are easy and fun to use. In this hour we looked at the Airbrush, Paintbrush, Pencil, and Eraser tools. Brush shapes apply to all the tools, not just to the Paintbrush. You can alter the brush shape or its behavior by double-clicking the Brushes palette to open the Brush Options dialog box. You learned to activate the Airbrush, Paintbrush, Pencil, or Eraser by typing a single letter. Double-clicking the tool in the Toolbox opens its tool options palette. You learned about some of the tool options and how they affect the quality of the brush stroke.

Q&A

Q Can I make a custom brush that's not round?

A Sure. You can even make part of your image into a custom brush. Use the rectangular Marquee tool to select a portion of an image. (You can use the Pencil tool to draw a particular brush shape, if you want.) With the marquee active, select Define Brushes from the Brushes palette menu. The new brush appears on the Brushes

7

palette. Double-click it to set its spacing option. Set Anti-aliased to make the brush blend with the background image. When you're done creating brushes, choose Save Brushes from the Brush Options palette menu to save your current brush set.

Q How do I make my brush strokes look like a watercolor?

A Easy. Just click the Wet Edges checkbox. Leave it unchecked if you prefer completely opaque paint.

7

Hour **8**

Digital Painting

Now that you know a little bit about brushes and painting tools, you need to know how to choose some colors to paint with. One of the nice things about digital paint is that it doesn't get under your fingernails. Also, you don't have to clean out your paintbrushes afterward. In this hour, we're going to learn about choosing and applying color. There are several ways of applying colors, and we'll also discuss Blending modes, which affect the way colors (and layers) interact with each other.

Foreground and Background Colors

At any given moment while working with Photoshop, you have two colors available. Only two? Don't worry—that's really kind of misleading. Perhaps it's better to say that you have two colors *active*; a foreground color and a background color. The foreground color is the one that you use to paint, to fill or stroke a selection. It's the color that's currently for your brush or pencil. (You'll learn about filling and stroking later on when we talk about paths.) The background color is the color Photoshop uses when you erase or delete a selected area on the background layer. You might think of it as the color of the canvas under your painting.

Selecting Colors

The fastest and easiest way to select color is to use the foreground or background swatch in the Toolbox (see Figure 8.1). The color swatch to the upper left is the foreground color, and the one to the lower right is the background color. You can set either color by clicking in its swatch.

 Swatches are those two little squares of color at the bottom of the Toolbox, not trendy wristwatches.

Figure 8.1
The foreground and background colors.

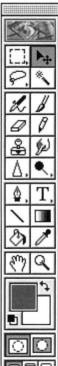

Foreground color

Default color

Swap colors

Background color

The small icon to the lower left of the swatches, that looks like a miniature version of the swatches, resets to the default colors (black and white). The little curved arrow to the upper right of the swatches toggles between background and foreground colors.

8

TIME SAVER

Here are a couple of quick keyboard shortcuts for you. You can reset the default colors by pressing D. Press X to toggle between the background and foreground colors.

To change the color of either of these swatches, double-click it. This opens the color picker that you selected in the Display & Cursors Preferences dialog box. If you haven't made a choice, the Photoshop Color Picker is selected by default. Your other choice is either the Apple or Windows Color Picker, depending on which operating system you use. The following examples use the Photoshop Color Picker.

The Color Picker

Photoshop's Color Picker enables you to select a foreground or background color in any of several ways. Figure 8.2 shows the Color Picker dialog box. You can click the color spectrum to select a color or drag the triangle up or down, click the large swatch (the color field) to select a color, or enter numbers in any one of the color model boxes.

Figure 8.2

The Color Picker.

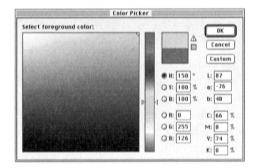

By default, the Color Picker opens in HSB model (Hue, Saturation, and Brightness), with the Hue radio button active. This makes the color field show you all of the possible saturation and brightness ranges of the particular hue that's selected. If you click anywhere in the color field you'll see the Saturation and Brightness numbers change, but the Hue setting will remain the same.

JUST A MINUTE

Just to remind you:

Hue = Color, measured as location on the color wheel in degrees.

Saturation = Strength of the color measured as percentage from 0% (gray) to 100% (fully saturated color).

Brightness = Relative lightness of the color measured as a percentage from 0% (black) to 100% (white).

If you click the Saturation button, the color field changes to something similar to the one in Figure 8.3. It's showing you all of the possible hues at the designated saturation value. If you click anywhere in the color field, the other numbers change, but the saturation remains where it was.

Figure 8.3

The Saturation color field.

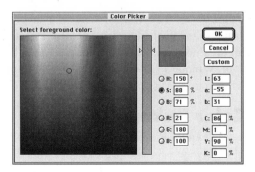

HSB mode is the one artists generally prefer because it's easy to understand. You're not stuck with it, though. Feel free to select RGB as a working mode. This is the model that governs how your computer displays color (it uses red, green, and blue, just like a projection television, for instance).

It's a little bit more complicated to choose a color in the RGB mode. When you click the Red radio button, the color you see in the color field is just as likely to be blue or green. Here's where the spectrum slider and the numbers start to make a difference. Remember, in this model, colors are made from three components, red, green, and blue, in amounts from 0–255. Pure red has a value of 255 R, 0 G, and 0 B. If you set those numbers in the Color Picker, as I have in Figure 8.4, the pure red will be way down in the lower-left corner of the color field. Colors representing mixes of green and blue with the red will fill the rest of the field.

Figure 8.4

The selected color is mixed with percentages of the other two primaries.

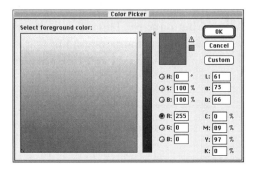

The best way to learn this color mode is to work with it. Open up your color picker and click a color. Then watch the numbers as you click a different one. Explore the different radio button settings and their color fields.

The Color Palette

The Color Palette has several advantages over the Color Picker when you're working in Photoshop. First of all, you can leave it open on the desktop, so you can change colors without having to go through all the fuss of double-clicking a swatch in the Toolbox, finding the color,

8

and then okaying your choice. For those of us who are mathematically challenged, there are fewer numbers to contend with, and the ones you see, as in Figure 8.5, are logically related to the sliders. By default, it opens in HSB mode, but you can set it to grayscale or whichever color model you prefer to work in, by using the pop-out menu as shown in the figure.

Figure 8.5
The Color Palette and its menu.

The menu also gives you access to a dialog box, shown in Figure 8.6, that enables you to reset the color bar at the bottom of the Color Palette window, according to the color model you are working with. If your work will be printed and you want to avoid using colors that are "out of gamut" (can't be achieved with CMYK inks), you can set the color bar to the CMYK spectrum and know that any color you click is printable.

Figure 8.6
If you're using your pictures on the web, stay with the HSB or RGB color bar.

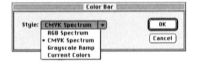

The Swatches Palette

Remember when I said at the beginning of the hour that Photoshop gives you several ways of choosing colors? Well, here's the easiest one of all…the Swatches palette works like having a child's box of watercolors on your screen (see Figure 8.7). You simply dip your "brush" in a color and paint with it. To choose a foreground color, click the one you want. To choose a background color, (Option-click)[Alt-click] the color you want to use.

Figure 8.7
The Swatches palette, and its pop-up menu.

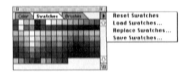

The Swatches palette, by default, opens with the current system palette. You can choose colors from the color picker to add to the Swatches palette, or you can select a color system, such as PANTONE, Focoltone, Trumatch, or Toyo, and have an additional 700–1000 or more *process color* (printing ink color) swatches appended to the palette. You can also add custom color to it using the Eyedropper tool described in the next section.

To add new colors from the color picker onto your palette, use the following steps:

1. Click the foreground color swatch in the Toolbox.

2. Use the color picker to select the desired color and click OK.

3. Open the Swatches palette (Window➧Show Swatches).

4. Using the tab in the lower-right corner of the Swatches palette, drag the window out so that it resembles the one in Figure 8.8.

Figure 8.8

Adding a new color to the Swatches palette.

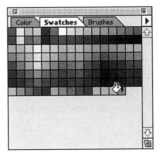

5. Move your cursor into the space below the existing swatches. It changes into the Paint Bucket tool.

6. Click and the new color is added.

7. If you press Shift, you can add the new color anywhere you want, replacing whatever swatch you click.

If you use a lot of the same colors over and over, and they are not represented in any of the palettes that ship with Photoshop, just elect to save a palette. Choose Save Swatches from the Swatches palette menu. This saves you time and the headache of having to reselect all your favorite colors each time you open Photoshop.

The Eyedropper Tool

You've seen the Eyedropper appear when you moved the pointer over a color swatch or over the color bar in the color palette window. Its function, quite obviously and intuitively, is to pick up a bit of whatever color you touch it to, making that the active color. What's neat about this tool is that is works in the same way on a picture—you can pick up a bit of sky blue, grass green, or skin and not have to try to identify a match for it with the color picker. The

Eyedropper tool is extremely helpful, especially when you are retouching a picture and need to duplicate the colors in it. Click it on any spot in the image and the color underneath its tip becomes the new foreground color. Use (Option-click)[Alt-click] to select a background color instead. If you drag the Eyedropper across an image, the swatch color changes each time the Eyedropper touches a new color.

Remember that the Eyedropper, like all of the tools, is active only at its "hot spot," in this case right at the tip.

TIME SAVER

The Eyedropper Options palette, shown in Figure 8.9, lets you decide how much of a sample to pick up with the Eyedropper. You can take a single pixel sample, or average a 3×3- or 5×5- pixel color sample.

Figure 8.9

The Eyedropper Options palette.

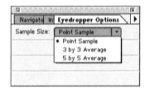

You can convert any other painting tool (except the Eraser) into the Eyedropper to change foreground colors on the fly by pressing (Option)[Alt] while you're working.

To choose a foreground or background color with the Eyedropper, and save it as a swatch, follow these steps:

1. Click the Eyedropper tool.
2. Click the image at the spot where you want to capture the color. If you're saving a background color, (Option-click)[Alt-click] the color you want.
3. Open the Swatches palette, if it's not already open. Put the Eyedropper on any empty (gray) space in the palette. It will turn into the Paint Bucket.
4. Click once to put a swatch of the selected color into the palette.
5. Choose Save Swatches from the Swatches palette menu.
6. Follow the usual procedure to name your Swatch file and save it in Photoshop Goodies or whatever folder is convenient for you.

To load a saved swatch file, use the Swatches palette menu. Select Load Swatches. Locate the Swatch file you want to use, as in Figure 8.10 and click OK.

Figure 8.10

The swatches are identified with swatch icons.

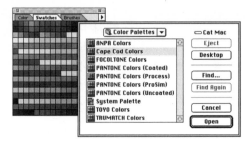

Blending Modes

In the real world, when you place a second brush full of paint over one that's already there, different things happen depending on the color of the paint you're applying, how opaque it is, whether the first layer is wet or dry, and so on. In Photoshop, you can control all of these factors by applying what's called *Blending modes.* You'll find them on a pop-up list in the Paintbrush Options window, shown in Figure 8.11. As you can see there are quite a few different ones. Let's take a quick look at the Blending modes and how they work.

Figure 8.11

Leave the Options window open while you work to make changes easier.

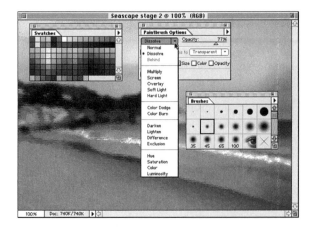

Let's suppose that we're working with only two colors. One is the *base* color, the one that's already in place. The second is the *blend* color, the one that we will be applying with each Blending mode enabled. We get a third color, a *result* that varies according to how we have blended the first two.

Here's what happens when you choose:

8

Figure 8.12
Normal: *This is the default mode. The blend color replaces the base color.*

Figure 8.13
Dissolve: *A random number of pixels are changed to become the blend color. Gives a splattered or "dry brush" effect.*

Figure 8.14

Behind: *Works only on transparent parts of a layer. You appear to be painting on the back of a sheet of acetate laid over the picture (not available if nothing is transparent).*

Multiply: *Multiplies the base color by the blend color, giving you a darker color. The effect is like drawing over the picture with a magic marker.*

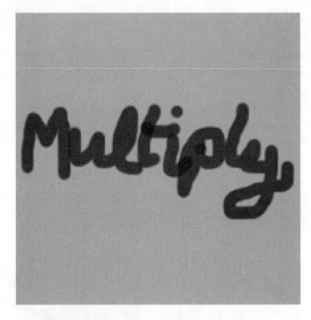

Figure 8.15

Screen: *Multiplies the base color by the inverse of the blend color, giving you a lighter color. The effect is like painting with bleach.*

8

Figure 8.16
Overlay: *Either multiplies or screens, depending on the base color. Preserves the highlights and shadows of the base color.*

Figure 8.17
Soft Light: *Darkens or lightens depending on the blend color. Effect is said to be similar to shining a diffused spotlight on the image. With a light blend color, has very little effect.*

Figure 8.18
Hard Light: *Multiplies or screens the colors, depending on the blend color. Effect is similar to shining a harsh spotlight on the image.*

Figure 8.19
Color Dodge: *Brightens the base color to reflect the blend color.*

8

Figure 8.20
Color Burn: *Darkens the base color to reflect the blend color.*

Figure 8.21
Darken: *Evaluates the color information in each channel and assigns either the base color or the blend color, which-ever is darker, as the result color. Lighter pixels are replaced, but darker ones don't change.*

Figure 8.22
Lighten: *Evaluates the color information in each channel and assigns either the base color or the blend color, whichever is lighter, as the result color. Darker pixels are replaced, but lighter ones don't change. This is the exact opposite of darken. (Had to switch background and foreground colors to show this effect.)*

Figure 8.23
Difference: *Compares brightness values in base and blend and subtracts the lighter from the brighter.*

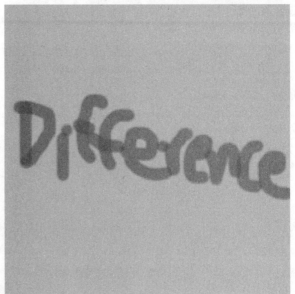

8

Figure 8.24

Exclusion: *Similar to the Difference mode, but with a softer effect.*

Figure 8.25

Hue: *Gives you a result combining the luminance and saturation of the base color and the hue of the blend color.*

8

Figure 8.26
Saturation: *Gives you a color with the luminance and hue of the base color and the saturation of the blend color.*

Figure 8.27
Color: *Retains the luminance of the base color, with the hue and saturation of the blend color. Useful for coloring monochrome images as it retains the gray levels.*

Figure 8.28

Luminosity: *Gives a result color with the hue and saturation of the base color and the luminance of the blend color. Opposite effect to Color blend mode.*

Tutorial: Using the Eyedropper and Paintbrush

Let's take a few minutes to do some practicing with the Paintbrush and Eyedropper. Pick out a picture that has lots of color, and open it in Photoshop. Then, do the following:

1. Before you begin, choose Save a Copy from the File menu and save a back-up copy of your picture, just in case you accidentally save a messed up version.

2. Open the Brushes palette and choose a medium-sized brush shape. Type B to activate the Paintbrush tool.

3. Put the brush on an area of dark color in the picture, as I have in Figure 8.29. Press (Option)[Alt]. The brush turns into an eyedropper and copies the dark color to the foreground.

4. Paint on the picture with the color you've just picked up. I added another tree to the picture shown in Figure 8.29.

5. Open the Color palette (Window➡Show Color) if it's not already open. Put your brush onto the Color bar at the bottom of the palette. It turns into an eyedropper.

Figure 8.29

Click to copy the color.

6. Choose another color and add something else to your picture. Use the same brush, or switch to the Pencil (type P) or Airbrush (type A). Experiment with colors and brushes until you feel comfortable with them. Be sure to try out some of the different Blending modes, too. See for yourself the difference between Multiply and Screen, and how Dissolve functions.

7. If you run out of space to paint, choose File➡Revert to go back to the original version of the picture and start over.

COFFEE BREAK

Can You Draw with a Bar of Soap?

As you get more used to using Photoshop, or any other graphics program, for that matter, you'll begin to realize that drawing with a mouse isn't really the best way to do it. As for the trackball and touchpad—well, they're even more difficult. They simply weren't designed for art work.

The natural way to draw is to pick up a pencil, pen, or brush and something to draw on. People have been doing it for thousands of years, all the way back to the ancient Sumerians who used a stylus and slab of wet clay, and the Egyptians who wrote and drew with squid ink and feathers on papyrus.

Today we have something much better—graphics tablets that work with Photoshop and other such programs. These consist of a flat drawing surface, tethered to the computer by a cable, and a stylus about the size and weight of a ball-point pen. The drawing surface is sensitized to "read" the motion and pressure of the stylus and send the input to the screen. A tablet such as the Wacom ArtPad II or Calcomp's Drawing Slate costs only about $150 and will save you a good deal of time and frustration. Try one at your friendly local computer store, and you'll be sold on it, too.

Summary

In this full hour, we covered the different ways that Photoshop gives you to choose and apply color to the picture. First, you learned the difference between the foreground color, which is the color that's on your brush or pencil, and the background color, which is the color of the canvas under the painting.

The Color Picker, Color palette, and Swatches palette all contain colors that you can paint with. The Color palette and Swatches palette are easier to use than the Color Picker because you can leave either one of them open on the desktop as you work. You learned to use the Eyedropper tool with the Paintbrush to choose colors from the palette or from the picture.

Finally, we covered Blending modes, the way that two layers of paint or images interact with each other.

Q&A

Q How can I know which Blending mode to apply?

A Obviously, it depends on the effect you're trying to achieve. You may not want the layers to blend at all. If so, use Normal. To lighten a color, use Screen. To darken, use Multiply. Beyond that, the best way to learn is to try different combinations until you get a look you like.

Hour 9

Moving Paint

Did you ever wonder why artists always have those paint-soaked rags lying around, and why they always have paint on their hands, under their fingernails, and all over their clothes? It's because you don't paint with just a brush, you sometimes paint with your finger, a piece of cloth, or some other tool that helps you blend the paint or lighten it or darken it just a little bit. In this hour, you learn the tricks that painters and darkroom technicians have been using ever since their respective media were invented.

Smudges

Smudge is the artist's term for blending two or more colors. In Photoshop, there are several ways of smudging. There are several ways of doing virtually anything in Photoshop. Be that as it may, the Smudge tool is the most obvious, and the quickest, way to blend something into a background.

Using the Smudge Tool

The Smudge tool looks and works like a finger. It picks up color from wherever you start to drag it and moves it in the direction in which you drag. Honestly, nothing could be much simpler. You do, however, have to use the Smudge Tool

Options palette to set the pressure of your smudging finger. At 100% pressure, the finger wipes away the paint if you smudge the background over the paint. If you smudge the paint over the background, you drag the full density of paint across the canvas. At 50%, the Smudge tool smears the paint. At 25%, the smear is smaller. Figure 9.1 shows these different smear pressures. Photoshop considers the Smudge tool to be a brush, so you can set the width of the "finger" by choosing an appropriate brush size from the Brushes palette.

Figure 9.1

Smudges at different pressure settings.

You can also use the Smudge tool to mimic finger painting. Check the Finger Painting checkbox to activate it. This option starts each stroke with the foreground color and smudges it into whatever is on the canvas. You'll find it quite handy if you need to blend some color into an existing picture, perhaps to hide something that's part of the original photo but that you'd rather do without. Figure 9.2 shows an example of finger painting. We used a small brush, and made sure the strokes followed the same direction as the water.

Figure 9.2

We needed to hide the bushes, so we smudged them out.

Setting Pressure Options

Pressure options and the Finger Painting option are set in the Smudge Tool Options palette, shown in Figure 9.3. Drag the slider to set the pressure, or type a single digit to set it to a multiple of 10%; type 4 to set to 40%, for instance.

Figure 9.3

The Smudge Tool Options palette.

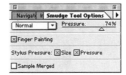

Check Finger Painting if you want to use the Smudge tool to add some smudged color as you drag. Otherwise, leave the checkbox empty. (Press and hold (Option)[Alt] to temporarily enter the Finger Painting mode.)

The Blending modes are listed on a pull-down menu. The Smudge tool doesn't give you all of the Blending mode options that you learned about in the last hour, but you can choose—aside from Normal—Darken, Lighten, Hue, Saturation, Color, or Luminosity. Of these, Darken and Lighten are obviously the most useful. The Darken and Lighten modes only affect pixels that are lighter or darker, respectively, than the beginning color. The Darken mode changes lighter pixels and the Lighten mode affects darker pixels.

Just a Minute

If the Smudge tool doesn't achieve the effect you intended, there's also a Smudge Stick filter, which you'll learn about in Hour 15.

Focus Tools

Now we turn our attention to the focus tools. These tools, Blur and Sharpen, are great for touching up images, fixing tiny flaws, and bringing items into sharper contrast. They can't save a really bad photo, but they can do wonders for one that's just a little bit "off." Sharpen can bring up the contrast to create the illusion of sharper focus, whereas Blur is most useful to rid the background of unwanted clutter and to de-emphasize parts of the picture that you don't want viewers to notice.

The Blur Tool

The Blur tool, simply put, creates blurs in images. By blurs I mean a softening or evening out of pixel values. Double-click the Blur tool in the Toolbox to select it (see Figure 9.4) and to bring up the Blur Tool Options palette (see Figure 9.5). When you are working with the Blur tool, you can temporarily select the Sharpen tool (and vice versa) by pressing (Control)[Alt].

Figure 9.4

The Blur tool.

Figure 9.5

The Blur Tool Options palette.

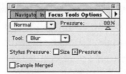

Options for the Blur and Sharpen tools are much the same as those for the Smudge tool described earlier. You have the same choices of Blending mode and the same pressure settings.

Figure 9.6 shows a close look at the Blur tool's effect. The picture of a ramshackle shed had a fence running right through the middle of it. A minute with the Blur tool merged the fence into the weeds and put the emphasis back on the shack. Figure 9.7 shows the picture before and after retouching.

Figure 9.6

The Blur tool in use.

9

Figure 9.7

Before and after blurring.

Make sure that as you blur you cover the entire area you intend to blur. A missed spot stands out. Also, don't forget that you can change the size of the Blur tool by choosing a different brush from the Brushes palette. For the Blur tool, I recommend using a brush with a soft edge, but not for the Sharpen tool. When sharpening, I prefer to use a small brush with hard edges so that I know exactly where I am. You'll also find it helpful to work on a magnified view of your picture, just so you have greater control of the tool.

COFFEE BREAK

Can You Believe Your Eyes?

One of the things you begin to notice as you become more accustomed to working with Photoshop is the use of image manipulation techniques in advertising and even in magazine and news editorial photos. You begin to recognize pictures that betray the work of a digital retoucher. You should also begin to examine them for technique and skill. Take note of the next automobile advertisement you see in a flashy, four-color magazine or brochure. Note the foreground. Check the highlights. Examine the reflections in the headlights. Do they look good? Too good? Almost all advertising images are retouched (mainly in Photoshop) and the people doing this are incredible professionals. Learn from them. Notice how the backgrounds fade or the trees blur or how the highlights appear. Not to foster any conspiracy, but evidences of Photoshop are all around you. Just keep your eyes open...

The Sharpen Tool

The Sharpen tool is the exact opposite of the Blur tool. Where the Blur tool softens pixel values, the Sharpen tool hardens and raises them by increasing the contrast between adjacent pixels. Because of their equal but opposite relationship, they share a space on the Toolbox, with a pull-out that lets you choose either one. You can also activate the Blur and Sharpen tools by pressing R (for Retouching). Press it a second time to toggle between the two. Figure 9.8 shows the shed again, with some sharpening applied to the structure. Compare it to the before picture in Figure 9.7.

Figure 9.8

Applying the Sharpen tool.

Sharpening is best done in very small doses. If you go over a section too much or have the pressure set too high, you can end up burning the color out of an image, which will probably make it look worse than it did initially. See Figure 9.9 for an example of too much sharpening.

Remember, too, that not even the magic of Photoshop can put back what wasn't there originally. Always work with the clearest, sharpest pictures you can manage. Rather than trying to salvage a bad scan, scan it again. If your photo is fuzzy all over, instead of trying to sharpen it, set it aside until we start working with filters (Hour 15).

Tutorial: Using the Focus Tools

Let's take a quick break here, and try out these tools. Open any convenient picture in Photoshop, and follow these steps:

1. Select the Zoom tool from the Toolbox and click the picture to zoom in. This gives you a magnification of 200%.

Figure 9.9

Too much sharpening.

2. Choose a soft-edged brush from the Brushes palette (Window➥Show Brushes).

3. Double-click the Blur tool in the Toolbox to open the Options palette.

4. Type 5 to set the pressure to 50%.

5. Make sure the Blur tool is selected, and drag it across the picture. Notice the effect (see Figure 9.10).

Figure 9.10

Using the Blur tool.

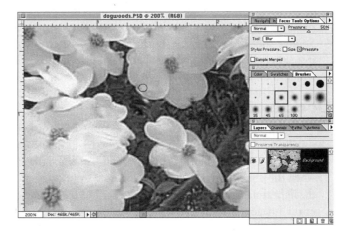

6. Switch to the Sharpen tool by pressing R. Choose a hard-edged brush. Drag it over a different part of the picture. Try to drag it along the edge of an object and note the effect.

Figure 9.11

Using the Sharpen tool.

7. Try sharpening the area you previously blurred. Can you restore it to its previous appearance? (Probably not.)

8. Now, just for fun, switch to the Smudge tool and see for yourself the difference between blurring and smudging in Photoshop.

9. Practice with these tools at different pressure settings and with different brushes. Use Revert to restore the picture if you run out of practice room.

The Toning Tools

Photoshop is primarily a digital darkroom program, so it makes sense that some of its most useful tools mimic the darkroom techniques that photographers use to lighten and darken portions of an image or to brighten colors. The toning tools include the Dodge, Burn, and Sponge tools. Dodging and burning are opposites, such as sharpening and blurring, but instead of affecting the contrast between adjacent pixels, they lighten or darken the area to which they are applied.

Dodge and Burn Tools

Dodging, in the photographer's darkroom, is accomplished by waving a dodging tool, usually a cardboard circle on a wire, in between the projected image from the enlarger and the photographic paper. This blocks some of the light and makes the dodged area lighter when the print is developed. It's also called "holding back" because you effectively hold back the light from reaching the paper. Use the Dodge tool when you need to lighten a small part of the image; for instance, to bring out the detail in an area that's in shadow. Photoshop's Dodge tool, shown in Figure 9.12, looks just like the darkroom version.

Figure 9.12

*The toning tools: Dodge,
Burn, and Sponge.*

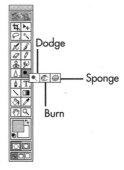

Dodge

Sponge

Burn

Burning has the opposite effect to dodging—instead of lightening a small area, it darkens the area. In the darkroom, burning is accomplished either by using a piece of cardboard with a hole punched out (the opposite of the Dodge tool) or by blocking the enlarger light with your hand so that it only reaches the area to be burned. Photoshop's Burn tool icon is a hand shaped to pass a small beam of light. Use the Burn tool to darken a small area of the picture without affecting the rest of it.

Notice the three choices on the pull-down menu in the Options palette (double-click the tool to open it, if it's not already open):

☐ Shadows

☐ Midtones

☐ Highlights

These options indicate the types of pixels that the tool affects. If you want to adjust the shadows, such as making them lighter and leaving the lighter pixels untouched, select Shadows. The default option for the Dodge tool is Midtones. This is a good choice when you want to affect the midtone pixels or when you are unsure of how to proceed. Select Highlights when you want to lighten already light-colored areas, leaving the darker areas untouched. Figure 9.13 shows the effects of dodging and burning on a typical photo.

Sponging

Surprisingly enough, sponging is also a darkroom trick. When a picture in the developing tray isn't turning dark enough, or looks to be underexposed or weak in color, the darkroom technician can often save it by sloshing some fresh, full-strength developing chemical on a sponge and rubbing it directly on the wet print in the tray. The combination of the slight warmth from the friction of the sponge and the infusion of fresh chemical can make the difference between a useless picture and an OK one. It's no substitute for a proper exposure, of course.

Figure 9.13

From the top: Original, Dodging applied to the rocks, Burning applied to the rocks.

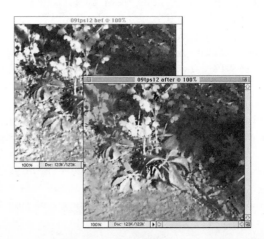

Photoshop's sponge does much the same thing. On a color image, it subtly increases (or reduces, versatile tool that it is) the color saturation in the area to which you apply it. On a grayscale image, the Sponge tool increases or decreases contrast by moving the grayscale level away from or toward middle gray. Figures 9.14 and 9.15 show before and after views of a woodland scene with the sponge applied.

Figure 9.14

Before using the Sponge tool...

Figure 9.15

…and after, using the Sponge in both Saturate and Desaturate modes.

JUST A MINUTE

Have you ever wondered what's meant by "middle gray?" If you consider the grayscale as going from 0% (white) to 100% (black), middle gray is the tone that's exactly 50%. In practice, highlights are anywhere from 0 to about 20–25%. Shadows are 70–100%. So, anything between a 25% gray and a 70% gray is considered a midtone.

These tools are great for fine tuning images and creating shadows or highlights. Use them in small doses to enhance the appearance of your images.

For this sort of precision work, I strongly recommend you change your cursors to Brush Size in the File➡Preferences➡Display & Cursors dialog box (see Figure 9.16). This enables you to see exactly what you are doing. Enlarging the picture is also helpful.

Figure 9.16

Setting the cursor to show the brush size.

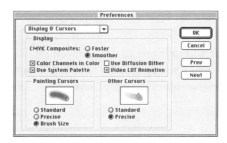

Tutorial: Using the Toning Tools

Find a photograph that has a good range of dark and light tones. Open it in Photoshop and prepare to use the toning tools on it.

1. Double-click the Dodge tool to select it and open the Dodge Tool Options palette.

2. Set the intensity to somewhere around 30% and choose a small, soft-edged brush, as we have in Figure 9.17.

Figure 9.17

This picture can use lots of help.

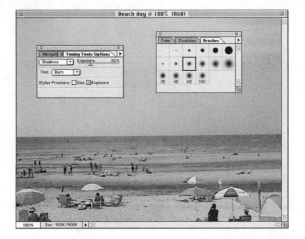

3. Find a dark area in your photo. Apply the Dodge tool. Press the mouse button and hold as you move the tool.

4. If one step wasn't enough, press the mouse button again and reapply the tool. Remember that the effects are cumulative; each time you press the mouse button you remove more of the dark tone (see Figure 9.18). Don't overdo it.

5. If you find that you have dodged too much and left a light spot, undo your last pass with the Dodge tool. If there's still a light spot, use File➡Revert, lower the intensity, and try again.

6. Now, find a light spot and press the letter O to toggle to the Burn tool.

7. Using the same method you used above to dodge, try darkening a light area. If you overdo, undo.

8. Press O to toggle to the Sponge tool. Set the pull-down menu in the Sponge Tool Options palette to Saturate. Find an area in your picture that could use more intense color and apply the sponge.

9

Figure 9.18
We dodged the umbrellas and the guy with the cell phone.

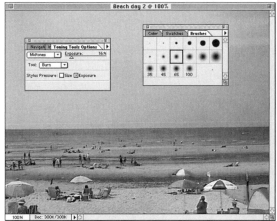

9. Choose Desaturate on the Sponge Tool Options palette menu. Now find an area that could use *less* color and use the Sponge tool to remove some. Again, if you go too far, use Undo or Revert if necessary.

10. Continue to experiment with these tools until you understand what they do and how to control them by changing the brush size and intensity.

Summary

Photoshop provides several different ways to move paint around, once you have applied it. The Smudge tool is useful for blending small areas of color. It has the same effect as dragging your finger through wet paint. Blur and Sharpen are two sides of the same coin, so to speak. One increases the contrast between adjacent pixels, whereas the other diminishes it. The toning tools, Dodge, Burn, and Sponge, are the digital darkroom equivalents of real darkroom tools and procedures. They can darken or lighten an image or change the color saturation, either adding more color or removing some. These tools are mostly used for retouching pictures that you have scanned or shot digitally, rather than for creating your own art.

Q&A

Q What's the difference between smudging and blurring?

A The main difference is in the way you apply them. Smudging, because you're moving the pixels from point A to point B, tends to show the direction of the move. Blurring decreases the contrast between adjacent pixels, so they seem to blend together visually but with no hint of movement.

Hour 10

Advanced Painting Techniques

Digital paint is so much easier to work with than the real kind. It doesn't smell, it never spills on the table, and there are no messy brushes to wash out when you're done. It doesn't get all over you and you don't even have to wait for it to dry. In Photoshop, you can either paint a picture from scratch, starting with a blank page and using it as if it were any other graphics program, or you can take an existing image and convert it into a painting. In the course of this chapter, we explore both ways of working.

When we talk about "paint" in the digital realm, we're talking, of course, about image manipulation that mimics "real life" painting techniques. Because we're imitating real life, you might think that we'd be limited in the number of painting techniques we can use—but this isn't the case. Under the broad category of painting, we can include colored pencil drawing, pastels, chalk and charcoal, and even neon tubing, as many of today's artists and art students are doing. Even though digital painting is the most spectacular part of Photoshop, as well as the most fun, you'll be amazed at how easy it is. More important, mastering Photoshop's painting tools takes you a long way toward becoming a more proficient digital artist.

Using Photoshop as a Graphics Program

Quite honestly, Photoshop wasn't designed to be a graphics program. It lacks some of the vector drawing tools that you find in Adobe Illustrator, CorelDRAW!, or Fractal Painter. It can, however, be used effectively for many kinds of graphics. Because of its plug-in filters, which you learn about later on, Photoshop can do some very remarkable things with graphics, most of which would be way beyond the capability of an ordinary painting or drawing program. Should Photoshop be your *only* graphics program? Probably not, if you need to do a lot of drawing. But for painting, digital darkroom work, and retouching, nothing can top it.

Simulating Different Media

One of the remarkable "tricks" Photoshop can do is to simulate the appearance of other media. The effect may be achieved through the use of a filter (we'll jump ahead a little in this hour and introduce you to some of Photoshop's "artistic" filters), by the use of the Smudge and Blur tools, or by choosing custom paint brushes and carefully applying paint with a particular Blending mode. You can either create a picture "from scratch," or you can start with a photograph and make it look like a watercolor, an oil painting in any of a half dozen different styles, or a construction of neon tubing. Whatever the method, the results will amaze you.

Watercolors

Artists who work in conventional media have a great deal of respect for those who choose watercolors. It's probably the most difficult medium of all to handle. You have to work "wet" to blend colors, but not so wet that the image turns to mud. Doing it digitally is much easier. Photoshop has a watercolor *filter* that converts a picture to a watercolor version of itself. You can find the filter in the Filters➡Artistic submenu, as shown here in Figure 10.1.

Figure 10.1
Watercolor is one of fifteen "artistic" filters.

10

NEW TERM *Filters*, in Photoshop terminology, are a set of instructions built into the program (or "plugged-in" as added features) that apply specific effects to your pictures. One of Photoshop's filters, for instance, converts your image to a pattern of dots. Another simulates flames shooting out of a selected object. There are dozens of filters available. Some come with the program, and others are sold by third-party vendors or distributed as shareware or freeware. In Hours 14–16, we talk more about what kinds of filters you can get, and where.

The Watercolor filter works most effectively on pictures that have large, bold areas and not a great deal of detail. Also, because it tends to darken backgrounds and shadows, it's best to start with a picture that has a light background. The photo in the figures that follow is a digital photograph of the ladder that encircles a water tank.

When you select the Watercolor filter (or any other Photoshop filter, for that matter), you open a dialog box similar to the one shown in Figure 10.2. The dialog box has a thumbnail view of your picture and a set of sliders that enable you to set the way in which the picture is converted. If you click the thumbnail image, you can slide it around to see the effect of your settings on different parts of the photo. Most Photoshop filters have dialog boxes and settings very much like this one. After you have tried even one, the rest will be just as easy.

Figure 10.2

Use the + and - symbols to zoom in and out on the thumbnail.

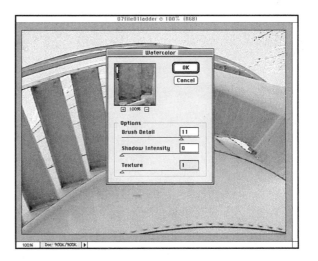

Filters can take anywhere from a few seconds to a minute or more to apply. If you don't see the effects of the filter on the thumbnail view immediately, look for a flashing underline beneath the percentage number under the thumbnail window. It flashes to tell you that the computer is calculating the filter effect. When the underline disappears, the filter is applied.

Brush Detail varies from 1–14, with 14 giving you the most detail and 1 being a sort of Jackson Pollock splatter effect. Depending on the nature of the picture you are converting and your own preferences, you may want to start experimenting with settings around 9–12. Shadow Intensity can be adjusted from 0–10, but unless you are looking for special effects, leave it at zero. The Watercolor filter darkens shadows too much, even at the zero setting. By the time you move it past 3–4, the picture's gone almost totally black. Texture settings vary from 1–3. These are actually quite subtle and you may wonder if they have any effect at all. They do, but are more noticeable combined with less detailed brush settings. In Figure 10.3, I've gathered samples of different brush detail and texture settings so you can see the differences.

Figure 10.3

All three texture settings have been applied to each sample brush setting.

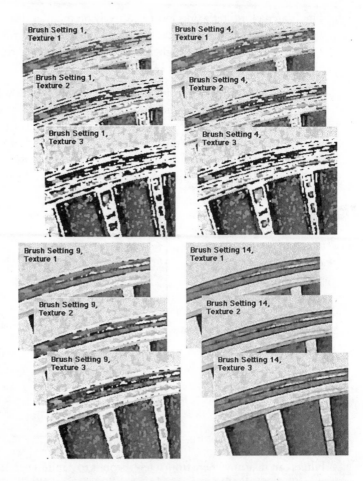

Tutorial: Converting a Photograph to a Watercolor

You might not want to convert all your photos into imitation watercolors, but some look really good with this treatment.

1. Find a picture that you think might look good as a watercolor. Open it in Photoshop and make any color adjustments you think necessary. (If you've forgotten how, turn back to Hour 6 to refresh your memory.) Remember not to let

the colors get too dark before you start applying filters. Photoshop filters, in general, tend to add more black to the image.

2. Choose Filter➟Artistic➟Watercolor.

3. In the Watercolor dialog box shown in Figure 10.4, use the sliders to choose a combination of texture and brush detail that you like. Move the thumbnail image to check details.

Figure 10.4

We've set the Brush Detail to 12 and Texture to 1.

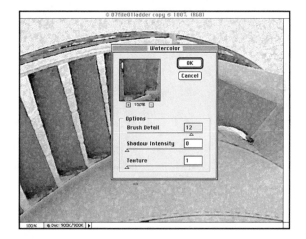

4. Set the Shadow Intensity to 0, unless you want a lot of black in the image.

5. When you're done, click OK to apply the changes.

Watercolors from Scratch

Sometimes you either don't have a photo of what you want to paint, or you just want to do it yourself. Perhaps you want a different style of watercolor than what's possible with the filter. If you work patiently and with some forethought, you can produce watercolors that you'd almost swear were painted with a brush on paper. Let's open a new page in Photoshop and do some painting.

You learned about working with the Paintbrush tool in Hour 7. As you remember, you can leave the Brushes and Paintbrush Options palettes open while you work so that you can switch from a large brush to a small one or change the opacity with just a click. I also like to open the Swatches palette and use it as a paint box to select colors, rather than going to the Color Picker each time. Please feel free to flip back if you need to refresh your memory about any of these things.

Transparency is one of the distinguishing features of "real" watercolor. In order to make a "synthetic" watercolor, you need to set the Paintbrush tool's opacity to no more than 75%. This means, because transparent is the opposite of opaque, your paint will be 25%

transparent, which is about right for watercolors. Try out the Paintbrush on a blank page and notice that, as you paint over a previous stroke, the color darkens. Click the Wet Edges checkbox for even more authentic brush strokes. This option adds extra color along the edges of a stroke, making it look as if the pigment gathered there, as it does when you paint with a very watery brush.

Watercolor artists painting on paper often start with an outline and then fill in the details. Figure 10.5 shows the beginnings of a watercolor painting of a flower. We've drawn the flower with its stem and leaves, and now we're working on filling in the leaves with a small brush. It's often easier to work in a magnified view when you're doing small details such as this.

Figure 10.5

Use brushes with soft edges.

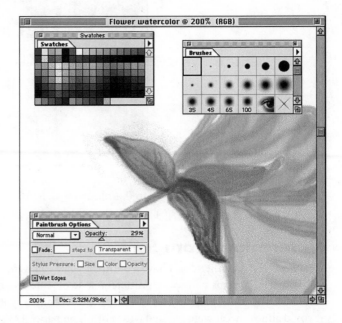

Another useful "trick" for creating a watercolor is to use the Eraser tool as if it were a brush full of plain water to lighten a color that you have applied too darkly. Use it at a very low opacity to lighten a color slightly, and at a high opacity to clean up around the edges if your "paintbrush" got away from you. Don't forget that the Eraser always erases to the background color. If you have been changing colors as you paint, make sure to set the background color to what you want to see when you erase.

10

TIME SAVER

For this kind of task, a pressure-sensitive graphics tablet, though not an absolute must, is certainly helpful. Drawing with a stylus is far more natural than drawing with a mouse or trackball, and the pressure-sensitive function permits you to make brush strokes that trail off like the real ones. Wacom and CalComp both make excellent graphics tablets.

Most real watercolors are painted on a heavily textured watercolor paper. If you would like yours to have the same grainy character, you can use the Texturizer filter, after your painting is completed, to add the watercolor paper texture to the picture. Don't apply it until everything else is done, though, because any further changes you make alter the texture. Figure 10.6 shows the Texturizer filter being applied. The Canvas texture comes the closest to replicating watercolor paper, especially if you scale it down some. I like to set it to about 70–80% with a relief height of 3 or 4. Use the sliders to set relief and scaling. I found that applying the same texture a second time with the light coming from the opposite direction gave me the best imitation of textured paper.

10

Figure 10.6

The direction of the light affects the shadows that make up the texture.

Oil Painting

Oil paint has a very different look from watercolor, and it's a look that Photoshop duplicates particularly well. The qualities that distinguish works in oil are the opacity of the paint, the textured canvas that adds a definite fabric grain to the image, and the thick, sometimes three-dimensional quality of the paint. In order to get the full effect in Photoshop, you may have to combine several different techniques. We'll start, as artists do, with underpainting.

Underpainting

When an artist starts an oil painting of a landscape or a seascape, she usually sketches out the subject with a few lines, often working with charcoal or a pencil to locate the horizon and major land masses. Then she dips a big brush in thinned-out paint and begins the process of underpainting. This blocks in all the solid areas; the sky, the ground, the ocean, and any obvious features such as a large rock, a cliff, or whatever else may be included. Underpainting builds the foundation of the picture, establishing the colors and values of the different parts of the image. It's much like building the foundation and framework of a house before you start stacking up bricks to make the walls. Underpainting puts down all of the basic structure of the picture before you go over it and add the details.

Photoshop's Underpainting filter looks at the image you're applying it to and reduces the image to the same sort of solid blocks of color. Figure 10.7 shows the settings we applied to a photo of a beach with some nice rocky cliffs in the background.

Figure 10.7

Underpainting gives you the basic elements of the picture, minus the details.

Using the Underpainting filter requires making some settings decisions. The Texture settings are exactly the same as in the Texturizer filter we used on the watercolor. Here, though, we want to bring out more of the canvas, so we would use a higher Relief setting and possibly a larger scale on the canvas. You can also paint on burlap, sandstone, brick, or on textures that you import. The Brush size setting ranges from 0–40. Smaller brushes retain more of the texture and detail of the original image. Larger brushes give a somewhat spotty coverage and remove all the detail. Texture coverage also ranges on a scale from 0–40. Lower numbers here reveal less of the texture, higher numbers reveal more. In underpainting, the texture is revealed only where there's paint, not all over the canvas.

To turn a scene into an oil painting, follow these steps:

1. As always, start by preparing the picture. Adjust the colors if necessary and crop as needed.

2. Choose Filter➡Artistic➡Underpainting to bring up the Underpainting dialog box.

3. Set the Brush Size to 3 and the Texture Coverage to 3. These settings retain most of the detail in the picture.

10

4. Set the Texture to Canvas and Scaling to 65%. You want to keep the Texture setting low so that it doesn't interfere with the detail you add to the picture later on.

5. Set the Relief to 8 and the Light Direction to Top. This shows just enough texture to establish that your painting is on canvas rather than stone.

6. Click OK to apply the filter. Figure 10.8 shows the results so far.

Figure 10.8

The scene with just the Underpainting filter applied.

10

Overpainting

The Underpainting filter leaves us with a somewhat indistinct picture, fine for some purposes but definitely unfinished. The way an artist would proceed is to go back and overpaint the areas that need detail. So that's what we'll do to complete this seascape.

Dissolve may be the most useful mode for working into our seascape. Use it, as shown in Figure 10.9, to stipple colors into the underpainting. Vary the brush size and opacity to add more, or less, paint with each stroke.

You can go on painting into this picture until it looks exactly like an oil painting, or you can use it as a basis to experiment with other filters and effects. In Figure 10.10, we've taken the seascape and applied the Smudge Stick filter (Filters➡Artistic➡Smudge Stick) to it. This filter, when used with a short stroke length, gives a nice paint-like texture to the picture. It does, however, also darken it quite a bit, so you may want to go back and adjust the curve again to bring back the sunshine. You can also increase the intensity to keep the picture from turning dark. This changes the smudge effect as well, however. Experiment with the settings until you find a combination that works with the image you're using.

Figure 10.9
*We've added white to the
surf and greens to the
shrubbery.*

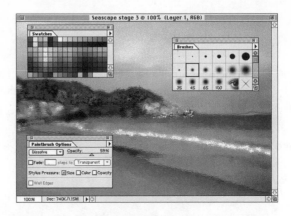

Figure 10.10
*The Smudge Stick adds
texture to large flat areas
such as the beach sand.*

Pencil and Colored Pencil

The Pencil tool has been part of every graphics program since the first ones hit the market. It's an extremely useful tool when you know how to use it properly. The first thing to learn about it is that by holding down the Shift key as you drag, you can draw neatly constrained straight lines; vertical, horizontal, or at a 45 degree angle. The second thing is that it can also serve as an eraser if you click the Auto Erase function in the Pencil Tool Options palette. With Auto Erase enabled, when you click the pencil point on a colored pixel, you erase it. Use this feature to clean up edges or to erase in a straight line.

The Pencil tool is great for retouching and drawing a single pixel-width line but difficult to use for actual drawing. It's easier to use if you set the screen to 200% so you can see individual pixels. Opening the Mouse control panel and setting the mouse acceleration to Slow also helps, but even better is to use a graphics tablet instead of a mouse.

If you want to get the look of a pencil drawing, without all the effort, try the Colored Pencil filter (Filters➡Artistic➡Colored Pencil) or the Crosshatch filter (Filters➡Brush

10

Strokes➡Crosshatch). The Colored Pencil filter, shown in Figure 10.11, creates a light, somewhat stylized drawing, from your original image. The Crosshatch filter, applied to the same image in Figure 10.12, retains much more of the color and detail, but still looks like a pen and ink drawing.

Figure 10.11

The Colored Pencil filter adds a light, airy, feel.

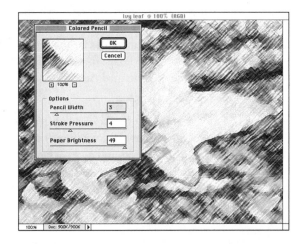

Figure 10.12

Crosshatching uses a different, more detailed drawing style.

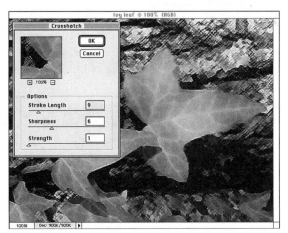

Chalks, Pastels, and Charcoal

Chalk and charcoal drawings date all the way back to prehistoric times. When the cave dwellers at Lascaux decided to decorate their walls, they used colored clays, chalk, and charcoal, with animal fat as a binder. Artists today use almost the same medium, except that the chalks are now compressed so well they don't need tallow. Natural birch charcoal is still considered the best of its kind. Chalk drawings in the real world can be found on virtually any surface, from grained paper to brick walls and sidewalks. Chalk drawings in Photoshop let you take advantage of the capabilities of the texture filters. Place your drawing on sandstone, burlap, or on a texture that you've imported.

Chalk and charcoal are linear materials, which is to say that they draw lines rather than large flat areas like paints. Choose your subjects with that in mind. You can, of course, apply shading as a pattern of lines or a crosshatch, and you can smudge to your heart's content. If you're drawing from scratch, start with a fairly simple line drawing and expand on it. If you're translating a photo or scanned image into a chalk or charcoal drawing, choose one that has strong line patterns and well-defined detail.

Chalk & Charcoal Filter

When you apply the Chalk & Charcoal filter, which is found on the Filter menu (Filter➡Sketch➡Chalk&Charcoal), you'll see that it reduces your picture to three colors, using a dark gray plus the foreground and background colors that you have set in the tool window. Chalk uses the background color and Charcoal becomes the foreground color. Areas that aren't colored appear in gray. You probably want to do some experimenting to find the "right" colors. It's a little bit counterintuitive because the foreground color is usually the lighter one, and this filter applies it to the darker areas of the image.

Figure 10.13 shows the Chalk & Charcoal dialog box, which controls how this filter works. In it you can set amounts for the chalk and charcoal areas. These sliders have a range from 0–20. Start somewhere in the middle and adjust until you get a combination that works for your picture. The stroke pressure varies from 1–5. Unless you want the picture to turn into areas of flat color, keep the setting at 1 or 2. Intensity builds up rather fast with this filter.

Figure 10.13

Move around in the preview window to see the filter's effects on different parts of the image.

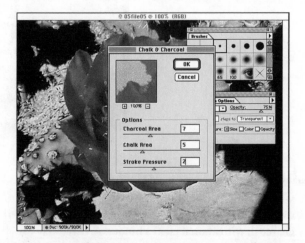

10

To convert a photograph to a chalk and charcoal drawing, follow these steps:

1. Open the image and then the Chalk & Charcoal dialog box (Filter➥Sketch➥ Chalk & Charcoal).

2. Set the Charcoal and Chalk areas to 10 or less. When you work with a filter for the first time, always start in the middle of the settings range, and increase or decrease as necessary.

3. Set the pressure to 1 or 2. Click OK if you like the view in the preview window, or experiment with other numbers.

4. Click OK to apply the filter. Figure 10.14 shows the filter applied to a picture of a chrysanthemum.

Figure 10.14

Choose colors that work with your subject.

10

5. Study the result. Decide what areas need touching up.

6. Select the Eraser tool and erase to bring up more of the background color.

7. Select the Paintbrush tool to apply more of the foreground color.

8. Use the Eyedropper to select the gray tone, if you need to apply more of it.

9. When you're satisfied with the drawing, save it.

The Smudge tool works nicely with chalk and charcoal. Use it exactly as you would to soften a line or blend two colors using your finger or hand on paper. Photoshop's Blur and Sharpen tools can also be used to define edges or to soften a line without smudging it.

After you apply the filter to the picture, you can go over it with the Paintbrush and Eraser tools, adding back important detail that was lost in translation or touching up as necessary. You can use the Eraser tool to apply the background color and the Paintbrush to apply the foreground color. In order to add more of the gray tone, however, we have to sample it with the Eyedropper tool so that we can paint it in. The gray is an arbitrary color used by this filter, and can't be adjusted.

Photoshop 4.0 includes 97 different filters! If you master one each week, within two years you'll know them all.

Just a Minute

Charcoal Filter

Use the Charcoal filter (Filter➡Sketch➡Charcoal) to convert an image to a good imitation of a charcoal drawing. Because charcoal doesn't come in colors, your charcoal drawings are most successful if you set the foreground to black and the background to white, or to a pale color if you want the effect of drawing on colored paper. The Charcoal dialog box, shown in Figure 10.15, enables you to adjust the thickness of the line from 1–7 and the degree of detail from 0–5. The light/dark balance setting ranges from 0–100 and controls the proportion of foreground to background color.

Figure 10.15

Experiment with these settings. Every image is different.

Figure 10.16 shows before and after versions of a portrait converted into charcoal and lightly retouched with the Paintbrush, Blur, and Sharpen tools. Using a graphics tablet instead of a mouse makes it easier to reproduce the filter's cross-hatched lines.

Figure 10.16

Retouching brought back the details that were lost in translation.

Before   After

10

Summary

Whew! This has been a very full and intense hour. Spend some time trying out these techniques before you go any further.

In this hour, you saw that digital painting is an area where Photoshop truly excels. You can either work "from scratch" or convert images that you upload as digital photos or scans or create in some other compatible program. After you have the image in Photoshop, the various filters and brushes enable you to turn your work into a good imitation of an oil painting, water color, or drawing. The "artistic" filter set includes filters that can do much of the conversion work for you. For best results, though, go in and touch up the picture after the filter has done its work. Choose tools and colors appropriate to the medium you're trying to imitate. Experiment, and if you find a technique or filter combination that works especially well, make notes on it. Yes, you can even write in this book! (Well, not if it's a library book...)

10

Q&A

Q How do you know which pictures will make good digital paintings?

A For digital watercolors, look for photos with large plain areas and not a lot of detail. In general, try lighter colored pictures because the Watercolor filter tends to darken images. Almost any "non-descript" picture will make a good oil painting. It helps if the subject is interesting or if there's a good deal of color.

Q Can I use more than one filter on a picture?

A You can, and many times you may want to, use a combination of several filters to achieve a particular effect.

Hour 11

Layers

You're almost halfway through. You've already learned a great deal about Photoshop, but there is, as always, more to learn. From this point on, most of it's fun stuff, too. Right now, we are going to discuss one of the most important aspects of Photoshop—layers.

At first, layers might seem confusing, even daunting, but don't worry—they're not as bad as they sound. In fact, they are exactly what their name implies—layers within one image—and each layer can be adjusted and edited separately from the others. That's what makes this feature so cool.

If it helps, think of it this way. Consider a Bugs Bunny cartoon. Imagine Bugs walking through the woods. The artists at the Warner Bros. studios created the backdrops and then drew Bugs on pieces of cellophane, which they laid over the background. They often put his body on one layer, his arms and legs on another, and as they cycled through the several sets of arms and legs they made the animated Bugs appear to move through the woods, or chase Elmer Fudd, who was on yet another layer or two of cellophane. There were limits, though. Too many layers, and the background turned gray, or the paint on the top cell cast shadows on the lower ones.

Photoshop has a capability similar to this animation technique, and you can create as many layers as you need, up to 100. You can hide layers, while you work on others. You can link layers together. You already learned how to use adjustment layers that enable you to make color and tonal corrections in your images. Now, you learn the rest of the story about layers.

Using the Layers Palette

Step one is to open a new page, and then to open the Layers palette by choosing Window➡Show Layers. The Layers palette is where you control your layers' behavior—creating, adding, deleting, hiding, and showing (see Figure 11.1). Think of the Layers palette as "command central" for working with layers. The small versions of your images on the left of the palette are called *thumbnails*. Each of these small rectangles displays a separate layer. For the moment, because we have not combined any images, you should have only one blank thumbnail in the Layers palette.

Figure 11.1

The Layers palette.

If the thumbnails are too small for your liking, choose Palette Options command Layers palette menu (the arrow in the upper-right corner of the palette), and check out Figure 11.2.

Figure 11.2

Optional thumbnail sizes.

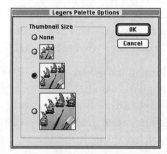

You can choose from three different sizes and also no thumbnail image at all. Remember that every image on your screen consumes a certain amount of the RAM available to run Photoshop. So if you can get by with the smallest thumbnail, try to. The smaller the thumbnail, the less space the palette takes up on your desktop. This is an advantage as you begin to work with three, four, five, and more images at a time.

11

Creating a New Layer

Now, let's make some layers. First of all, let's put something on the Background layer, just so we'll know where it is. Follow these steps:

1. Using the Airbrush and your biggest brush shape, choose any light to medium color and spray paint a large patch of color on the canvas.

2. Look at the background thumbnail. (It's the only one on the palette.) It should look something like Figure 11.3.

Figure 11.3

A colored background.

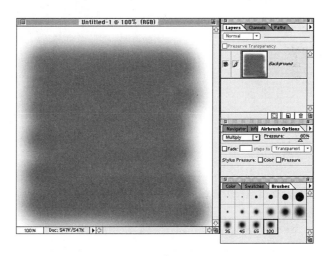

3. Click the small page icon at the bottom of the Layers palette. You've just added a layer! Now your palette should look like Figure 11.4.

Figure 11.4

Creating a new layer.

Let's pause here for a moment and take a close look at the new layer's thumbnail. Compared to the Background layer, it has a thicker black frame around it. The thick frame indicates that this is the *active* layer. Notice the box next to the thumbnail that contains a paintbrush. This also indicates the active layer—or the layer on which you can work. Paint all you want, but only the layer with the paintbrush receives the paint.

Changing the Active Layer

To change the active layer, click in the white space to the right of the icon (see Figure 11.5). If you try to click in the empty box where the paintbrush icon should appear, you end up with a chain icon, which indicates that the layers are linked. We'll look at this option in just a few pages, but for now it's not what we want.

Figure 11.5

Changing the active layer.

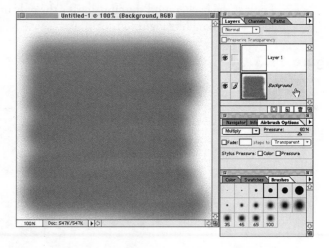

Try changing the active layer to the Background layer.

1. Click in the space to the right of the background thumbnail. Notice that the active layer frame turns black, and the paintbrush icon moves down.

2. Now, change the active layer back to Layer 1, by clicking next to its thumbnail. Let's put something on this layer.

3. Choose a medium paint brush and a color that contrasts with the background. At the left side of the canvas, write a letter A (see Figure 11.6).

Figure 11.6

Working in the active layer.

4. Use the Layer➡New menu to add Layer 2. (This is just a different way to do it.) For now, make no changes in the New Layer dialog box (see Figure 11.7). Just click OK to add the layer.

Figure 11.7

Using the New Layer
dialog box.

5. In the middle of the canvas, on Layer 2, write a letter B.

6. Use the Layer palette menu to add Layer 3. Figure 11.8 shows the menu. The dialog box looks just the same as the previous one. Click OK to add the layer.

Figure 11.8

Adding a layer from the
Layers palette.

7. Write C on Layer 3. Your screen should look something like Figure 11.9. You may have to expand the Layers palette to see all four layers.

Figure 11.9

Adding layers is as easy as
ABC.

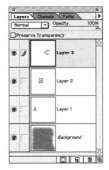

You can move, add to, or erase anything on the active layer, but doing so doesn't affect layers above or below it. If, for instance, you make Layer 2 the active layer, you can use the Move tool to slide the B around, but you can't move the A or C.

Moving Layers

You also can change the order of the layers.

1. Click to the right of the thumbnail of the active layer and hold. The active layer becomes highlighted with an outline.

2. While still holding the mouse button down, drag the layer up to the top of the stack. It becomes the topmost layer.

Hiding/Showing Layers

Another great feature of layers is that when you want to concentrate on one part of your image, you can hide all the other layers. To the left of the thumbnails are small icons that resemble eyes (see Figure 11.10). These indicate that a layer is visible. If you see the eye, you can see the layer. If you click the eye, however, the eye disappears and the layer becomes hidden.

Figure 11.10

Only the Background and Layer 3 are visible.

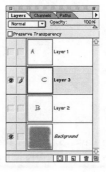

Click the eye icons next to Layers 1 and 2. They disappear, as do the corresponding layers. Click again and the icon reappears—with the layer.

Removing Layers

The simple way to remove a layer is to click to make it active and then click the small trash can icon at the bottom of the Layers palette. You can also select Delete Layer from either the Layer menu or the Layer palette menu. When you do this you see a warning box asking if it's really OK to delete the layer. If you (Option-click)[Alt-click], you can skip the warning. (The trash can deletes without the warning.) Undo brings the layer back if you have done nothing else in the meantime.

Working with Multiple Layers

You have seen how to create, move, and remove layers. But we still haven't really addressed the question of what they're good for. You use layers in many different situations. Whenever you are combining two or more images (in Photoshop terms, *compositing*), the elements you paste over the background image are added on separate layers. You can use the Layer palette to control precisely how these elements are combined and control the opacity of objects you

11

paste onto a layer or paint that you apply to it. (The layer is transparent, even if you set the paint on it to 100% opacity.) You can also control the blending modes that affect how one layer appears on top of another, just as you could when painting over an image or background.

Opacity

The Opacity slider at the top of the Layers palette controls the opacity of the active layer (see Figure 11.11). It can be adjusted from 0 to 100% by dragging the slider or by entering a value by typing "0" for 0%, "1" for 10%, "2" for 20%, and so on.

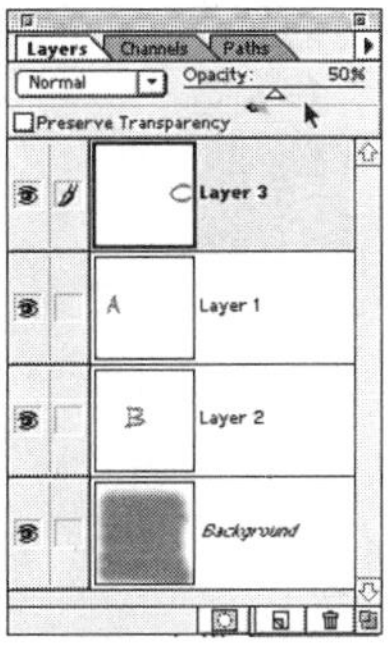

Figure 11.11

The Opacity slider is located at the top of the Layers palette.

Let's give the Opacity slider a try. You should still have the ABC document open on your desktop. Make Layer 3 active and drag the Opacity slider to about 50% (refer to Figure 11.11). Can you see the background through the C? Drag the slider down to 10%, and then to 0%. Then move it back to 100% again. Pretty cool, huh?

The Background layer cannot be affected by the opacity slider. It always remains at 100% opacity. There is, however, a way around this. There is a difference between the background of your image and what Photoshop sees as the *background* to your layers.

You can create a transparent background by opening a new canvas and selecting Transparent as the contents, as we have in Figure 11.12. When the canvas opens, you see a checkerboard pattern as a placeholder, indicating that there's nothing on the background layer. Now, anything we copy from another source and paste in goes on a new layer that can also be made transparent.

If I drag the background and some of the letters from the previous experiment into this new document, I can make the airbrushed background 50% transparent because Photoshop sees it as just another layer and not as a background. The advantage to this is that I can then arrange the layers so that one is on top of the semi-transparency and not affected by it, and the other layer is beneath it and is changed by it. In Figure 11.13, the layers are stacked with B on the top, then the background at 50% transparent, and C on the bottom.

Figure 11.12
Making a transparent background.

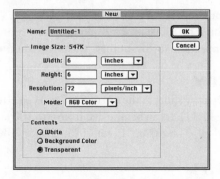

Figure 11.13
Each layer can have a different transparency.

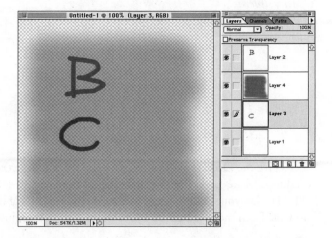

TIME SAVER

Use the Layer➡Arrange submenu to bring a layer forward or send it behind another. This menu also has transform commands to flip, rotate, scale, and distort a single layer.

Layer Blending Modes

In Hour 8, "Digital Painting," you learned about Blending modes and how they affect the way paint goes on. The same set of modes is available to you for blending layers, and the modes produce the same general effects, but only on the layers beneath the one to which you have applied the Blending mode. The layer in this case is the blend color, and the image below is the base color. As with the painting tools, the Blending modes are found on a pull-down menu on the Layers palette.

11

Just as a reminder, the Blending modes are:

- ☐ Normal
- ☐ Dissolve
- ☐ Multiply
- ☐ Screen
- ☐ Overlay
- ☐ Soft Light
- ☐ Hard Light
- ☐ Color Dodge
- ☐ Color Burn
- ☐ Darken
- ☐ Lighten
- ☐ Difference
- ☐ Exclusion
- ☐ Hue
- ☐ Saturation
- ☐ Color
- ☐ Luminosity

If you have forgotten how they work, flip back to Hour 8 to refresh your memory.

Linking Layers

If you click in the box on the Layers palette next to the eye icon, on any layer that's *not* the active layer, a piece of linked chain appears in the box. This indicates that the layer is linked to the active layer, meaning that if you move the contents of the active layer, the linked layers move with it. Figure 11.14 shows the Layers palette with linked layers.

Merging Layers

The more layers you add to an image, and the more effects you add to those layers, the larger your image file will become. If you have a large capacity hard drive and can back up to removable media, size isn't a problem.

It does, however, make a big difference if you want to use your files for anything else, such as publishing in print or on the web. The only format in which you can save a multilayered image is the Photoshop native format, which is great for Photoshop, but bad for other uses. For the web, you need to save as GIF or JPEG. For print, you probably need to save as TIFF. For any of these uses, you need to either merge layers or flatten the image when you're done working with it.

Figure 11.14

Layers linked to the active layer move with it.

Here's the difference between merging and flattening:

☐ Merging groups of layers, without flattening the entire image, conserves memory space but still enables you to work on the layers that you haven't finished. Merging Down merges a layer with the one below it. You also can merge just the visible layers, just the linked layers, and a clipping group by choosing the appropriate Layer➡Merge command.

☐ Flattening, on the other hand, compresses all visible layers down to one layer. Any layers that you have made invisible at the time of flattening are lost. To flatten an image, choose Layer➡Flatten Image, but make sure that you are done. At this point, all the layers are reduced to one.

You can use either the Layer menu or the Layer palette menu to merge or flatten layers, or the keyboard combination (Command-E) [Control-E]. Figure 11.15 shows the Layer menu with the Flatten Image command highlighted.

Figure 11.15

This compacts all the layers into one.

11

Summary

In this hour, you learned the mechanics of working with layers. You saw how to use the Layers palette and how to create, delete, and move layers. Layers are an important part of the Photoshop interface, and knowing how to apply them helps you a great deal, especially when you work with type and composite images later on.

Q&A

Q How can I convert a background to a layer?

A The easy way is to rename it. If you double-click the Background layer in the Layers palette, you open up its dialog box. By default, it appears as Layer 0. If you click OK, it's renamed and won't be the Background layer.

Q Can I add a Background layer to a page that doesn't have one?

A Yes. If there's no Background layer, use the Layer dialog box pull-down menu. At the very bottom of it is the Background option. This creates a Background layer. If it's not present in the menu, you already have a Background layer.

11

Hour 12

Using Masks

Masks can be your best friends when you're working on a complicated picture. They can also be a darned nuisance because there are several different kinds of masks you can apply to your image, and they do somewhat different things. So, you not only have to create a mask, you have to know ahead of time what you want the mask to do for you, and then you have to apply the right kind of mask.

NEW TERM So, what exactly *is* a mask? In a sense, any selection you make is a mask because it permits you to do something that affects only the selected area, effectively masking anything that's not selected. Masks let you change one part of a picture without changing all of it.

You can select a single flower from a picture of a garden and change its color without changing everything else. You can also delete the selection, which permanently masks it. Masks can cover the part of the picture you don't want to change, much like masking tape covers the woodwork you don't want to paint when you're painting the walls.

The confusion about masks comes from there being so many different types. You can have layer masks, mask channels, transparency masks, clipping paths and clipping groups, and Quick Masks. All can be used to isolate an area you want to protect while you make changes to the rest of the picture.

Applying Masks

Masks can hide a selected object or the background and can be opaque or semi-transparent. (If the mask were totally transparent, it wouldn't be a mask.) In Figure 12.1, if I want to change the background color, I need to mask the box. The easiest way to do this is to use the Magic Wand to select the background. By selecting the background and not the box, it is masked. If I wanted to change the color of the box, I could again use the Magic Wand to select the background, and then choose Select➡Inverse to invert the selection.

Figure 12.1

Selecting the background.

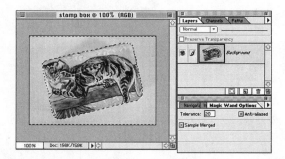

This is the most basic kind of masking. It's not always perfect, though. In Figure 12.2, you can see that the Magic Wand didn't really give us a very smooth mask. The background color appears to have leaked into the box on the left side, just by the cat's paw, and there's a bit in the upper right that got masked and shouldn't have. What's needed is a way to edit the mask.

Figure 12.2

Color change with bad masking.

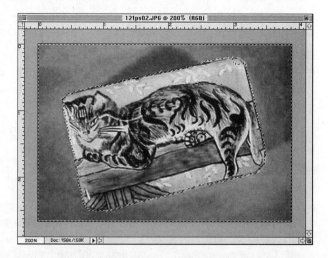

12

Using Quick Mask

Photoshop provides a very quick and easy way to make a temporary mask that can, in fact, be edited. It's called Quick Mask, and one of its advantages is that you can see both the image and the mask at the same time. You can start with a selected area and use the Paintbrush tool to add to it or take away from it, or you can create the mask entirely in Quick Mask mode. Let's apply a Quick Mask to the box.

To create a Quick Mask, follow these steps:

1. Using whatever selection tool seems appropriate, select the part of the image you want to change. It's okay if your selection isn't perfect.

2. Click the Quick Mask button at the bottom of the Toolbox (see Figure 12.3).

Figure 12.3

The Quick Mask button.

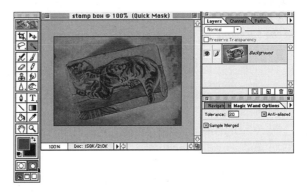

3. A color overlay appears on the protected area indicating the mask, which is to say, the area *not* selected. (By default, the mask is 50% opaque red, imitating a piece of the rubylith film that artists use to mask photos for retouching.)

4. If the mask needs editing, as this one does, select an appropriate paintbrush size from the Brushes palette and select the Paintbrush or type B to activate it.

5. Painting with black adds to the mask. Painting with white (or erasing) takes it away. Notice that the foreground and background colors changed to black and white when you entered Quick Mask mode. (If, for some reason, they didn't, type D for Default.) Painting with gray gives you a semi-transparent mask. Figure 12.4 shows the edited mask.

6. When the mask is edited to your satisfaction, click the Standard mode button in the Toolbox (to the left of the Quick Mask button) to return to your original image. The unprotected area, (in our case, the background) is surrounded by a selection marquee. Now we can apply any change we want to make to this area without affecting the area that we masked (see Figure 12.5).

12

Figure 12.4

*The mask, touched up
and ready to use.*

Figure 12.5

*I added a texture and
changed the background
color.*

7. When done making changes, type (Command-D)[Control-D] to deselect the area
   and get rid of the mask.

TIME SAVER

> If you need a straight edge on your mask, use the Line tool to draw a
> single pixel line. As long as you are in Quick Mask mode and are
> drawing with the foreground color when you draw the line, it appears in
> the mask color.

Layer Masks

Layer masks enable you to hide and reveal parts of layers, as well as apply special effects, such
as filters, in a controlled and precise manner. Layer masks, like Quick Masks, can be edited.

To make a layer mask, select an area of the image to mask and click the New Layer icon at
the bottom of the Layers palette to make a new layer. Then click the Layer Mask icon to make
the new layer into a mask. When you do, a layer mask thumbnail appears next to the image
thumbnail. Figure 12.6 shows an example. Black indicates the portions of the layer that are
covered and white shows the parts that are revealed. If the mask has been made to be semi-
transparent, the partially masked areas would be shown in gray.

Figure 12.6

Layer 1 masks everything but the sky and Layer 2 masks everything but the boat hull.

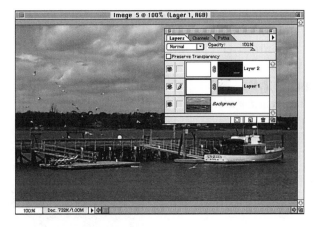

Notice the links between the two thumbnails, indicating that the mask is linked to the layer. After you create the mask, you can edit it by making the mask layer the active layer. The foreground and background colors revert to the defaults, and you can apply black to add to the mask or white to remove parts of it. To see the actual size and shape of the mask as you're working, select the part of the image to be masked, and then go to the Layer menu. Select Layer➡Add Layer Mask and choose either Hide Selection or Reveal Selection, depending on whether you're masking the area around the selected piece of image, or the image itself. Figure 12.7 shows the menu.

Figure 12.7

The Layer menu.

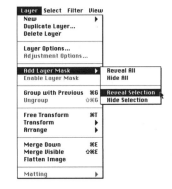

Hide Selection hides the area you have selected so that you can work on the rest of the image. If you look at Figure 12.8, you can see a layer mask for the sky in the boat picture. The black section of the layer mask is the actual mask.

With this mask, we can protect the sky and work on the rest of the picture. Reveal Selection obviously does just the opposite of the first command, Hide Selection. This command hides everything on a layer *except* that area within the marquee selection. The other commands, Hide All and Reveal All, work a little differently. These, as the names suggest, are based on the entire layer.

Figure 12.8

Black is masked, and white is editable.

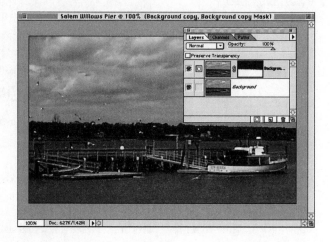

Each layer can have only one layer mask. If you need to do additional masking, activate the layer and apply Quick Mask.

JUST A MINUTE

The business of making masks can seem confusing, so let's take the process step by step. To add a mask to a layer, follow these steps:

1. Open the Layers palette, if it's not already active.
2. Select the layer to which you want to add a mask.
3. To hide the entire layer, Choose Layer➡Add Layer mask➡Hide all.
4. To make a mask that hides or reveals a selected area, first make the selection on the active layer.
5. Choose Layer➡Add Layer mask➡Hide Selection *or* Layer➡Add Layer mask➡Reveal Selection, whichever is appropriate for your needs.

Take some time now to open a picture and practice applying masks. Try Quick Mask first, and then make a selection and turn it into a layer mask. If you practice these skills while they're fresh in your mind, you'll remember them later on when you need to do a quick color change, or preserve an object while changing its background.

12

Editing Layer Masks

If you click the Layer Mask thumbnail in the Layers palette to make it active, you see the mask icon appear in the small square to the left of the layer thumbnail. This indicates that the mask is active. Select a painting tool and paint the mask with black to add to it. Paint with white to subtract from the mask. Paint with gray to make the layer partially visible. The mask thumbnail displays your changes. Figure 12.9 shows a mask being edited. I switched the view to the larger thumbnail to make it a little easier to see what I was doing. Just as a reminder, you can do this by choosing Layer Options from the Layers palette menu.

Figure 12.9

I've painted white over part of the black mask to make an A.

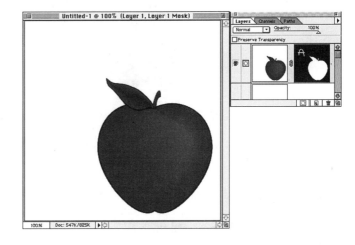

To edit the layer instead, either click its thumbnail, or go to the Layer palette menu and select Disable Layer Mask. This option puts a large X through the mask thumbnail so that you know it's inactive (see Figure 12.10).

Figure 12.10

The mask is temporarily disabled.

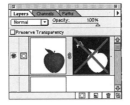

TIME SAVER

Choosing Layer➡Disable Layer Mask enables you to get rid of the effects of the layer mask temporarily. When you want it back, just choose Layers➡Enable Layer Mask and you are back in business.

Removing the Layer Mask

There are two ways for you to get rid of the layer mask when you are done with it or you want to start over. The first way, possibly the easiest, is to drag the layer mask icon found in the Layers palette onto the small trash can icon at the bottom of the window (see Figure 12.11).

Figure 12.11
Trashing a layer.

Trash icon

You also can get rid of a layer by choosing Layer➡Remove Layer Mask. Whichever way you prefer, you are presented with the following box in which you are prompted to apply the effects of the mask or discard the mask without applying it (see Figure 12.12).

Figure 12.12
Apply, Discard, or Cancel.

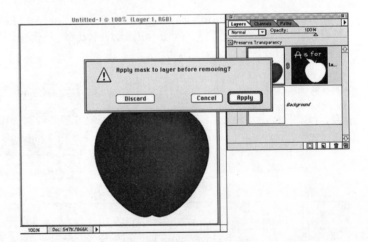

COFFEE BREAK

Channels Demystified

Even though a detailed explanation of channels and how to use them is somewhat beyond the scope of this book, a few words about channels may prove helpful to you at this point. Photoshop creates color information channels when you open a new image. An RGB document starts with four channels; one for each color and the composite that merges them. These are akin to the color separations used in four-color process printing. You can also create additional channels, called *alpha channels* in Photoshop parlance, that hold information about the masks you create for the image.

Channel thumbnails can be viewed in the Channels palette, which shares a window with the Layers palette. Click the Channels tab to open it. The composite is listed first, and then the color channels, and finally the masks or alpha channels show up at the bottom of the list. If you have made several layer masks, you may need to use the scrollbars or resize the palette to see them all. As with the layer thumbnails, you can increase the size of the channel thumbnails to see them more easily. You can also click the eye icons in the Channels palette to hide, or show, single channels in the image window. This is the function of the Channels palette that you will use most. It's often helpful to arrange the Channels palette so that you view the mask and the color composite (RGB or CMYK) channel together. By default, individual channels display in grayscale, but you can change this to see them in their own color by choosing File➡Preferences➡Display & Cursors and checking Color Channels in Color.

Masks and the Channels Palette

The mask that you add to an image creates a new channel in your image. Channels are Photoshop's way of storing color and mask information (refer to the "Channels Demystified" coffee break for more information about channels). If you add a mask to a layer and select Window➡Show Channels, you see something like the example in Figure 12.13

Click the eye icon to the left of the mask in the Channels palette and the mask appears as red, representing rubylith. The main reason for displaying the mask this way is that you can now edit it full screen, rather than by poking around and trying to see what you are doing in a tiny thumbnail. Figure 12.14 shows edits to the mask as an alpha channel.

There are other ways of creating masks, too. If you browse through Photoshop's documentation, you will find references to clipping paths and clipping groups, and to transparency masks. Unfortunately, they're beyond the scope of this book. Use the masks you have learned about in this hour. They'll serve you well in just about any situation that needs masking.

12

Figure 12.13

The Channels palette with a layer mask at the bottom.

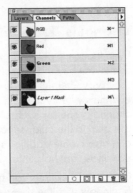

Figure 12.14

Use the Paintbrush and Eraser to edit the channel mask.

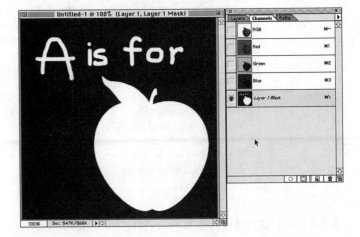

Summary

In this hour, we looked at using masks. Masking enables you to apply changes selectively, while protecting parts of the picture that you don't want to change. You learned about the Quick Mask function and how to edit a mask with the Paintbrush and Eraser. Then you learned about layer masks and how to turn a layer into a mask. Finally we looked at editing a channel mask, which is an easy way of painting and erasing parts of the mask.

Q&A

Q My picture has a lot of red in it, and the red mask is hard to see. Is there a way to change it to some other color?

A Of course. If you're working in Quick Mask mode, double-click the Quick Mask icon on the Toolbox to open the Quick Mask Options dialog box. If you're

12

working on a layer mask, (Control-click)[Option-click] to open a context menu
that gives you access to the Layer Mask Display Options dialog box. In either one,
you can set the color and amount of opacity for your mask. In the Quick Mask
Options dialog box, you can also set a radio button to determine whether the
selection or the mask is indicated by the colored area.

12

Hour 13

Paths

Congratulations! You're halfway through, which is to say that you've seen only half of what Photoshop can do.

Early on, you learned about selections and how selecting part of an image isolates that part so that you can work on it and not on the entire image. Last hour you learned about converting selections to masks to protect the parts of your image that you don't want to work on.

The problem with selections is that as soon as you remove the selection, it's lost forever. The only way to reselect something is to use the appropriate tools (Marquee, Lasso, or Magic Wand) and make the selection all over again.

Paths solve this dilemma. With paths (also called clipping paths), you can create and *save* specific selections for future use. The paths are saved right within the Photoshop file, sort of like a layer. Also, paths can be useful when you want to create complex shapes using the Pen tool.

Let's start by exploring the two different ways to create paths and then go into techniques for editing and using them in Photoshop.

Creating Paths

You can follow either of two paths for creating paths:

☐ Create the path directly from a selection you've already made.

☐ Create the path from scratch by using the Pen tool and drawing the path by hand.

Paths via Selections

Depending on the image at hand, this can be the easiest and quickest way to create a path. You simply make a selection and convert it to a path.

Let's look at an example. Figure 13.1 shows our test image, an open book on a flat-color background. If you want to isolate the book from the background, you can do so by selecting the book.

Figure 13.1

Our test image; we want a clipping path that outlines the book.

As you remember, selecting can be accomplished by using a number of tools. For this image, the Magic Wand is perfect because the background pixels are roughly the same color. Simply set the Magic Wand Tolerance to about 25 (so you're sure to get all the background pixels), select the background, and then invert the selection (Select➥Inverse) so that the book image is selected (see Figure 13.2).

Figure 13.2

The book is now selected.

13

Now that you have a selection, follow these steps to convert it to a path:

1. Make sure that the Paths palette is visible. If not, choose Window➡Show Paths.

2. Select Make Work Path from the Paths palette menu (see Figure 13.3).

Figure 13.3

The Paths palette menu.

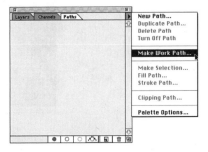

3. The only thing to set in the Make Work Path dialog box is Tolerance (see Figure 13.4). Tolerance refers to how closely Photoshop follows the outline of your selection in creating the path. The smaller the tolerance, the more exact the path is.

Figure 13.4

The Make Work Path dialog box.

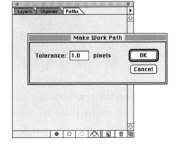

For this image, I first tried a Tolerance setting of 5 pixels. As Figure 13.5 shows, the results were unacceptable. Photoshop was too flexible and approximate in creating the path at this setting. You can see that the smoother line of the path does not follow the outline of the book closely enough.

When this happens, I simply reach for my favorite Photoshop command: Undo. Undo the path conversion and try a lower Tolerance setting. After some experimentation, I found that a value of 1 pixel worked quite well (see Figure 13.6).

CAUTION

Be aware that complex paths can be resource-intensive. More complexity means more points, angles, curves, and so on. The result can mean slower processing of the image, bigger files, and possible problems when printing. It is definitely something to be aware of.

Figure 13.5

When the path doesn't match the selection to your satisfaction, Tolerance is set too high.

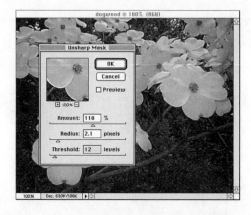

Figure 13.6

When Tolerance is set correctly, the path matches the selection satisfactorily.

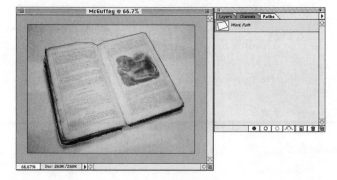

4. Note how the path also appears in the Paths palette. Photoshop has named it Work Path. You can rename the path by simply double-clicking it in the Paths palette. In the Save Path dialog box that appears, type the new path name and click OK (see Figure 13.7).

Figure 13.7

Rename paths by using the Save Path dialog box.

13

Although renaming paths isn't required, it's a good idea, especially if your Photoshop document will eventually have multiple paths in it. If you don't rename a path after saving it, and then create a second path, the second path *replaces* the first path in the Paths palette. Don't worry: Both paths still exist, and you can still recover the first path by selecting it and choosing Save Paths from the Paths palette menu. But if that seems like too much hassle and confusion to you, rename each path as you create it!

Paths via the Pen Tool

Sometimes making a selection is too difficult or requires too much work on a particular image. In that case, consider using the Pen tool and drawing the path by hand.

If you've used vector-based illustration programs, such as Adobe Illustrator or Macromedia FreeHand, you already know about *Bézier*-based drawing tools such as Photoshop's Pen tool. If you haven't used these kinds of tools before, you should know right up front that it takes a little practice, but the payoff is worth the effort.

 A *Bézier curve* is a curve defined by three points: one on the curve and two outside the curve at the ends of handles that you can use to change the angle and direction of the curve. If this sounds like gibberish, don't worry, you'll see some examples.

The best way to learn how to use the Pen tool is to play around with it in a new Photoshop document, so that's what we're going to do in this tutorial.

1. Create a new Photoshop document big enough to move around in; 6×6 inches sounds good. A plain white background looks good.

2. Select the Pen tool. Also make sure that the Paths palette is visible.

3. Click somewhere near the left-hand edge of the image. This is where your path begins. (Notice that Photoshop immediately creates a path called Work Path in the Paths palette. This path can be renamed the same way as in the previous section.)

4. To draw a straight line, move your cursor and click somewhere else. You've just created a *corner point*, which means that Photoshop connects the two points with a straight line (see Figure 13.8).

5. To continue the path but now with a curved line, move your cursor to the middle bottom of the window and then click and drag leftward. You'll see a curve immediately appear and change as you drag it (see Figure 13.9). You've just created a *smooth point*, which means that Photoshop creates a smooth curve where two curved line segments meet.

13

Figure 13.8

A simple click creates a corner point and a straight line.

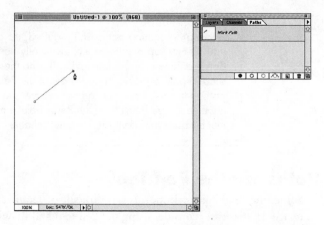

Figure 13.9

A click-and-drag action creates a smooth point and a curved line.

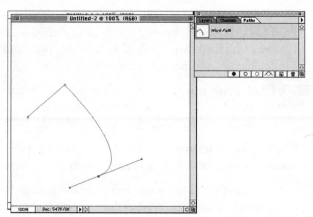

6. To make this clearer, draw another smooth curve. Move your cursor to the center of the window; then click and drag to the right and a bit down. Again, a smooth point and a curve are created (see Figure 13.10).

   The point you created in Step 5 creates a nice smooth curve between the point you just created and the point you created in Step 4. That's what a smooth point is all about.

   As you have no doubt noticed, creating smooth points also results in the appearance of two *handles* for each point. These handles can be used to change the angle and direction of a curve after you've initially established it. You learn more about them later in the "Editing Paths" section later in this chapter.

Okay, that's the basics: straight lines via corner points and curved lines via smooth points. But there's more that you have to know about each one to use them effectively.

Figure 13.10

Click and drag to create another smooth point on the same path.

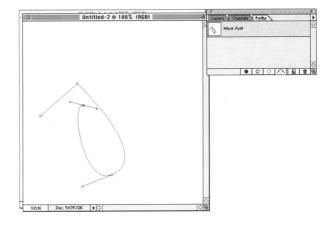

Corner Points

Corner points are easy. No matter what kind of line is coming into a corner point, the result is always an angle, not a curve. If a curved line comes into a corner point, it's the smooth point at the other end of that line that affects the line's angle (see Figure 13.11).

Figure 13.11

Corner points surround a smooth point.

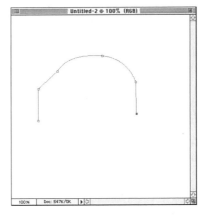

TIME SAVER

If you want to constrain corner points so that they appear only at 45- or 90-degree angles, hold down the Shift key while you click to create the point.

Smooth Points

As you saw in the first Pen tool example, the behavior of smooth points is a bit more complicated and takes some getting used to. A smooth point will always try to create as smooth a curve as it can between two meeting lines (see Figure 13.12).

Figure 13.12
Smooth points do their utmost to create curves out of any situation.

There is a less smooth kind of curve you can create when you need it. It's called a *sharp curve*, and here is how you create one:

1. In a new Photoshop document, begin a path with an initial point.

2. Create a smooth point as you normally would, making one curve.

3. Move the pointer so that it's exactly over the smooth point you just created. Hold down the (Option)[Alt] while you click and drag the mouse in the direction of the bump in the new curve. Release the key and mouse button. Your screen should look similar to Figure 13.13.

Figure 13.13
Creating a sharp curve. The rightmost line is what I just created by using the (Option)[Alt] key.

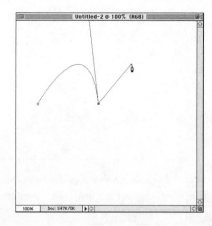

4. Move the cursor to where you want the line to end; then click and drag in the opposite direction you dragged in Step 3. Figure 13.14 shows the resulting sharp curve.

13

Figure 13.14

The final sharp curve.

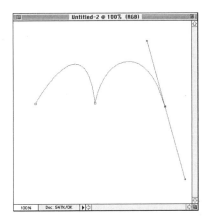

Previewing the Path

When you're creating all these points and lines, there's a preview feature that can be very helpful. Double-click the Pen tool in the Toolbox to bring up the Pen Tool Options palette. The only option here is called Rubber Band. Activating this feature enables you to preview both straight lines and curves before you click to create them. Experiment to see this feature at work.

Completing the Path

To complete a path, you have two choices: close the path by connecting the final point to the initial point, or leave the path open.

A closed path means you have created a loop, so the final path has no beginning or end. To close a path, use the following steps:

1. Create a path by using whatever points you need.
2. After the last point, move your cursor so that it appears on top of your initial point. You'll see a small circle next to the Pen pointer.
3. Click to create a final corner point or click and drag to create a final curve (see Figure 13.15).

An open path means the path has a beginning and an end. Figures 13.10 through 13.14 have all been open paths. To end a path that you want to keep open, use the following steps:

1. Create a path by using whatever points you need.
2. After the last point, click the Pen tool in the Toolbox. The path now has an end.

   The next time you click in the image, you start a new path instead of continuing your previous path.

13

Figure 13.15

Closing a path with a final corner point click.

Another Way to Make Paths

There's also another way to create a path from a selection. Make a selection, then click the Make Work Path button at the bottom of the Paths palette (see Figure 13.16). Photoshop creates the path using the existing Tolerance setting. Don't forget to rename the path using the Save Path dialog box!

JUST A MINUTE

> Saying that you've created "a path" is a little misleading. Actually, the path that you see consists of a number of subpaths that Photoshop has created. But for our purposes, they act as a single path. One thing to remember is that any path you create is not really *part* of the image. That is, you aren't changing the actual image at all. Think of it as adding a new layer to an image, like a layer of clear acetate that helps you manipulate an image better, but doesn't necessarily alter it in any way.

Figure 13.16

Here I've created a new path around the flower. Photoshop uses the same 1-pixel setting I used earlier.

13

Editing Paths

Most of the time, the initial path you create, whether produced by converting a selection or drawing with the Pen tool, won't be perfect. It's often too difficult to get the selection just right or the lines and curves perfectly placed on the first try. You probably realized this while following the previous steps in this chapter.

Fortunately, you can easily alter paths after they are created. And, once again, you use the Pen tool (and its associated tools) to do this.

The Path Tools

First, let's look at the various path tools available in Photoshop. Click and hold on the Pen tool (see Figure 13.17).

Figure 13.17

Photoshop's path tools.

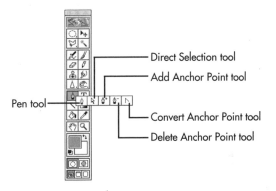

Direct Selection tool

Add Anchor Point tool

Pen tool

Convert Anchor Point tool

Delete Anchor Point tool

☐ **Pen tool:** You already know this tool intimately. It's used to create new paths.

☐ **Direct Selection tool:** This is the tool to use for selecting and moving points and handles. Hold down the (Command)[Control] key while using any other path tool, and this tool is temporarily in use.

☐ **Add Anchor Point tool:** Use this tool to add points to a path.

☐ **Delete Anchor Point tool:** Use this tool to cut points from a path.

☐ **Convert Anchor Point tool:** Yes, you can even change the *type* of point after you have initially created it. For example, you can turn a corner point into a smooth point, a smooth point into a sharp curve, and so on. You'll learn more about this tool in the next section.

You can switch between these tools in one of two ways: either by clicking and holding down the Pen tool in the Toolbox so that the other path tools appear, or by pressing P on the keyboard, which cycles through all the path tools.

13

Basic Path Techniques

Here are a few basic techniques for navigating through and using paths:

☐ To select a path, click its name in the Paths palette, just as you'd click a layer to activate it. Selected paths show up in your image, as you'd expect.

☐ To deselect a path, click another path name or click elsewhere in the empty area of the Paths palette. This makes the path disappear in the main window.

☐ To delete a path, select the path in the Paths palette and drag it to the Trash Can button at the bottom of the palette, just as you'd delete a layer.

☐ To create a new path, you can do one of three things: simply start drawing the path in the main image window; choose New Path from the palette's pull-down menu; or click the Create New Path button at the bottom of the palette.

☐ To duplicate a path, select the desired path in the palette and drag it to the Create New Path button. This works in the same manner as duplicating a layer does.

Using Paths

So what can you do with paths after you've gone to all the trouble of creating them? In Photoshop, you can use paths to remember selections that you want to use repeatedly. You can also fill a path area or define the color, border, and so on of the outline of the path. Paths indicate selections or lines, but they don't actually appear on your canvas unless you add some paint to make them show up. You can fill a path, stroke it, or both. Stroking adds a stroke of paint over the path. Fill places a color or pattern inside the path.

CAUTION

> When you fill a path, you are adding pixels to the active layer of your picture. Make sure that the layer you want to put the paint on is the active one.

Turning Paths into Selections

In Photoshop, paths are most useful as permanently saved selections. This can be incredibly helpful when you think you might want to reuse a specific selection later. When in doubt, create a path so that the selection is always available!

You already learned how to convert a selection to a path. Here's how to convert a path into a selection:

1. Create a path through whatever means suit your fancy.
2. Activate the path you want to convert by clicking it in the Paths palette.

3. Choose Make Selection from the Paths palette menu.

4. In the Make Selection dialog box that appears, you can set the tolerance of the selection that Photoshop creates (see Figure 13.18). The higher the Feather Radius setting, the less exact the selection is.

Figure 13.18

The Make Selection dialog box.

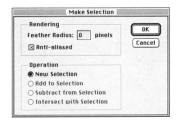

5. Click OK, and you'll see the path turn into a selection.

Filling a Path

Filling a path means just what you'd expect. Select a path, choose Fill Path from the Paths palette menu, and you get the same kinds of options you get for filling a selection (see Figure 13.19). In the Fill Path dialog box, you can choose a color, a pattern, or a snapshot to fill the area with. You can also choose a Blending mode, opacity percentage, optional transparency, anti-aliasing, and a feathering value (everything you already learned about in previous hours).

Figure 13.19

The Fill Path dialog box.

Stroking a Path

Stroking a path means affecting the outline of the path, not the entire area enclosed within a path. Select a path and then choose Stroke Path from the Paths palette menu. The dialog box enables you to choose the tool you want to use, from Pencil and Paintbrush to Blur and Sponge.

Whatever tool you pick, Photoshop uses that tool's current settings to create the result. So, for example, if you want to airbrush the path outline with only 60% pressure, make sure that value is set in the Airbrush Tool Options palette *before* you select Stroke Path (see Figure 13.20).

Figure 13.20

The Stroke Subpath dialog box.

There are shortcuts for filling and for stroking. Hold your mouse pointer over the buttons at the bottom of the Paths palette, and you'll see the options.

Summary

The path is a magical Photoshop feature that has many applications in your daily Photoshop existence. You can use paths as permanent Photoshop selections that can be reused anytime, as methods to fill or stroke part of an image, as a way to convert areas of an image or work on an image in Illustrator, or as clipping paths to be exported into a page layout program. Photoshop provides an array of tools and options for creating paths: You can do so by converting a selection you have already made, or by drawing a path from scratch by using the Pen tool. You can also edit existing paths with the assorted path tools.

Q&A

Q If I need to draw a square box inside my picture, how would I use the path tool to do it?

A Select the Path tool and draw the shape you need. Then, select the path you've drawn, and choose Stroke subpath from the Path palette menu. This gives you a line in the shape of the path. To fill it in, select Fill Subpath. The dialog boxes that appear enable you to choose a color.

13

Hour **14**

Filters That Improve Your Picture

I don't know whether Photoshop's creators pioneered the idea of filters or just took the ball and ran with it. In either case, they've given us a wonderful tool for altering the all-over appearance of a picture. Some of Photoshop's filters are strange. Some are beautiful. Some are merely useful, and those are the ones we'll look at in this hour.

The title for this hour's lesson doesn't really tell the story. Presumably, you wouldn't apply a filter that *didn't* improve your picture. What would be the point? It might be more correct to say that the filters we'll be looking at fix common photographic problems.

Sharpening Filters

One of the most common problems is the out of focus picture. There are many reasons why a picture might be fuzzy. The subject or the photographer might have moved slightly. Perhaps the camera wasn't focused correctly. Or possibly the picture was taken with an inexpensive camera with a poor quality plastic lens. Some of these problems are easier to compensate for than others.

If a photo is really way out of focus, there's not much that can be done to bring it back. If it's just a little bit soft, Photoshop can at least create the illusion of sharper focus. It does this with a set of filters called Sharpen. As with all the filters described in this chapter, they're found on the Filter menu (see Figure 14.1).

Figure 14.1

The Filter menu.

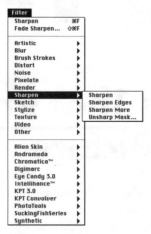

Sharpen and Sharpen More

The first two sharpen filters, Sharpen and Sharpen More provide different amounts of the same function. They work by finding areas in the image where there are significant color changes, such as at the edges of an object. Whenever such an area is found, Photoshop increases the contrast between adjacent pixels, making the lights lighter and the darks darker. Figure 14.2 shows three views of a piece of a photo. The first example is "before" sharpening. The second example has had Sharpen applied, and the third, Sharpen More.

JUST A MINUTE

These filters, unlike most of the ones you'll encounter, don't have dialog boxes that let you determine how they are applied. The amount of sharpening is preset.

Figure 14.2
Before and after sharpening.

Original photo

Sharpen filter

Sharpen More filter

If you don't enlarge the picture too much, the effect looks quite good. But if you take a close look, as we have in Figure 14.3, you can see that it's really quite artificial looking.

Sharpen More is the same effect as applying the Sharpen filter twice to the same picture. Keep in mind that you can do this, any time a filter has less than the desired effect. The easy way to apply the same filter again is to type (Command-F) [Control-F]. This keyboard shortcut applies whatever filter and filter settings (if any) you applied last.

Try the Sharpen filter on one of your own pictures and see what you think. Does it help? Try the Sharpen More filter also. These are great for adjusting slightly out of focus photographs or scans, but don't rely on these filters too much. They can't add what is totally missing from

14

the image—namely focus and good contrast. They can, however, help a picture that is just a little bit off.

Figure 14.3
Sharpen More magnified to 300%.

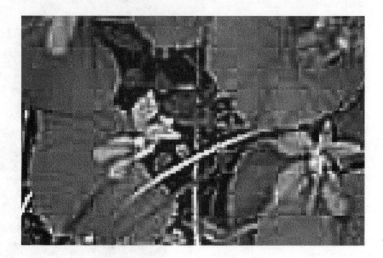

Sharpen Edges

Sharpen Edges is a truly useful filter. It doesn't affect the whole image, so you don't get as much of that harsh blocky effect as with Sharpen More, but Sharpen Edges sees and enhances the contrast at whatever it perceives to be an edge. Figure 14.4 shows a before and after version of a bunch of flowers. Sharpening the edges has a slight but noticeable effect on the quality of the photo.

Unsharp Mask

Unsharp masking is a traditional technique used in the printing industry for many years. It is probably your best bet for precision sharpening. It corrects blurring in the original image or scan as well as any blurring that occurs during the resampling and printing process. The Unsharp Mask works by locating every two adjacent pixels with a difference in brightness values you have specified, and increasing their contrast by an amount you specify. It enables you to really control the sharpness of an image.

Set the amount of sharpening you need in the Unsharp Mask dialog box (see Figure 14.5). The Radius control sets the number of surrounding pixels to which the sharpening effect is applied. I suggest that you keep the Radius setting fairly low—around 2.0. The Threshold setting controls how much alike pixels must be to be sharpened. The lower the setting, the more similar pixels have to be. The higher the setting, the greater Photoshop's tolerance of difference. (Of course, as always, feel free to go wild and try all of the settings. That is the best way to learn.)

14

Figure 14.4

The Sharpen Edges filter.

Before

After

Figure 14.5

The window lets you see what effect your settings have.

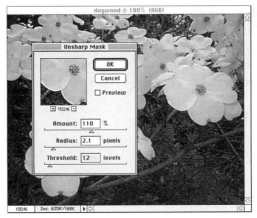

Many Photoshop experts recommend always applying the Unsharp Mask filter to every image that you process, whether it's going to be printed or used on the web. (I personally don't like to say "always" or "never" because there can be exceptions to any rule.) You should probably try it on every image to see whether or not you like the effect.

14

Photoshop filters aren't restricted to Photoshop. Other Adobe products, such as PageMaker and Illustrator, can use them also. Even Macromedia's Director can employ certain Photoshop filters.

Blur Filters

The Blur filters (Filter➡Blur) are useful tools when you want to soften the effects of a filter you have just applied or of brushstrokes in a painting. Blurring can gently smooth a harshly lit portrait, or, when used on a selection instead of the whole image, it can throw an unwanted background out of focus, making it less obtrusive. The Blur filters include

- ☐ Blur
- ☐ Blur More
- ☐ Gaussian Blur
- ☐ Motion Blur
- ☐ Radial Blur
- ☐ Smart Blur

Blur, Blur More

The two basic blur filters, Blur and Blur More, do exactly as their names suggest. Blur is very subtle. Blur More is only a little less so. Figure 14.6 shows a comparison of the two against a non-blurred original. As you can see, the changes are minor. Blurring doesn't make much difference, but it can smooth out wrinkles in a portrait or soften a hard edge. As with the Sharpen and Sharpen More filters, these aren't adjustable.

Figure 14.6

You have to look carefully to see the effect.

No blur
Blur
Blur more

Gaussian Blur

You can apply the Blur filter several times in order to get the effect you want, or you can move on to Gaussian Blur (Filter➡Blur➡Gaussian Blur), which is more controllable. The Gaussian Blur filter uses a mathematical formula (the Gaussian Distribution Equation or bell curve) to calculate the precise transition between each pair of pixels. The result is that most of the blurred pixels end up in the middle of the two colors or values, rather than at either end of the spectrum, producing a generalized blur that neither darkens or lightens the image. We'll use the Gaussian Blur filter later on to create drop-shadow effects.

The Gaussian Blur dialog box, shown in Figure 14.7, lets you determine exactly how much blur to apply by setting a Radius value from 0.1–255. You can also use it to anti-alias the edges of an object, and to blur shadow areas when you want to create a drop-shadow effect. Even at fairly small settings, the Gaussian Blur filter has quite a dramatic effect. Anything over 5.0 would make the image incomprehensible.

Figure 14.7

Smaller numbers give you less blur.

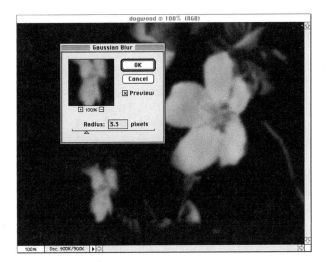

The Gaussian Blur filter is a useful retouching tool when applied to an area within the picture that you want to de-emphasize. The photo in Figure 14.8 was shot at a wildlife park in Canada. The tiger looks very happy, lying in his patch of sunshine, but we can also see the chain link fence behind him and the wire-wrapped tree he's leaning against. It would be a better picture if we got rid of these reminders of civilization. Obviously, we don't want to blur the tiger's stripes. So, rather than applying the blur to the whole image, we need to select the fence and tree. Clicking the Magic Wand tool on the area in question selects it, and then we can adjust the blur radius until the fencing disappears.

14

Figure 14.8

Selective blurring can hide flaws, too.

Careful inspection shows that although the Blur filter took out most of the fence, there are still a few spots on the tree where we can see chain links. A quick application of the Blur tool, with pressure set to 75%, blends these in, and the tiger appears to be back in the wilderness again.

TIME SAVER

> Use the Blur filters when you have a large area to blur. Use the Blur tool when you just want to soften a small area. It's more controllable, in terms of the degree of focus change it applies.

Radial Blur

The Radial Blur filter can be interesting if you carefully choose how to apply it. It gives you two choices: Spin and Zoom. Spin gives you a blur that looks as if the image is spinning around its center point. Zoom theoretically gives you the effect of zooming the camera into or away from the image. Imagine looking at a picture that was taken while the photographer was running (Zoom) or doing a somersault (Radial). It's almost enough to make you seasick. These filters aren't especially useful except for special effects, but they are fun to play with.

Figure 14.9 shows the Radial Blur dialog box. In it, you can set both an amount for the blur effect (from 1–100) and a quality level (Draft, Good, or Best). Amount refers to the distance that the pixels are moved to create the blur. You can see the difference in the window as you set the blur amount. You can also use the same window to determine a center point for the blur effect.

The Quality Level settings determine the manner in which the blur effect is calculated; you can choose Draft, Good, or Best. Figure 14.10 shows a comparison of the three different quality levels on a single image. As you can see, there's very little difference in quality between

Good and Best. The biggest difference, in fact, is not in the image quality but in how long it takes Photoshop to compute and apply the blur in each mode. Best can take quite a long time, if the image is complex and if your computer is an older model.

Figure 14.9
*The same dialog box
applies both Zoom and
Spin.*

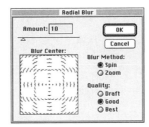

Figure 14.10
*From left to right: Draft,
Good, and Best.*

Smart Blur

The Smart Blur filter (Filter➡Blur➡Smart Blur) is probably the most useful one of the bunch, especially for image editing and photo repair. It blurs everything in the image, or selection, except the edges. Smart Blur calculates the differences between color regions to determine boundaries, and it maintains these boundaries while blurring everything within them. It's the perfect filter when you need to take 10 years off a portrait subject's face or smooth out the texture in a piece of cloth without losing the folds.

Figure 14.11 shows the Smart Blur filter dialog box and Figure 14.12 shows before and after views of the filter applied to a portrait. You can set the Radius and Threshold to determine how much blur is applied, and also the Quality, as shown earlier, to determine how the effect is calculated.

The Smart Blur filter has three modes:

☐ **Normal mode:** The preview window shows the effects of the blurring.

☐ **Edge Only:** Shows you the outlines that Smart Blur is working with.

☐ **Edge Overlay:** Shows the outlines as black lines on top of the image.

You can use the Edge Overlay or Edge Only to help you determine what threshold to set. Convert the mode back to Normal before you click OK to apply the effect.

Figure 14.11
*If you overdo the blur,
the face starts to look like
a plastic mask.*

Figure 14.12
*On the left: before; on the
right: after.*

Motion Blur

When we see lines drawn behind a car, a cat, or a comic strip character, we instinctively know that it or he is supposed to be in motion. Those lines represent "motion blur," which is actually a photographic mistake caused by using a slow shutter speed on a fast subject. The image appears blurred against its background because it actually traveled some distance during the fraction of a second that the camera shutter was open. In the early days of photography, motion blur was a common occurrence because shutter speeds were slow and film sensitivity was not great. Today, motion blur is unusual unless the photographer has planned to try to capture it this way on purpose, by using the least sensitive film available or using a small lens opening and a correspondingly slower shutter. If you want to try to approximate the effect of motion blur, however, Photoshop gives you a tool that can do it.

14

The Motion Blur filter (Filter➡Blur➡Motion blur) can add the appearance of motion to a stationary object by placing a directional blur for a predetermined distance. In the Motion Blur dialog box shown in Figure 14.13, you can set both the distance and direction of the blur according to how fast and in what direction you want the object to appear to be traveling. Distance sets how much of a blur is applied—or how far the original image is "moved." Angle sets the direction of the blur. To adjust, drag the radius icon or enter precise values into the field next to it. The trick, however, is to select the right area to which to apply it. To get a convincing blur, you need to blur the space where the object theoretically was, as well as where it theoretically has moved to.

Figure 14.13

Using the Motion Blur filter is tricky at best.

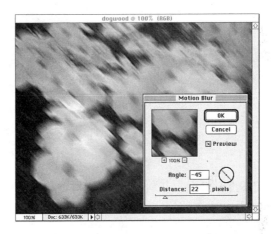

The Motion Blur filter doesn't do much for most pictures. After all, the camera shake blur is the kind of thing we try to avoid, not add. But for some special effects, and for doing tricks with type, it has interesting possibilities. Figure 14.14 shows one possible use. Adding motion blur gave us a much zoomier zoom. But we could even take this further.

This time I took the word apart, cutting and pasting each letter to a different layer. I then applied a different (increasing left to right) number of pixels to each motion blur, from 6 pixels on the Z to 24 pixels on the M. The resulting zoom, which you can see in Figure 14.15, almost seems to be sliding into the screen.

TIME SAVER

The type used in this exercise was generated with Adobe Type Twister, a wonderful little program that lets you do all sorts of strange and occasionally beautiful things to typography. If you do any web publishing or desktop publishing, you ought to have it available. You can buy it from your friendly software dealer, and it's often bundled with Adobe fonts or drawing programs.

14

Figure 14.14
You can't Zoom standing still.

Figure 14.15
Using layers lets you apply different filters or different degrees of filter to the same image.

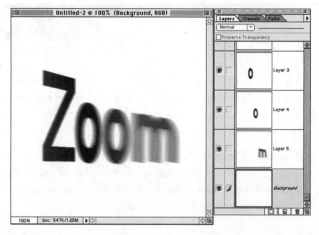

Fading Your Filters

Filters are cool, but sometimes they just do a little too much to the image. Many, such as the Motion Blur filter are variable. You can set their effects to be as subtle or dramatic as you wish. Others, such as Blur and Sharpen, don't have dialog boxes and don't give you the opportunity

14

to apply any less than the full amount of effect that Photoshop thinks is right. Well, Papa Photoshop *doesn't* always know best. But you do have an option.

You can apply a filter and then choose Filter➡Fade to fade the effect anywhere from 1–99%. You can also use the Fade box to set a Blending mode for the fade effect. Even more important, in the same dialog box, shown in Figure 14.16, you can fade whatever you last did. Painted something but the color was too strong? Fade it 50%. That's quicker than redoing it with a different color. Overdid an image color adjustment? Fade it. Experiment with this feature. It can save you tons of time.

Figure 14.16

The Fade dialog box.

To fade a filter effect or color adjustment:

1. Apply the filter or make the color adjustment (Image➡Adjust).
2. Choose Filter➡Fade. If you're working on a selection, rather than the whole image, don't deselect it.
3. Set the preview option so you can see the effect of the fade.
4. Drag the slider to adjust the opacity.
5. Choose a Blending mode other than normal if you want a particular effect.
6. Click OK. Deselect the selection to merge it.

Summary

Photoshop's filters are the tools that make the program a "must have" for anyone working with photos. In this hour, we looked at the Photoshop filters that can help you "rescue" a bad photo or bad scan. The sharpen filters can restore the apparent focus in out-of-focus photographs by increasing the contrast between adjacent pixels. The most useful of these is the Unsharp Mask filter, which enables you to set the parameters for how it finds and adjusts contrasts.

Blur filters come in several varieties and are most useful for putting unwanted parts of the picture out of focus and for softening hard edges. The Motion Blur filter lets you create the illusion of movement in stationary objects and do interesting things to type.

Fade works with filters and other Photoshop tools to decrease the effect of your action by a percentage you can set.

14

Q&A

Q What's the difference between the Blur filter and the Blur tool?

A You can apply the Blur tool as if it were a paintbrush to as small an area as you
want. (The Blur tool was covered in Hour 9.) The Blur filter blurs the entire image
or selection evenly.

Q If I change my mind about applying a filter, can I stop the process?

A To cancel the filter as it's being applied, press (Command- . (period))[Esc]. To
Undo a filter, press (Command-Z)[Control-Z].

Hour 15

Filters to Make Your Picture Artistic

In Hour 10, you saw how Photoshop's filters can help imitate other media. We looked specifically at the Watercolor, Colored Pencil, Charcoal, and Underpainting filters. But those are still just the tip of the iceberg. Under the general heading of artistic and sketch filters, there are about thirty different filters that can be applied alone or in combinations to turn your so-so picture into a masterpiece. In this hour, we will run through the alphabet of the artistic, brush stroke, and sketch effects. You will be amazed, boggled, confounded, delighted, ecstatic…

JUST A MINUTE

I've deliberately left out the step-by-step instructions in this chapter. All of these filters are applied in the same way: Filter→Artistic→ and so on. Use the dialog box and its preview window to judge the effects of the filter as you change the settings. The key to success with any of these filters is to experiment until you get the effect you want. If you don't like what you see when you apply it to the whole picture, undo or revert.

Artistic Filters

Artistic filters apply a certain amount of abstraction to your image. How much depends on the kind of filter and to an even greater degree on how you set the filter's variables. Many of these filters ask you to set Brush Size, Detail, and Texture. Brush Size affects the thickness of the line. Detail determines how large a "clump" of pixels must be in order for the filter to, in effect, notice it and apply its changes. Texture, not to be confused with the Texturizer filter, adds a random smudge here and there in your image.

Most of Photoshop's filters have a preview window in which you can see the effects of changing the settings before you apply the filter. To move the image inside the preview window, click it. The cursor turns into a hand, enabling you to slide the picture around to see the effect on specific parts of the image. If you change settings and the preview doesn't change right away, you see a thin line between the plus and minus symbols beneath the magnification amount number. This line tells you that Photoshop is calculating the changes to apply. Click the plus or minus symbol to see a reduced or enlarged view within the preview window.

For the sake of consistency, we'll apply all of the artistic filters to this picture of the Fisherman's Wharf sign. See Figure 15.1 for the unfiltered view.

Figure 15.1

Basic, non-artistic photo.

Colored Pencil

The Colored Pencil filter goes over the photo with a sort of cross-hatched effect (see Figure 15.2). It keeps most of the colors of the original photograph, though any large flat areas are translated to "paper" color, which you can set to any shade of gray from black to white or to

15

15

any color you like. The Colored Pencil dialog box, shown in Figure 15.3, asks you to choose a pencil width and stroke pressure.

Using a narrow pencil (low number) gives you more lines. Greater stroke pressure picks up more detail from the original picture. In Figure 15.2, we used a small pencil and heavy pressure. In Figure 15.4, we've reversed these, using a pencil width of 22 and a stroke pressure of 2. As you can see, the result is quite different.

Figure 15.2
The Colored Pencil filter.

Figure 15.3
Colored Pencil filter settings.

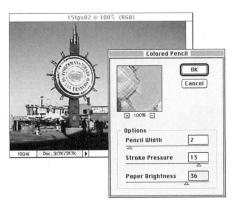

TIME SAVER

The main trick to remember when using the Colored Pencil filter is that any large light areas will be filled with the background color. Choose colors before you apply the filter, and select a light background color if you want to keep the tonal balance of the original.

Figure 15.4
More pencil, less pressure.

Cutout

The Cutout filter is one of my favorites. It can reduce your picture to something resembling a cut paper collage or a silk screen print. It does so by averaging all of the colors and shades and converting them to just a handful. You can decide how many by setting a number of levels from 2 to 8 in the filter's dialog box. You can also set Edge Fidelity (1–3) and Edge Simplicity (1–10) in the dialog box, which is shown in Figure 15.5.

Figure 15.5
The Cutout dialog box.

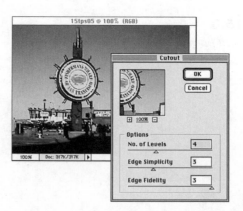

Low Simplicity and high Fidelity settings produced the picture in Figure 15.6, which seems to be the most pleasing variation for this filter and photo combination. It's important to experiment with different settings every time you apply a filter to a new photo. What works

15

with one picture may be totally wrong for another that is more, or less, complicated. Still, in one combination or another, this filter manages to make almost any picture look good.

Figure 15.6

The Cutout Filter applied to the image.

Dry Brush

Dry brush is a term used by watercolor painters to denote a particular style in which the brush is loaded with heavily concentrated pigment and dabbed, rather than stroked, on the paper. Figure 15.7 shows the Dry Brush filter's dialog box, in which I set a small brush and high amount of detail. The result is shown in Figure 15.8.

Figure 15.7

The Dry Brush dialog box.

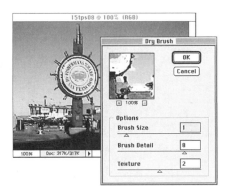

This filter both darkens and reduces the detail in the picture. It works best when applied to light photos with large flat areas. If your picture is dark to begin with, you may not be happy with the results of the Dry Brush filter.

Figure 15.8

*This filter can be very
exciting when applied to
the right picture.*

Film Grain

One of the reasons that many commercial photographers are turning to high resolution
digital photography is to get away from the problems caused by film grain. Film grain is the
inevitable result of applying a layer of chemicals to a piece of plastic. When a picture is
enlarged a great deal, you see the graininess of the chemicals as specks in the picture. Why
Photoshop's creators decided this was an effect worth achieving is beyond me. But it can add
an interesting texture quality to your pictures if you apply it carefully. This is an effect that
should be applied to selections, rather than to the whole photo. Figure 15.9 shows what
happens when it's misapplied.

Figure 15.9

*Bad use of Film Grain
filter.*

15

Notice how it picks up the shading in the sky. It makes the picture look gritty. A better use is shown in Figure 15.10. Here, I have applied the grain just to the background, keeping the shiny peppers untouched. The contrast in textures makes the picture more interesting. This used the following settings: Grain -4; Highlight area -2; Intensity -8.

Figure 15.10
Better use of the Film Grain filter.

Fresco

Fresco is an Italian term for a mural painting done on a wet, freshly plastered wall. Photoshop's Fresco filter has little resemblance to the classical fresco works by such artists as Botticelli or Michaelangelo. It's an interesting filter, however, and possibly useful. You need to be careful not to let the picture get too dark, as the Fresco filter adds a good deal of black to the image in the process of abstracting it. Figure 15.11 shows an example.

Neon Glow

It's hard to understand how this filter got its name. It has no resemblance to neon. What it does, as you can probably tell in Figure 15.12, is reduce the image to a single color negative and add highlights around the edges of objects. It applies the background and foreground colors plus a third "glow" color. You can choose a "glow" color in the dialog box and specify the width of the "glow." If you use a very light color or gray, it can produce an interesting, sort of watermark effect.

TIME SAVER

Applied to a landscape, the Neon Glow can give you an spaced-out, surrealistic effect. It doesn't do much for portraits, however.

Figure 15.11
A fresh approach, if not exactly a fresco.

Figure 15.12
The Neon Glow filter.

Paint Daubs

The Paint Daub filter adds an interesting square crosshatch texture to the image. You can set Brush Size and Sharpness, and choose among several brushes. Figure 15.13 shows the Wide Blurry brush. Experiment with the settings on this one. Some work much better than others.

15

TIME SAVER

This filter looks great with most kinds of landscapes and still life. If you use the Simple brush and keep the settings small (less than 10), it turns an ordinary portrait photo into an extraordinary one. If you like the works of Andrew Wyeth, you will like this filter.

Figure 15.13
The Paint Daub filter.

Palette Knife and Plastic Wrap

When a painter uses a palette knife, the result is large areas of smudged color that blends interestingly at the edges. This filter, alas, doesn't do that. Instead the Palette Knife filter reduces the picture to blocks of color by grouping similar pixels and averaging them. The result is not very interesting and not worth reproducing.

Plastic Wrap is another filter that probably should have been left in the bit bucket (the programmer's trash can). It places a gray film over the whole picture and then adds white "highlights" around large objects. It's supposed to look as if you had covered the scene with plastic film. Instead, it looks more like you'd poured liquid latex over it.

Poster Edges

Here's a filter that *is* worth playing with. Poster Edges locates all of the edges in your image, judging by the amount of contrast between adjacent pixels, and posterizes them, placing a dark line around the edges (see Figure 15.14). Unfortunately, it also breaks up large flat areas such as the sky in our sample picture. Use it on selected areas for best results.

Figure 15.14
The Poster Edges filter.

Rough Pastels

Rough Pastels is a terrific filter. Its interface is a little bit more complicated than the others because you can specify texture as well as the stroke length and detail. Figure 15.15 shows its dialog box. Choose from the textures supplied or import one from another source. (You can create textures and save them as Photoshop documents, then open them and apply them as textures through this dialog box or the Texturizer filter's dialog box.)

Figure 15.15
The Rough Pastels dialog box.

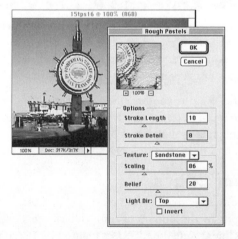

The Stroke Length and Stroke Detail settings seem to give the best results in the middle of their respective ranges, but, as always, experiment to see what works best for your image. Figure 15.16 shows this filter applied to our San Francisco picture.

15

Figure 15.16

The Rough Pastels filter on Sandstone.

15

The Rough Pastels filter works well with almost any kind of subject. On portraits, it adds a nice, "artistic" feel, while eliminating wrinkles. On still life and landscape pictures, it gets rid of unnecessary details and adds texture. Try it. You'll like it.

Smudge Stick

This is a tricky filter. On light-colored areas, the Smudge Stick filter adds a subtle, rather spotty texture that can be quite nice. On dark areas and lines it adds a smudge, making the lines heavier and edges blurry. Figure 15.17 shows an example.

Figure 15.17

The Smudge Stick filter.

Because of the way this filter treats light areas, it doesn't usually look good on portraits. The subject's nose and forehead tend to become either spotty or flat white. Neither is desirable.

Sponge

Have you ever tried painting with a sponge? It's a technique that's taught in some of the finer preschools and kindergartens. Basically, you dab a sponge into poster paint and then dab it on the paper. The results can be very nice, especially if you skip the poster paint and go straight to Photoshop's Sponge filter. On large, flat areas, this filter gives a pretty good imitation of a coarse, natural sponge (the kind they sell in the Sponge market in Key West). In areas of detail, the sponge is a smaller one. You can, in fact, set the brush size, definition, and smoothness in the Sponge filter's dialog box. One possible result is shown in Figure 15.18.

Figure 15.18
The Sponge filter in action.

Underpainting

The Underpainting filter, which you saw in Hour 10, the chapter on imitating media, reduces everything to a somewhat grayed-out, paler, and soft-focused version of itself. Use it as an intermediate filter on the way to an effect, rather than by itself. Used alone, the Underpainting filter makes the image too indistinct.

Instead, first apply the Underpainting filter to a photo to reduce the detail and soften the image. Then apply another filter, perhaps the Cutout or Smudge Stick filter, to add back some definition and texture.

15

Watercolor

There are, as you saw in Hour 10, ways to make a photo look like a watercolor. Unfortunately, applying the Watercolor filter isn't necessarily one of them. Figure 15.19 shows this filter applied to our sample image. The look isn't really watercolor, but it may have some uses.

This is another filter that can turn your picture very dark. It's best used on light subjects.

Figure 15.19

The Watercolor filter.

TIME SAVER

Some of these filters take a while to apply. There's a lot of math involved in recalculating all those pixels. Depending on the speed of your computer, the process may take anywhere from half a minute to several minutes. When you apply a filter that requires a lot of math, you'll see a progress bar onscreen to let you know that something is happening. You can speed things along by making sure that Photoshop is the only open application.

Brush Stroke Filters

For some strange reason the brush stroke filters aren't artistic filters. Artists use brushes, don't they? But the creators of Photoshop isolated these eight filters as the brush stroke set. What do they do? Let's take a look. Figure 15.20 is a picture of a Cape Cod waterfront, before applying the filters.

Figure 15.20
Breakwater, Dennisport, MA.

Accented Edges

Best if applied subtly, this filter enhances the contrast of edges. The Accented Edges dialog box enables you to choose edge width, edge brightness, and smoothness. Figure 15.21 shows the filter applied. As you can see in the figure, it helps bring out the detail and texture.

Figure 15.21
The Accented Edges filter.

15

Angled Strokes and Crosshatch

These filters give a crosshatched effect similar to, but darker than, the one applied by the Colored Pencil filter. Angled Strokes is less dramatic than Crosshatch. Figure 15.22 shows both.

Figure 15.22

Angled Strokes (left) and Crosshatch (right).

You could use either of these to simulate a pen and ink or scratchboard effect. They're more successful when applied to pictures that don't have strong diagonal lines to start with.

Dark Strokes

This filter, unfortunately, is only useable if you set the Black Intensity to 0 and the White Intensity to 10 in the Dark Strokes dialog box. Otherwise, it tends to turn the whole picture black. Figure 15.23 shows you a carefully balanced application of dark strokes.

I haven't found very many situations in which I'd choose this filter. Perhaps you'll like it. As they say, "different strokes for different folks."

Ink Outlines

The Ink Outlines filter places first a white line and then a black line around every edge that it identifies. You can set stroke length and intensity in the dialog box.

Applied to a still life or landscape, the Ink Outlines filter can give you the look of an old woodcut. Applied to a portrait, however, this filter adds warts, blobs, and other undesirable effects.

Figure 15.23
The Dark Strokes filter.

Figure 15.24
The Ink Outlines filter.

Spatter

The Spatter filter did nice things to the rocks in our sample picture but thoroughly messed up the horizon. This is a filter that's potentially useful but needs to be applied to selections rather than to the whole picture. Best applied in small doses…

15

Figure 15.25
Angled strokes on the left.

Sprayed Strokes

Sprayed Strokes looks like Spatter, but is less messy. The interesting thing about this filter is that you can control the direction of the spray. Figure 15.26 shows what it does to our picture.

Figure 15.26
The Sprayed Strokes filter.

Sumi-e

Sumi-e is Japanese for brush painting, but this looks like the work of a crazed Sumo wrestler, rather than a Zen master. This filter turns any area with any sort of detail almost completely black, even at the lowest settings. Forget this one.

Sketch Filters

Photoshop has fourteen different filters lumped under the heading of "Sketch." Some, such as bas relief, must have landed there by default. They have little or nothing to do with the process of sketching. Others, such as Conte Crayon or Chalk & Charcoal, are definitely sketch media. Figure 15.27 shows the sample image for these filters.

Figure 15.27
Wild rose.

Bas Relief

The Bas Relief filter uses the foreground and background colors to create a low relief rendering of your picture. If you choose colors carefully, it can look like copper foil, hammered metal, or carved stone. Figure 15.28 shows the result.

Chalk & Charcoal

With the Chalk & Charcoal filter, which reduces the image to three tones, you need to set the foreground to a dark color and the background to a light one. The third color, by default, is a medium gray, so choose colors that work with it. This filter can produce really beautiful drawings. Figure 15.29 shows the filter applied.

15

Figure 15.28
Use a dark background color for best results with the Bas Relief filter.

15

Figure 15.29
The Chalk & Charcoal filter.

Charcoal

The Charcoal filter does much the same thing as the Chalk & Charcoal filter but uses only the foreground and background colors. It's also more difficult to control because there are only two colors. Experiment until you are satisfied.

Chrome

The Chrome filter appears to be a close relative to the Plastic Wrap filter described previously. It's only slightly more successful. As you can see in Figure 15.30, any resemblance to real metal is purely coincidental.

Figure 15.30
The Chrome filter.

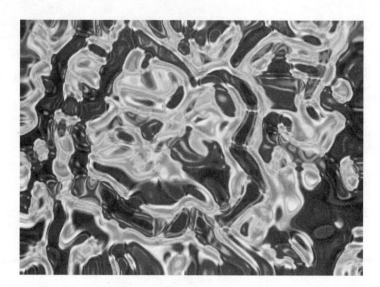

Conte Crayon

I *love* this filter. It's done good things to every picture I have ever used it on. The Conte Crayon filter works like the Chalk & Charcoal filter described earlier, but with the addition of background textures and using the same interface you saw in the Rough Pastels dialog box. Figure 15.31 shows the rose rendered in conte crayon on a canvas background.

Graphic Pen, Halftone Pattern

These two filters do very similar things. Both reduce the image to whatever foreground and background colors you have set. Graphic Pen then renders the image in slanting lines, whereas Halftone Pattern renders it in overlapping dots. Neither is particularly useful.

Note Paper, Plaster

I don't understand the name of this effect. I'd have called it Stucco, or maybe Flocked Wallpaper, but not Note Paper. See for yourself in Figure 15.32. The Note Paper filter uses the background and foreground colors, plus black for a shadow effect. Interesting, but Note Paper? The Plaster filter is very similar, but smooth instead of grainy. It has the look of wet, runny, freshly poured plaster.

15

Figure 15.31

The Conte Crayon filter.

15

Figure 15.32

The Note Paper filter.

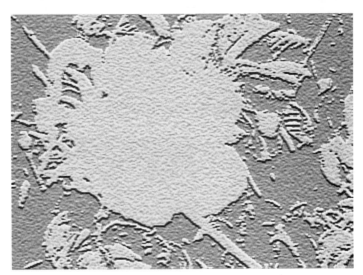

Photocopy, Reticulation, Stamp, Torn Edges

These four filters can be grouped together. They all, like many of the filters in this set, convert the image to a two color copy of itself. Stamp loses most of the detail, attempting to replicate a rubber stamp, not very successfully. Photocopy keeps most of the detail, giving the somewhat confusing image in Figure 15.33. Reticulation adds dot grain to the Stamp filter, so it looks as if you stamped the picture on coarse sandpaper. Torn Edges is the stamp filter again, only with the edges of the image roughened.

Figure 15.33
The Photocopy filter.

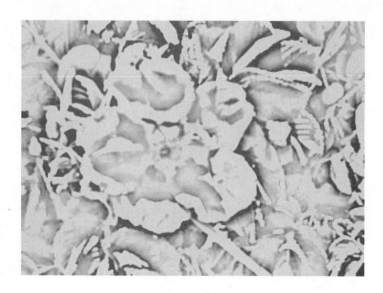

Water Paper

The last one in the sketch set is a strange filter. Once again, I don't know how they named it. To me, it looks more like needlepoint, at least in the background. Unlike most of the filters in the sketch set, it keeps the colors of your original picture, adds a vertical cross-hatching in the background, and softens what it identifies as the subject of the picture. Figure 15.34 shows this filter applied to the rose.

Figure 15.34
The Water Paper filter.

15

Summary

None of the filters described in this chapter will produce a work of art from a really lousy photo. The old proverb about silk purses and sow's ears applies. These filters can, however, when carefully and thoughtfully applied, elevate an ordinary picture to something quite extraordinary. Photoshop's filters are well worth taking the time to master. I hope you take a familiar picture and work through the filter sets as we've done in this hour so that you can see—in color and enlarged—exactly what they can do.

Q&A

Q How do you decide which filter to try?

A As you've seen, you can't always judge a filter by its name. If you're looking for an "art" effect, decide first whether you want full color or limited color. For the latter, look at the sketch filters. Consider how abstract you want to get.

Cutout and Conte Crayon are both successful with most pictures.

Hour **16**

Filters to Distort and Other Funky Effects

So far, the Photoshop filters we've seen have been more or less useful. They've corrected a fuzzy image or blurred a distracting background. Or they've done something to turn your photo into an imitation drawing, painting, or mixed media construction. In this hour, we'll play with some filters that are mostly for fun. These filters distort, stylize, and pixelate your picture. Most of these are meant for special effects. They're not for every day, but you may find one or two that are actually helpful.

The key to success with these filters is to try as many different combinations of settings as you can with each filter and each new image that you bring into Photoshop. When you encounter a filter that relies on background and foreground colors, try several different color combinations. Try a dark background and light foreground, and then reverse them. It's simple enough to do if you click the double-headed arrow next to the color swatches in the Toolbox.

Distort Filters

Distort filters run the gamut from gentle glassiness to image destroying twirls and even more. Want to make your picture look like it's going down the drain or being blown off the page? These are the filters for you. In this section, we try out filters on this picture of a cypress tree on the beach (see Figure 16.1).

Figure 16.1
Monterey Bay, CA.

The Diffuse Glow Filter

Not all of the distort filters actually distort. The Diffuse Glow filter adds a gentle haze of your background color over the lighter areas of the picture. This creates a glow that blends into the image. Hard to say why it is in the distort family of filters, but it is cool nevertheless.

The controls are as follows: Graininess, Glow Amount, and Clear Amount. I suggest, for realism, keep the graininess setting low. The higher, the greater the graininess. Try to balance the Glow Amount and Clear Amount. In Figure 16.2, I put a surrealistic green haze over the picture.

Displace

The Displace filter is one of several Photoshop filters that require the use of a *displacement* map, which works like a texture map. You'll find a collection of these in the Photoshop Plug-ins folder. After you set the amount of displacement in the dialog box, you're asked to choose a filter. Figure 16.3 shows a partial list of filters, and Figure 16.4 shows the results.

NEW TERM   *Displacement maps* are images or patterns that are saved in the Photoshop format, and applied as part of a mathematical formula that moves each pixel in the original image according to the values in the displacement map.

Figure 16.2

The Diffuse Glow filter.

16

Figure 16.3

Choosing a displacement map.

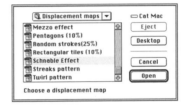

Figure 16.4

The Displace filter.

The Glass and Ocean Ripple Filters

I decided to lump the discussion of these two filters together because of the similar effects they have on an image. Both filters create displacements that make the image seem as if it is being seen through glass or water.

The Glass filter, shown in Figures 16.5 and 16.6, offers you a greater amount of control. You are able to select type of texture, such as frosty, tiny lens, or canvas, and you also may load a texture of your own. Just select Load Texture from the pull-down menu at the bottom of the dialog box.

Figure 16.5
The Glass filter.

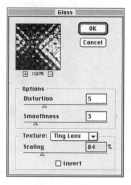

Figure 16.6
The application of the Glass filter.

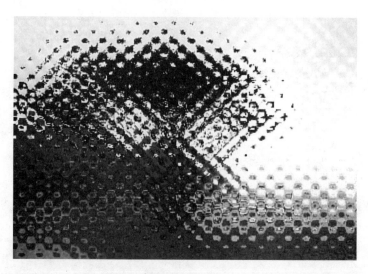

Use the Smoothness slider to increase the fluidity of the image. Keeping the Distortion low and the Smoothness high creates a subtle effect. Try the opposite for a much more distorted image.

16

The Invert button at the bottom of the dialog box replaces the light areas of the texture with dark areas and vice versa.

The Ocean Ripple filter is quite similar. It creates an effect that makes your image appear as though it is underwater. It is an effective filter and easier to use than the Glass filter because it has only two options in its dialog box.

Pinch, Spherize, and ZigZag

These again are lumped together, not because they do the same thing, but because their interfaces are so similar. Figure 16.7 shows the dialog box for the Spherize filter.

Figure 16.7

The Spherize filter's dialog box.

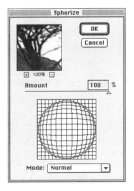

Keep an eye on the grid provided at the bottom of the box as you drag the Amount slider higher or lower. It can give you a good indication (as can the Preview box) of what is going on in the image. See the final version in Figure 16.8.

Figure 16.8

The Spherize filter.

This is a tough filter to master, but a good one to have in your bag of tricks. The Spherize filter can be very useful on occasion, but don't try to force it. If it doesn't look right, try something else.

Also, you can use a negative amount in the Amount slider to generate a hollow instead of a bump. And if this doesn't satisfy your needs, try the Pinch filter, which is essentially the opposite of the Spherize filter. Instead of making things appear to billow outward, this filter makes them seem to scrunch in. There's another similar filter, the ZigZag filter, which does very neat pond ripples, as well as a sort of pinwheel effect. Try them for special effects or to create distortion in reflections.

The Shear Filter

You can tell a great deal about most filters just by their names, but this isn't one of them. The Shear filter warps images vertically. Click and drag the line in the dialog box, shown in Figure 16.9. Watch the preview. You also can add more control points on the curve by clicking it at different areas. These control points are like joints. They enable you to redirect the motion of the curve.

Figure 16.10 shows the results of the results of the Shear filter. We've blown the tree quite a bit sideways.

Figure 16.9

The Shear filter's dialog box.

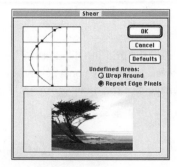

The Twirl Filter

The Twirl filter does precisely what its name suggests—it spins an image. You can control the amount of spin with the slider within the dialog box. So far, I have not found very many subtle uses for this filter, but if you can, go to it. It creates wonderful, kaleidoscopic effects, and can also be used to simulate a swirling drain (see Figure 16.11).

16

Figure 16.10
The Shear filter applied.

Figure 16.11
The Twirl filter applied.

Pixelation Filters

When one is "pixilated," according to my dictionary, he's inebriated, but in a charming, bemused, whimsical, and pixieish way. Pixelation in Photoshop can be equally whimsical and bemusing, if applied to the right subjects. Misused, it turns everything into a bunch of dots. Pixelation happens when similarly colored pixels are clumped together to form larger units, which may be square (pixel-shaped) or round, or rounded off by anti-aliasing to whatever form they take. It happens, unasked for, if you're printing a picture at too low a resolution. You end up with large pixels forming jagged shapes that look like they've been built out of a child's plastic block set.

When it is controlled, the effect can be quite interesting. Photoshop includes a set of Pixelation filters that produce different effects all based on the notion of clumping together similar pixels. It's best to apply these effects to simple subjects and to those with strong contrasts, such as the example in Figure 16.12.

Figure 16.12

Yellow fruit, unfiltered.

CAUTION

Most of the pixelate filter set looks best if the effect is applied as small as possible. Otherwise, the crystals, facets, and so on, get so big the image becomes unrecognizable.

Crystallize

The Crystallize filter is intended to make your picture look as if the colors were facets on a large crystal. In Figure 16.13, I've applied the Crystallize filter at a cell size of 8. It adds reasonable distortion without destroying the fruit shapes. In Figure 16.14, I pushed the cell size up to 50, destroying the picture. You can even set the cell size as high as 300, but it turns the entire picture into one or two cells.

16

Figure 16.13
The Crystallize filter applied.

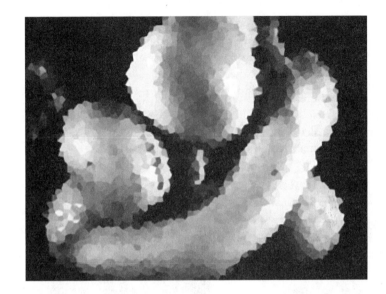

16

Figure 16.14
Same filter, over applied.

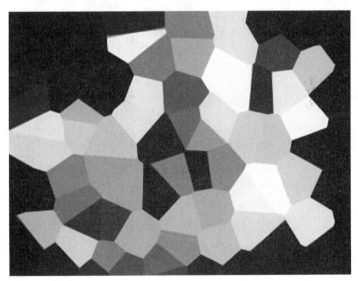

Pointillism and Mosaics

As a former art student, it's fun to go back and recall the first time I was introduced to the work of Georges Seurat. It was a revelation (especially coming out of studying some of the "sloppier" French impressionists) to see these dabs of paint all neatly clustered to form elegant scenes from a distance, and up close form equally elegant abstract patterns. It would be nice if the Pointillism filters did the job as neatly and scientifically as M. Seurat. They don't.

This is, however, one case where the smallest setting doesn't work as well as some of the larger ones. I first tried the picture using 3 pixels as the dot size. I got a spotty picture, as I expected, but it looked more like video noise than pointillism. Using a slightly larger dot size produced an image a little closer to what I was looking for. But when I tried a much larger size, around 25, I ended up with baseballs. Figure 16.15 shows all three effects.

There's a Mosaic filter in the pixelate effects, but all it does is make larger pixels out of the smaller ones. The result is the sort of thing they use to hide the faces of the people being arrested on all those late night police shows (see Figure 16.16).

Figure 16.15
Cell sizes: 3, 8, and 25.

16

Figure 16.16
Alleged perpetrator.

16

Stylizing Filters

The stylize filter family offers some wonderful effects. They are very creative and can be used to add *final effects* or touches to an image. In this section, we touch on the most interesting of the filters, the Find Edges filter, Glowing Edges filter, Trace Contour filter, and the Wind filter.

Find Edges, Glowing Edges, and Trace Contour

These three effects sound as if they should look alike. They actually do look somewhat alike, with Glowing Edges and Find Edges being much more dramatic than Trace Contour. Find Edges removes most of the colors from the object and replaces them with lines around every edge contour. The color of the lines depends on the value at that point on the original object, with lightest points in yellow, scaling through to the darkest points, which appear in purple. It makes the picture look like a rather delicate colored pencil drawing of itself. Find Edges becomes more interesting if you apply it more than once to the same object. Figure 16.17 shows a picture of a flower with the edges traced twice.

Figure 16.17

The first tracing lacked character, but doing it again made the lines heavier.

Unfortunately, there's no way to set the sensitivity of the Find Edges filter. In practical terms, this means that you have to prepare the picture before you trace it. Begin by despeckling so that Photoshop won't attempt to circle every piece of dust in the background. If you don't want the background to show, select and delete it, or select your object and copy it to a separate layer first.

Glowing Edges is more fun, first because it's prettier, and second, because you can adjust it to have maximum impact on your picture. Glowing Edges turns the edges into brightly colored lines against a black background. The effect is vaguely reminiscent of neon signs. You can vary the intensity of the color and the thickness of the line.

In Figure 16.18, I've applied Glowing Edges to the basket of fruit we used earlier. It works especially well with "busy" pictures with lots of edges. The more it has to work with, the more effective the filter is.

The Trace Contours filter does precisely that. It traces the contours of shapes in your picture. Figure 16.19 shows it applied once to the fruit photo. Trace Contours also works better on some pictures if you apply it several times. The Trace Contour dialog box has a slider setting for the level at which value differences are translated into contour lines. When you move the slider, you are setting the threshold at which the values (from 0–255) are traced. Experiment to see which values bring out the best detail in your image. Upper and Lower don't refer to the direction of the outline. Lower outlines specifies where the color values of pixels fall below a specified level; Upper outlines tells you where the value of the pixels are above the specified level.

16

Figure 16.18
Some of the color remains, but the background goes black.

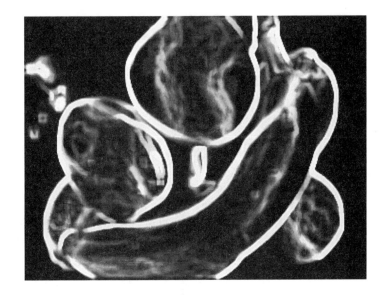

16

Figure 16.19
The fruit is identifiable, but not very interesting.

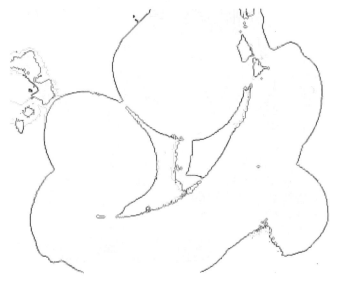

This filter by itself is not of much use. It offers no control. You select the command, and there is no ensuing dialog box, only an effect. This filter can, however, be the starting point for a number of effects. After finding the edges, for example, try inverting the image with Select➡Invert. Also, try using some of the artistic filters we looked at in the previous hour.

TIME SAVER

You'll get more interesting results from many of these filters if you apply them a second or third time to the same picture. Because you only have one level of Undo, be sure to save your work just before you start applying the filter, so that you can use the Revert command if you don't like the results of the filter.

The Wind Filter

The Wind filter creates a neat directional blur that looks, strangely enough, like wind. You can control the direction and the amount of wind in the dialog box (see Figure 16.20). This is a great filter for creating the illusion of movement and for applying to type. It works best when applied to a selected area, rather than to the entire picture.

Figure 16.20

The Wind filter and its dialog box.

Emboss

Honestly, the Emboss filter doesn't do much for most photos. It turns an image into a bas relief, though not as well as the Bas Relief filter does. In the process, it converts the image to medium gray. But like the Wind filter, it works very well on type. You can adjust the shadow angle and amount in the dialog box. Figure 16.21 shows a piece of embossed type.

Figure 16.21

Embossing.

Emboss!

Occasionally, you come across a photo, like this portrait of a lion, that almost begs to be turned into a corporate logo or advertising image. In such cases, the Emboss filter can do wonders toward making the picture just abstract enough to be useful. In working with this photo, I found that the angle at which the filter is applied can make a major difference. The following figure shows two different angle settings applied to the same picture (see Figure 16.22). The height and amount settings were the same for both.

16

Figure 16.22
Embossed lions.

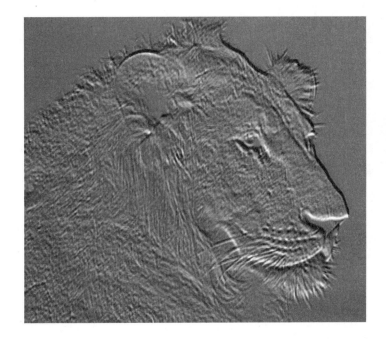

16

Combining Filters

Some people like things plain. I'm not one of them. I want the whipped cream, marshmallow, nuts, and cherry on my ice cream, and I'm seldom satisfied with using just one Photoshop filter. And with an arsenal of 99 different Photoshop filters, (plus dozens of third-party add-ons) why shouldn't we take advantage of as many as possible? In the remaining few minutes of this hour, we'll look at some interesting combinations.

Texturizer

You can add a texture to any photo, no matter what you have already done to it. The Texturizer filter (Filter➡Texture➡Texturizer) places a pattern resembling canvas, burlap, brick, or sandstone over your image, making it look as if it's on paper with that texture. The canvas texture is particularly nice if reduced in scale. Figure 16.23 shows a photo of a lion, first treated with the Colored Pencil filter and then texturized.

Dry Brush and Smudge Stick

The Dry brush filter added a nice "painterly" quality to the lion portrait. Figure 16.24 shows the single filter applied to it. In Figure 16.25, I added the Smudge Stick over the Dry Brush, and came up with what I think is an even more interesting result.

Figure 16.23

The Colored Pencil and Texturizer filters applied to an image.

Figure 16.24

Dry brushed lion.

16

Figure 16.25

Lion, drybrushed, and smudge sticked.

16

The possibilities are endless. If you can imagine a style or treatment for a picture, chances are excellent that Photoshop can do it. As a final picture, and final filter combination, here's how you can turn a photo into instant stained glass. Start with any picture that has reasonably large areas of light color. Figure 16.26 shows my original picture, a somewhat fuzzy close-up of a dogwood flower.

Figure 16.26

Unfiltered dogwood.

To turn this picture into stained glass:

1. Apply the Crystallize filter (Filter➡Pixelate➡Crystallize) with a moderately large cell size. I used 30 as the cell size in Figure 16.27.

Figure 16.27
Cyrstallized dogwood.

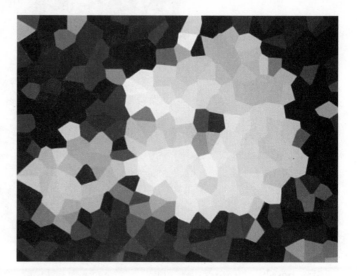

2. Next, apply the Ink Outlines filter (Filter➡Brush Strokes➡Ink Outline with the Stroke length set to about 4 and the light and dark intensity balanced at about 15. Figure 16.28 shows the result; a reasonable rendering of a stained glass window. You can, of course, draw in any lines that Photoshop didn't trace completely, and you can go over the "glass panels" and change their colors if you want.

Figure 16.28
Stained glass dogwood.

16

At the risk of sounding like a broken record, let me leave you with a final reminder to keep on experimenting. You never know what a filter or combination will do to a particular picture until you try it. The way that Photoshop calculates the filter effects means that some filters can look very different according to the kind of picture to which they are applied. You can't always predict what will happen, but the unexpected effects are frequently wonderful.

Summary

This hour has been devoted to some of Photoshop's stranger filters: the Distort, Pixelate, and Stylize filters. They're not for everyone, and certainly not for every image, but they're fun to play with and can occasionally create some interesting and unusual effects—even some beautiful effects. Filters can add interesting dimensions to type, also.

Don't hesitate to add a second filter over the first. Many times the second filter, or second application of the original filter, can turn a ho-hum picture into something marvelous. At worst, you can always Undo.

Q&A

Q Why do some filters have ellipses after their names, whereas others don't?

A There are two kinds of native Photoshop filters. The ones with an ellipsis (…) open a dialog box with parameters to set before the filter is applied. The filters with no ellipsis are one-step filters. You have no control over the way the filter is applied. When you select a one-step filter from the menu, it's applied. Period. You can apply it a second time to double the effect.

Hour 17

Adding Type to Pictures

If a picture's worth a thousand words, how many more is it worth if we add words to the picture? Well, never mind... The fact is, though, that sometimes you have to add type to a picture for one reason or another. Photoshop's Type tool isn't the simplest or the most versatile you'll ever encounter, but it does at least enable you to paste the text onto the image. From there you can convert the letterforms to paths and fill them with images, apply filters, or use any of a variety of other tricks. Let's start with the basics.

The Type Tool

Text appears in whatever the foreground color is. If you want a specific color, it's easier to change it before you start the process of text creation. After you have a color chosen, select the Type tool from the Toolbox. Photoshop's type tool is represented by the letter T on the Toolbar. When you click it, you see the familiar I-beam cursor that means you can insert text. Position the cursor where you want the text to start on the page, and then click. Surprise! Photoshop doesn't place the cursor there for you to start typing. Instead it opens a dialog box, as shown in Figure 17.1.

Figure 17.1

The Type Tool dialog box.

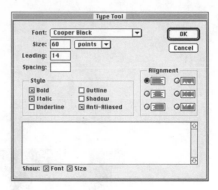

Pop-up menus within the dialog box let you choose a font from those you have installed and let you set the size, leading, alignment, and other attributes. The window at the bottom of the box is where you can see what you're typing. The blinking cursor line indicates that you're ready to type. Once you start, your word(s) appear in the window. If there's more text than the box can display, you see scrollbars at the side of the window, as in Figure 17.2.

Figure 17.2

Working in the Type Tool dialog box.

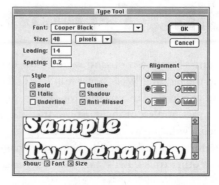

After you have entered the words and set the type attributes, you must click OK or press Return (Mac only) to position the type. Type always appears on a new layer.

TIME SAVER

If you check the show font and show size boxes (which I definitely recommend), you can see the type in its assigned font and size.

After the type is placed onscreen, you can have some fun with it. Apply filters to your heart's content. Pour paint into selected letters. Select the type and distort it. Figure 17.3 shows a few of the things you can do.

17

Figure 17.3
Filtered, stretched, and distorted type.

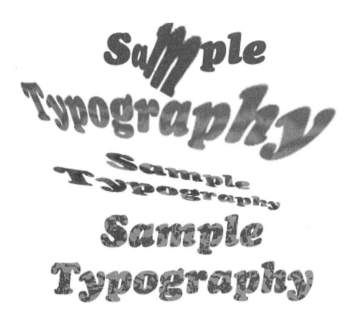

17

Filters are most successful on bold type. Thin, delicate letters tend to get lost. Skip the shadow effect in the Type Tool dialog box. There's a better way...

Drop Shadows

As soon as you start looking for drop shadows, you'll find them everywhere: in magazines, television ads, web sites, and in every other form of media you can imagine. Everyone is discovering that as soon as you put a shadow behind some text or an image, it takes on an added dimension that really makes it pop forward into view. It's a nice and easy special effect for giving something more visual weight and making people pay attention.

Some tips for using drop shadows effectively:

☐ Don't use them all over the place! If you use too many shadows, then everything pops forward equally and you've lost the benefit of using shadows to give attention to one particular object.

☐ Make sure all your shadows look alike! If you're going to use shadows on multiple objects in the same area, make sure the shadows all go the same way, and make sure the "depth" of the shadow is appropriate. If the shadows are all different and haphazard, people will notice (see Figure 17.4).

☐ Don't make the shadows too dark. It's easy to go overboard and create deep, saturated shadows that overwhelm what's supposed to be getting all the attention: the foreground image. Keep them light and subtle.

Figure 17.4

Which side looks better? If you can't tell, read the second tip again.

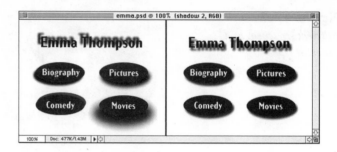

Basic Drop Shadows

Okay, let's get down to business and create a cool drop shadow:

1. Create a new Photoshop document with a white background. (Mine is 400 pixels wide by 200 pixels tall.)

2. On a new layer (Layer 1), type the text you want, or place the graphic (see Figure 17.5). (Make sure the Layers palette is showing by choosing Window➡Show Layers.)

Figure 17.5

The original art in need of a drop shadow.

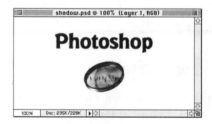

3. Duplicate Layer 1. In the Layers palette, click Layer 1 and drag it down to the bottom of the palette until the Create New Layer button is selected, then release the mouse button (see Figure 17.6). You'll get a new layer called Layer 1 copy.

4. I find it easier to remember what the layers are if I rename them. So double-click Layer 1 copy in the Layers palette and rename it Shadow.

5. Now click the Shadow layer in the Layers palette and drag it down just below Layer 1 (see Figure 17.7). If you don't do this, the final shadow appears on top of the graphic, which obviously won't look right!

6. Make sure the Shadow layer is still the active layer, and select the entire canvas (Select➡All). Then select the Move tool and quickly hit the left and right arrow keys, in any order. This selects just the graphics themselves, not any of the surrounding empty space (see Figure 17.8). It's a trick for selecting objects that's worth remembering.

17

Figure 17.6

*Duplicating the original
layer.*

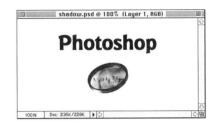

Figure 17.7

*Reordering the layers so
that the shadow is
underneath.*

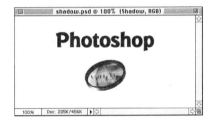

Figure 17.8

Selecting the objects.

7. Fill the selection with black by choosing Edit➥Fill. You can pick any color for the
   shadow, but shadows cease to look like shadows if you use bright colors. If you
   make Layer 1 temporarily invisible (click the eye in the Layers palette), you can see
   that your images are now entirely filled in (see Figure 17.9).

Figure 17.9

*The objects are filled
with black.*

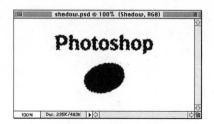

8. Use the arrow keys to move your new shadow one pixel at a time. Let's move it 8 pixels down and 6 to the right for this example. Now deselect the shadow with the Move tool still selected (see Figure 17.10). Just to remind you, deselect by pressing (Command-D)[Control-D].

Figure 17.10

*The shadow gets offset
from the original image.*

TIME SAVER

I find that shadows work better if they're *below* the original image, that is, moved down instead of up when they're offset. When the shadow falls downward, the object looks more like it's popping up.

9. Now for the magic step. Choose Filter➡Blur➡Gaussian Blur. In the ensuing dialog box you can choose different Radius settings and see what each one looks like. As long as the Preview checkbox is checked, you see your temporary result in the main image window as well as in the dialog box window (see Figure 17.11). I like a setting of 4 pixels for this image, so I typed 4 and clicked OK.

Figure 17.11

*The magical Gaussian
Blur dialog box.*

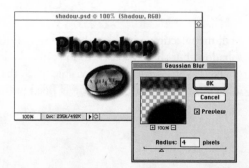

17

10. There's your drop shadow! You can still change it, of course. If it's too dark, for example, you can do one of two things:

   ☐ Adjust the Opacity slider in the Layers palette.

   ☐ Choose Image➡Adjust➡Brightness/Contrast and adjust the Brightness setting.

11. Also, you can still move the shadow, even after you've blurred it. Simply select it like you did in Step 6 and move it where you want it (see Figure 17.12).

Figure 17.12

The final drop shadow.

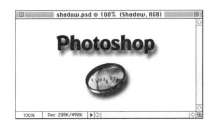

Drop shadows can by tricky. When it looks right, you'll know it. Trust your eyes to tell you what looks realistic and what looks fake. And be willing to experiment with settings. Try making your shadow twice as blurred as your original setting or twice as far offset. You might be surprised!

Drop Shadows on Varying Backgrounds

Of course, drop shadows don't have to occur just over white or solid-color backgrounds. You can have a drop shadow fall over a texture, an image, or anything else that strikes your fancy. Let's look at an example:

1. First, we create the Photoshop image. The important thing to remember is to create a *new layer* for each element you want to have a drop shadow (see Figure 17.13). For a refresher on layers, refer back to Hour 11.

Figure 17.13

The original image before drop shadows.

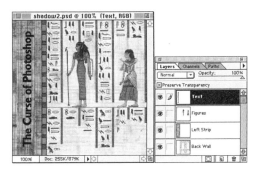

2. Let's add a shadow to the text first by following the steps as in the previous section. For my shadow, I offset the shadow 4 pixels up and to the right and gave it a Gaussian Blur with a Radius setting of 3 pixels (see Figure 17.14).

Figure 17.14

A drop shadow applied to the text.

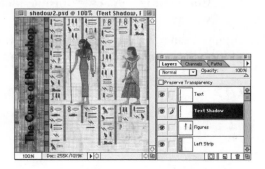

Notice how you can actually see the texture of the background right "through" the new shadow. The result is a pleasant, realistic effect. You can make even more of the background show through by adjusting the Opacity slider in the Layers palette. Give it a try.

3. Now let's create some depth in the background. I want the left-hand vertical strip to look like a step up from the main background. So I'll add a drop shadow just like I added under the text—same treatment, same settings. Also, make sure that you don't move the shadow down to the right. Otherwise, you will not have the shadow at the top of the strip, unless that is what you want.

4. Finally, let's make the figures pop out from the background. I want these to pop forward more than the left-hand strip or the text, so I offset these shadows 8 pixels and apply a Gaussian Blur of 8. The resulting shadows are still a little dark, so I adjust the Opacity slider to 90%. Figure 17.15 shows the final image. Notice again how the background shows through the shadow, making the image more realistic.

Figure 17.15

The final image with drop shadows.

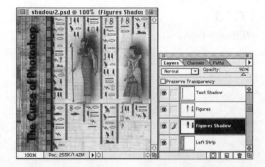

17

COFFEE BREAK

> ### Tasteful Typography
>
> There are thousands of typefaces available to you. Buy them in CD-ROM collections, download them online, use the ones that come with other applications, and so on. Trying out wild typefaces can be so much fun that you may lose sight of the goal—to communicate. Before committing to a design, print out a sample page and hold it up at full arm's length. If you can't read it easily, maybe even with your reading glasses removed, try to figure out why and consider tweaking the design. It may be a simple matter of making the type larger or giving the lines of type more space (leading). You may need to rethink your background or add an outline. A drop shadow may help or may make matters even worse. Try combinations of different type and image treatment.
>
> Avoid using the outline and shadow type attributes for anything but extremely limited circumstances. In the early days of the Macintosh, these styles were included for fun. Today, they simply brand your work as non-professional. Even worse, they're hard to read. The pros don't use underlining very often, either. The underline habit comes from the old manual typewriter days when no other typographical tool was available to give emphasis to words. Use bold or italic type styles instead.

Filled Type

Half the battle is finding a picture to work with. The other half is finding a nice fat typeface that leaves plenty of room for your pictures to show through. Let's say I'm working on a logo for a company called Cloud Nine. The first thing I do is to flip through my photo files in search of some good looking clouds. I opened the picture in Photoshop, cropped it, and punched up the contrast a little bit more.

Then I selected the Type Mask tool by pressing the letter T twice. Now the cursor looks like the familiar I-beam type insertion cursor. Clicking it on the clouds opens the Type Tool dialog box. (Before clicking, I made sure that the horizontal line on the cursor—the type baseline—is where it should be, low enough to catch the clouds.)

I chose Cooper Black from my font list, making it bold as well for a few extra pixels worth of width. The word "Cloud" is typed as large as possible to fit in the area. Figure 17.16 shows this step.

When I close the dialog box and return to the picture, I have selection paths in the shape of the letters. Figure 17.17 shows how this looks on the screen.

Figure 17.16

Enter the words in the type box.

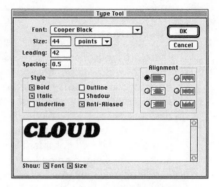

Figure 17.17

The letters are active paths.

After making sure the letters are centered over the clouds I want to capture, I copy the selection and paste it to a new layer. It's important to copy and not cut. If I use the cut command, I leave holes in my original picture, and that's no good because I have another word to grab from it. First, though, I adjust the color in the picture. The first clouds were pink, as at sunset. These are more blue. Repeating the Type tool process, I enter the word "Nine" and take a different section of clouds.

The next step is to get rid of the original picture because I don't need it any more. But the lettering does need background. Clouds would probably be appropriate, so I start by adding another layer and pouring it full of light blue paint. I also have to pour paint into the interior of the closed letters O and D. After making sure that my foreground color is white and my background color is an appropriate blue, I choose Render Clouds from the Filter menu. Figure 17.18 shows the result.

The rendered clouds just don't look very impressive, and there's not enough contrast against the lettering. I can make the clouds stand out a little more by adjusting the contrast and color balance. I can also put a drop shadow behind the lettering. And, if that's not enough, I can select the letters, make a border around them using Select➡ Modify➡Border, and then fill the border with white. Figure 17.19 shows the final logo after all of these tricks.

17

Figure 17.18
More clouds.

Figure 17.19
Photoshop puts me on cloud nine.

Summary

Photoshop doesn't have all the type capabilities of a more traditional graphics or desktop publishing program, but you'll probably never need them. Its Type tool is clumsy compared to some of its other tools. Getting the letters into the picture, however, is only the beginning. After you have the type on the page, you can apply all of Photoshop's filters, Blending modes, and tools to it. If you want to set type, use a program such as PageMaker. If you want to do strange and wonderful things to type, Photoshop has all the tools you need.

Q&A

Q **I have a lot of fonts installed, and it takes forever to scroll down the list to find the one I want. Any suggestions?**

A Use a font management program such as Suitcase or Master Juggler to sort your fonts into suitcases. Keep a suitcase for serif type and a separate one for sans serif faces, one for display faces, and one for special purpose fonts such as Handbill, StarTrek, or Wild West. Only open the suitcases with fonts you're likely to need.

17

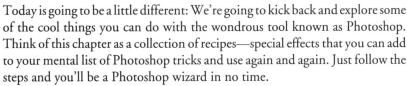

Hour **18**

Special Effects

Today is going to be a little different: We're going to kick back and explore some of the cool things you can do with the wondrous tool known as Photoshop. Think of this chapter as a collection of recipes—special effects that you can add to your mental list of Photoshop tricks and use again and again. Just follow the steps and you'll be a Photoshop wizard in no time.

Here are the special effects covered in this chapter:

- ☐ Glows
- ☐ Lighting effects
- ☐ Reflections

JUST A MINUTE

Very detailed instructions are given in this hour, and I use very specific settings along the way. It's important to realize that as you create these special effects with your own images, my settings might not be the best settings for you. Different resolutions, sizes, and colors call for different settings. So when you see specifics, feel free to play with them a bit and see if you can get even better results with your artwork.

That's the real secret of getting better and better at Photoshop: *Never stop experimenting!*

Glows

The glow, an easy special effect, is essentially a drop shadow that isn't offset at all from the original object and is often in a color other than black.

Let's create a basic glow around some text:

1. In a new Photoshop document, fill the background with black. With a deep blue as your foreground color, use the Text tool to add some text on a new layer (see Figure 18.1).

Figure 18.1

The original text, sans glow.

2. Duplicate the layer, as you would for a drop shadow, but instead of filling the selected area with black, fill it with a bright yellow. *Don't* offset this yellow layer from the original text layer.

3. After deselecting the yellow area, apply the Gaussian Blur filter. Try a setting of 5 or so (see Figure 18.2). Cool results, eh?

Figure 18.2

Glowing text.

TIME SAVER

If you want an extra-large glow, expand the yellow area before moving to Step 3. An easy way to do this is to choose Select➥Modify➥Expand and enter the number of pixels to which you want the selection to grow. After clicking OK, make sure to fill the new, larger selection with yellow as well.

This technique just scratches the surface of glow effects. Try all sorts of settings and colors. Experiment with the brightness and size of the glow. Try other blur filters for glows that imply movement or dimension. Have fun!

Lighting Effects

Lighting effects refers to a whole range of special effects all related to how objects are lit. By illuminating objects in a unique way, you can change the entire feel of an image, drawing attention exactly where you want it.

Our primary tool, as you might expect, is Photoshop's Lighting Effects filter.

1. Start with an original image. Perhaps this is an image that is fairly "flat" as far as brightness is concerned. Perhaps it's an image that looks too two-dimensional for its content (see Figure 18.3).

Figure 18.3

Our original image, in need of some special lighting.

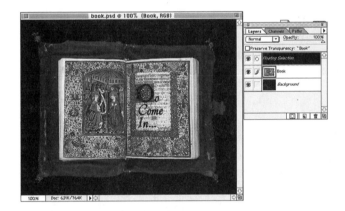

In our example image, the "book" is on a separate layer from the background, so both can be lit separately.

2. Make sure the Book layer is active, then select just the book. The Lighting Effects filter works only if you have something selected for it to work on.

3. Choose Filter➞Render➞Lighting Effects to bring up the Lighting Effects dialog box. Under the Style pull-down menu near the top, select Soft Spotlight (see Figure 18.4). You'll see the preview of your image in the right with the new spotlight effect.

Figure 18.4

The Lighting Effects dialog box.

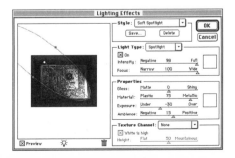

4. Although Photoshop ships with a number of neat default settings, it's fun to play around with the various sliders and values. Don't be intimidated by the number of choices here. For one thing, I don't like how the spotlight is currently falling to the lower right of the image. I want it to shine onto the middle.

To change the direction and/or shape of the spotlight, simply grab the handles around the oval you see in the left side of the dialog box. You can move them around as you wish. You can even move the center point. Move everything around so it looks something like what you see in Figure 18.5.

Figure 18.5

Moving the spotlight manually.

5. Okay, not bad, but the spotlight is too intense and too bright. Play around with the Intensity slider a bit and settle on a value of 50.

6. Now it looks like the non-lit parts of the image are too dark. The overall lighting needs to be brought up a bit, so adjust the Ambience slider up to 35.

7. One more thing: Light doesn't always have to be white. For this image, a softer, more yellow light is more appropriate because of the yellows and reds already in the image. Click the white square to the right of the Intensity slider, and up comes the Color Picker (see Figure 18.6). Find a subtle yellow by setting the RGB values to 240, 255, and 200 respectively.

Figure 18.6

Changing the color of the light.

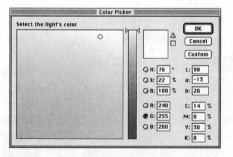

18

8. Click OK to approve the color, and look over the Lighting Effects dialog to make sure you like the preview image (see Figure 18.7).

Figure 18.7

All the settings are finally as I want them.

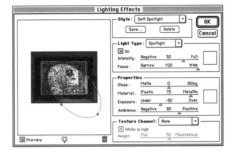

9. Click OK, and after a little processing time, the final image emerges (see Figure 18.8).

Figure 18.8

The book with a warm spotlight highlighting the area you want to focus on.

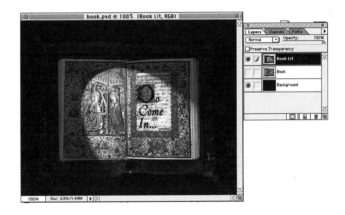

If you like, you can also add lighting effects to the black background as well to add a further sense of depth to the image.

Reflections

If you often find yourself combining various images in Photoshop (and I predict you will), you can't simply toss the images together and have it look realistic. As we've seen, effects such as shadows are essential to create a realistic-looking environment. Creating reflections is another technique for doing this.

Let's look at an example to see how you can add reflections to your toolkit of special effects:

1. Let's say you have a cat that you want to insert into an image you've created. First, use the various selection tools to extricate the cat from its original photographic background. Then place the cat (on its own layer, of course) into the new image (see Figure 18.9).

Figure 18.9

The cat in his new environment.

The effect isn't very realistic. It looks as though the cat and background came from two different sources (which they did; but you don't want it to be so obvious!).

2. To start working on a reflection of the cat in the floor tile, duplicate the cat layer (refer back to the "Drop Shadows" section for details). In the Layers palette, move this new layer (name it Cat Reflection) below the original cat layer because you want the reflection to appear "underneath" the cat.

3. With the Cat Reflection layer active, select Layer➡Transform➡Flip Vertical. This flips the reflected cat onto its head.

4. Select the cat reflection and use the Move tool to move it down. (Hold down the Shift key as you move the selection so that it moves straight down and not at all horizontally.) Move it down so that the "two cats" precisely meet without any tile visible between them (see Figure 18.10).

Figure 18.10

The cat flipped and moved down into place.

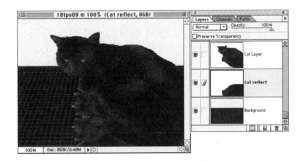

It looks like a reflection, right? Well, sort of. If the tile floor is *perfectly* reflective, like a mirror, which obviously no floor is.

5. To make the reflection realistic, some of the tiles have to show through, just as we saw with drop shadows. Deselect the cat reflection so the image is easier to see as a whole. Then adjust the Opacity slider in the Layers palette until the reflection looks more realistic and blends in with the floor (see Figure 18.11). My floors are freshly waxed, so I took Opacity down to 40%.

Figure 18.11

With opacity reduced, the reflection looks much more realistic.

If you're satisfied with the reflection as it is now, then you're done. Unfortunately, I'm picky and seldom satisfied. The reflection still looks too perfect to me. No floor is that smooth.

6. To introduce a little "dirtiness" into the reflection by blurring it slightly, use the Gaussian Blur filter. A setting of 1 pixel was used to get the effect in Figure 18.12.

Figure 18.12
The reflection is now slightly blurred, which is what a realistic floor does to reflections.

Okay, now it's looking good. The cat image is now interacting with the floor image, creating a realistic effect. There's just one more thing bugging me: the wall behind the cat. Shouldn't the cat and wall interact? Shouldn't the cat be casting just a bit of a shadow on the wall? I think so.

7. Create a drop shadow. Duplicate the original cat layer, select the new cat, and fill it with black. Don't forget to send it behind the cat.

   Instead of offsetting the whole shadow, however, you need a perspective shadow. The bottom of the shadow should match the bottom of the original cat, and the top of it should be cast above the cat onto the wall.

8. To stretch the shadow, select Layer➡Transform➡Distort. Grab the top middle handle that appears and drag it upward to about what you see in Figure 18.13. Double-click within the box to approve the change.

18

Figure 18.13

Stretching the cat's shadow onto the wall.

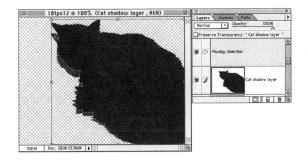

9. Deselect the shadow. Obviously it's too dark and too sharp.

10. Time for another Gaussian Blur. We want a really fuzzy shadow, so it looks like the cat is being illuminated by ambient light, not a specific light source. A value of 12 pixels looks good.

11. Finally, grab the Opacity slider and move it down to 60%, so the shadow looks lighter and the wall texture shows through a bit (see Figure 18.14).

Figure 18.14

The finished image, with reflection and shadow.

18

The image now looks like one piece instead of three disparate images thrown together. That's what special effects such as reflections can do for you.

Summary

A "special effect" isn't about specific instructions and narrowly defined settings—it's about experimenting with all that Photoshop has to offer and being pleasantly surprised by new discoveries. As you use Photoshop's features (especially its filters) more and more, you'll uncover an endless stream of special effects. This hour has given you just a small taste of what's possible.

Have fun creating your own special effects!

Q&A

Q How would you place a reflection in water?

A Much the same way that we did on a tile floor, except that I'd apply an appropriate ripple filter to the reflection, as well as blurring it. Depending on the kind of water, you may want to apply the blur first and then the ripple, or vice versa. Try both and see which looks more realistic.

18

Hour **19**

Photoshop Plug-ins and Add-ons

By now, you have seen, if not used, most of the 99 filters that came with your copy of Photoshop. There couldn't possibly be any more, could there? Well, Photoshop is like those fashion dolls or action figures that kids of a certain age demand. You can't just buy Batman and Robin or Barbie. You need the Batmobile, Stately Wayne Manor, Barbie's Dream House, yacht, and RV... After you see how much fun you can have with the basic filters, you'll want Eye Candy, KPT and Convolver, Photo Tools, and at least several dozen of the latest shareware filters, too. And the list goes on.

You've probably also considered buying a graphics tablet and more RAM (you can never have too much). And maybe you need a faster computer to make all these tools work a little more efficiently. You don't have to have any of these things, but for the next hour, let's pretend we're kids in a candy store. We'll sample everything possible.

Where to Get Them

Commercial plug-in sets, such as the KPT, Chromatica, and Eye Candy packages described in this hour can be found in mail-order catalogs or at your friendly local computer dealer. You can generally download demo versions from the publisher's web sites, and upgrade by phone.

On the other hand, you needn't spend a lot of money. It often amazes me how many talented and generous people there are who not only write useful software, but then turn around and give it away or sell it for such a pittance that they might as well be giving it away. I am speaking, of course, of shareware, and the authors who spend many long nights polishing a program, and then upload it to CompuServe, AOL, or the web. If you go searching in appropriate areas for Mac or Windows software, you should find plenty of new and useful Photoshop plug-ins.

TIME SAVER

I did a Lycos search for "Photoshop filter," and got back a list of hundreds of sites triggered by that combination of keywords. Here are some good ones to get you started:

```
http://www.alienskin.com
http://the-tech.mit.edu/KPT/
ftp://ftp.asi.com/pub/photoshop/
```

How to Install Them

Few things could be simpler than installing an individual filter. Drag it into the Photoshop filter folder if you're using a Mac, or follow whatever procedure is necessary to do the same on a Windows machine. If you purchase a set of filters, such as Alien Skin's Eye Candy, there's an installer included that automatically places the filters where they belong. Installed third-party filters appear in the filter list after Photoshop's native filters. Figure 19.1 shows my current collection.

19

Figure 19.1

The Filter menu.

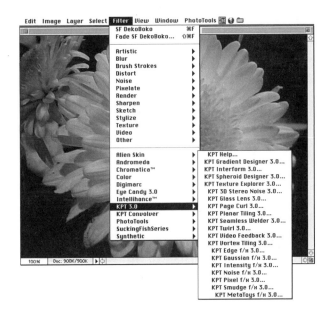

Kai's Power Tools

Kai Krause is a legend in the field of computer graphics. He's the guiding genius behind Kai's Power Tools, Bryce, Convolver, Vector Effects, Final Effects, Goo, Soap, and probably many goodies yet to be announced. Power Tools 3 (also known as KPT), the current edition, comes with an "Explorer Guide" rather than a manual. There's much to explore, but as Kai says in a foreword, you really don't need to read the book. The interfaces are designed to be as intuitive and as interesting as possible. There are excellent help screens available within each filter. (Look for a question mark and click it.) The goal of these filters, along with doing interesting things to your photos, is to do interesting things to your mind and to your way of working with the computer.

Lens f/x

One of the coolest and most useful of Kai's tools is the Lens. If you think Swiss Army Knife, and turn it into a magnifying glass that does tricks, you'll have the beginning of an understanding of the Lens f/x. The tool is shown in Figure 19.2. Each of the lines, bumps, and buttons on it does something. Clicking the words Lens f/x opens the menu of effects available with this tool, enabling you to switch without going back to the Photoshop screen. Effects that the Lens applies are: Pixel, Gaussian, Noise, Edge, Intensity, Smudge, Glass Lens, and Twirl.

Figure 19.2

Kai's Lens f/x tool.

The gray marks along the left side, along with the two red balls on either end, control the intensity and opacity of the effect you're applying. The left side handles intensity and the right opacity. Clicking either ball and dragging up increases the percentage, whereas dragging down decreases it. The third ball, when present, controls the directionality of the effect. Clicking and dragging this one applies that direction to the effect if it's an effect that can be directional. In the figure, we're using the pixel effect, which treats the image as if it were composed of grains of sand. These can be blown around and scattered, so directionality is available.

The top button is the Preview button. It toggles your view through the lens between the center of the image and whatever the lens happens to be on top of. You can drag it all over the image to preview the effect on different areas. You can also drag it across the rest of the screen to see what your menu bars, trash can, or recycle bin looks like with the effect applied. The lower button is the reset button. It returns all the settings to their defaults. The gauge directly below the reset button is the options gauge. Pressing it opens the menu listing options for applying the effect. You have, generally speaking, the same options you have when applying any other Photoshop effects: Normal, Darken, Lighten, Multiply, and so on. Remember that after you apply a KPT effect, you can still go back and fade it using Photoshop's Fade settings.

When you have adjusted the effect the way you want it, click the small green dot at the bottom right of the lens to apply it. If you decide you don't want it, click the red dot instead to cancel and return to the regular Photoshop screen.

TIME SAVER

Try combining KPT effects with the regular Photoshop filters. If you combine, for instance, Photoshop's Glowing Edges filter (Filter➡Stylize➡ Glowing Edges) and the KPT Twirl Kaleidoscope effect, you can create beautiful stained glass window patterns.

19

Texture Explorer

This is Kai's texture generator. It comes with a library of default textures, all of which are generated mathematically, hence they demand little in the way of memory or hard drive space. The Texture Designer interface is somewhat intimidating at first glance. The large square on the right is the source texture, and the squares surrounding it hold derivative textures, all recompiled each time you make a change. As you can see in Figure 19.3, you can use your own image as the source for texture generation. Clicking any of the initial 16 derivative textures makes it the source, and 16 new variations are generated, and so on until you get tired of clicking. If you find one you like, you can protect it by clicking it while pressing (Option)[Alt]. This puts a red line around it, protecting it and keeping it from changing when you next change the source texture.

Figure 19.3

The Texture Explorer.

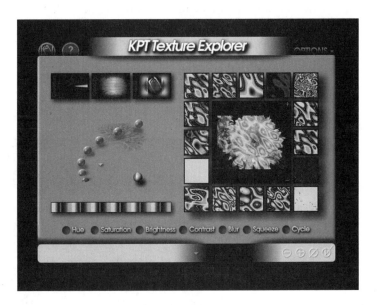

The collection of red and/or aqua balls on the left is the Mutation Tree. (Note the shadow of a tree beneath.) These balls represent the degree of mutation that the filter adds each time you create new texture sets. The bottom-most ball applies minimal mutation, and so on, up the tree to the top ball, which is maximum mutation. This gives you results that don't even remotely resemble the source. Clicking the balls on the mutation tree results in new mutations based on the same source.

The multicolored globe changes the gradients used to generate colors for the derivative textures. Each time you click the color ball, Explorer applies a different gradient. The strip below it shows the current gradient. Clicking the strip brings up a pop-up menu that lets you select a preset from hundreds that are included.

19

The words at the bottom of the screen each represent a control that affects the gradient on which your texture is based. You can change any of these by clicking and dragging right or left.

The three small windows near the top of the screen represent rotation, opacity, and glue. The rotation window lets you rotate your source texture by clicking and dragging. The opacity window lets you adjust the opacity of the gradient, making it more or less transparent, by clicking and dragging left or right. When you double-click the same window it cycles through the sample backgrounds so that you can see the results of applying your texture to different kinds of images.

Spheroid Designer

This interface is a little weird. According to the book, it "...may seem like a bunch of balls dropped into a pile of mud...," but it is "...actually a bunch of spheres dropped onto an old, stale brownie." Hey, those are Kai's words, not mine. Weird, yes. Powerful, you betcha. The spheroid designer gives you pseudo 3D modeling power in what's really only a two-dimensional program. You can take an image, convert it to a relief, and turn it into one, several, or hundreds of spheres, balls, little roundish things—whatever. Figure 19.4 shows the spheroid designer in operation.

Figure 19.4

Kai's Spheroid Designer.

The sample sphere at the center shows the work in progress. It's the equivalent of a preview window. The four smaller clusters of spheres around it are the light sources you can apply to your sphere. Click the larger ones to turn them on and use the small, marble-sized ones to

19

control the color, position, intensity, and highlight intensity of each light source. As with any of Kai's tools, clicking the logo lets you see the effect in full-screen form. Figure 19.5 shows the chrysanthemum spheres applied over the original image.

Figure 19.5

Adding spheres to the picture.

The three balls at the lower left of the screen control the curvature of the sphere, the glossiness and amount of ambient light around it, and the opacity. Clicking and dragging on these balls changes their settings.

TIME SAVER

Some of these operations can take a great deal of memory. If you can't place your sphere over the background you want to, close that file and save it to a new, blank screen. Then you can merge the two images later.

There are many more dots and balls and other goodies to click in this interface. The clustered balls determine how many spheres you generate. The mutation tree in the upper-left corner of the screen, as in the texture generator, gives you random variations on your sphere. You can set bump polarity, height, rotation, and zoom with the four small dots below and to the right of the bump map panel. The best way to figure out what the various buttons and dots do is to experiment. You won't get bored with this tool, and even if you do nothing else for a week, you won't discover all its possibilities.

More Tools

There are other KPT tools that do interesting and occasionally useful things. Glass lens adds distortion to an image. Gradient designer does what its name implies, but being one of Kai's tools, it does so with an interesting and unique interface. Page curl makes your picture look as if it came from an old, dry book. Seamless welder creates images that wrap around a 3D object with no visible seam. Twirl sends your picture through a tornado, variable as to intensity and direction. It also contains the kaleidoscope filter that makes your pictures look as if you're seeing them through an actual kaleidoscope. Figure 19.6 shows a sample of the twirl effect applied to the flower.

Figure 19.6

Twirl is fun.

KPT Convolver

If those initials seem familiar, they should. Convolver is another Kai creation. You could think of it as Power Tools' more practically minded brother. Convolver has two functions: corrective and creative. If you only use it for one of these, you'll be happy with your investment, but you'll be missing half the fun. The good thing about Convolver is not so much what it does, though it's extremely powerful and definitely useful. Its biggest feature is that it brings all the tools together. When you're tweaking an image, you don't have to keep going back to the menu to get new tools. Everything's right there. If changing the saturation affects something else, you don't have to go very far to fix it.

Figure 19.7 shows Convolver in Tweak mode. (Your other two choices are Explore and Design.) The large central diamond is the preview window, and the smaller one above it is called the Current Kernel Tile and is used to select a portion of the image to mutate in Explore mode. Along the right side of the screen are the image controls. To apply one, click its button and drag right or left. Numbers appear in the bar below the preview window to tell you what settings you're using. Most of these tools can be applied as a negative as well as a positive.

19

Saturation, for instance, starts at 100% when you first click the button. Dragging left lowers the saturation to amounts less than 100%, whereas dragging right raises it. How high? I stopped after 3200%.

Figure 19.7

Making multiple adjustments with Convolver.

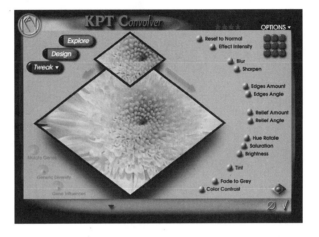

TIME SAVER

Exploration is its own reward with Convolver, but there are more tangible ones as well. To encourage you to poke around, the program includes some hidden tools. They're called stars, and the idea is that you get one after you've shown you really use the program. Each one adds a new tool when you're ready to apply it. It takes a while to work up to all five stars.

Design mode uses the image controls in pairs, taking the central diamond and breaking it into fifteen windows, each representing a combination of two image control effects in a different degree of variation. That sounds confusing, but it should become clear when you look at Figure 19.8.

You'll notice an arrow along each axis of the diamond and a label denoting one of the effects. There are nine different options for each axis, and considering that they can go positive or negative, that makes eighteen possible settings for each axis. Multiply that by fifteen tiles of variations, and ten degrees of intensity for each setting, and you end up with a lot of options. The difference between Design mode and Tinker mode, other than the difference in the interface, is that Design mode has the image effects divided into logical pairs, whereas in Tinker mode you can adjust them individually.

One of Convolver's best features is the multiple Undos. You can undo—and of course, Redo, by pressing (Command-R)[Control-R]—up to 200 levels of change.

19

Figure 19.8
Convolver in Design mode.

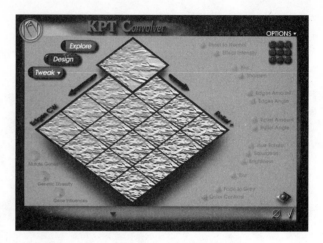

Explore mode is the creative side of Convolver. It applies new mutations based on some combination of colors and textures every time you click the mouse. Although it's not especially useful for cleaning up a poor-quality photo, it could turn something you don't care for into a work of art.

Alien Skin's Eye Candy

Kai's not the only one who invents interesting plug-ins for Photoshop. The guys over at Alien Skin have come up with a set of goodies called Eye Candy (formerly called Black Box). Some of the Eye Candy effects are probably not for everyday use, unless your day job is designing covers for a science fiction magazine. Others, however, such as drop shadow and perspective shadow, could be very useful.

The Alien Skin interface changes according to the effect you're applying, but the basic screen, shown in Figure 19.9, remains the same.

Figure 19.9
Alien Skin's Eye Candy.

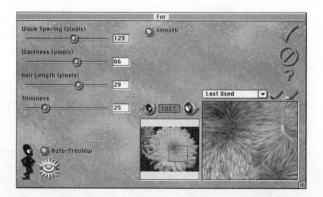

19

In this example, the chrysanthemum is having a bad hair day. Fur is one of the 21 Eye Candy effects, along with Smoke, Fire, Jiggle, Squint, Swirl, and a lot more.

Applying many of these effects requires first selecting an area to which the effect will be applied or adding a layer for it. A few, such as Antimatter, simply do their thing. Antimatter's thing is to invert the brightness without affecting the colors or saturation value. Darks become light and lights become dark.

Creating Glass Distortion

Possibly the most useful of the Eye Candy effects is Glass. In Figure 19.10, we're looking at one of my favorite scenes through a sheet of bumpy glass. The glass effect is achieved by simulating three different effects: reflection, refraction, and light filtering. To use the Glass distortion effect, follow these steps:

Figure 19.10

Using Glass distortion.

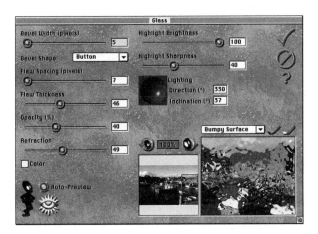

1. Start with a simple image. Glass works best on uncomplicated photos. Select the Glass filter from the Eye Candy list.

2. Set the bevel width. This controls both the width of the smooth outer edge of the glass and the apparent thickness of the glass. Larger values, used with high refraction, make your glass seem thicker. Smaller values, with low refraction, make the glass appear thinner.

3. Flaw spacing and Flaw thickness create the ripples in your glass. Smaller spacing increases the frequency of flaws, whereas larger thickness makes them more obvious.

4. Use the color box to select a color or shade of "dirt" for the glass. A very light gray suggests a dusty window without affecting the colors of the original picture. Use the Opacity slider to determine how much of a color tint is applied to the glass. Higher values add more color. Lower values enable the picture to show more clearly.

5. Set the smoothness. Higher values remove small ridges in the bevel.

6. Refraction is the most important control for "glassiness." It controls the amount your picture is warped by the glass. The scale runs from 0–100%, but only the low end of it lets your image remain intelligible. Setting refraction past 50% reduces the underlying photo to vague shapes.

7. Highlight brightness and sharpness affect only the white highlights that appear on the "bumps." Higher values here give a glossier effect. Direction and inclination can be set by typing numbers into their boxes or by dragging the ball around until the lighting looks right.

8. Watch the effect of each change in the preview window as you make it. When you like what you see, click the check mark to confirm it and return to Photoshop, or press Return. If the overall effect is too much, undo it and lower the settings or use Photoshop's Fade command to moderate it.

As is true of any of these tools, the more you explore, the more you learn about working with it.

Extensis PhotoTools

PhotoTools is a comprehensive set of plug-ins that makes working with Photoshop easier and more pleasant. It includes a version of Intellihance (a "smart" filter for exposure correction), and it has several other goodies as well. The first thing PhotoTools does is to add another menu to your screen, with its own options and filters.

The main goodie, PhotoBars, adds toolbar functions to Photoshop. Instead of fishing through menus or popping out the palettes in the Photoshop Toolbox, you can just click a tool icon at the top of the screen to get the command or tool you want. More to the point, you can customize the Toolbox to the way you work: Keep stuff hidden that you don't use often, for example, or put the buttons you press again and again in easy reach. And then there's SmartBars, which automates the process of building a toolbar for you by tracking your work, and assembles a list of the buttons and commands you use. Then, with a single click, you can turn the list into a toolbar. In Figure 19.11, SmartBars is running, and the PhotoBar toolbar is installed.

Figure 19.11
Extensis PhotoTools.

19

SmartBars makes a list of the tools you used on an image. When you're finished with it, you can look at the list and decide whether you want it as a custom toolbar for future projects. If so, you can save it by clicking in the PhotoBar menu and giving it a name. You can also edit it or add more tools using the Toolbar editor. You can even generate custom icons for my favorite filters. Maybe a picture of Kai?

PhotoText

If there's one reason to buy PhotoTools, it's the type tool, PhotoText. As you probably noticed, Photoshop doesn't have a whole lot of flexibility or even real WYSIWYG interface on typography. PhotoText makes up for this lack by letting you place type over a picture while you're typing it. The PhotoText window is shown in Figure 19.12.

Figure 19.12

PhotoText is terrific!

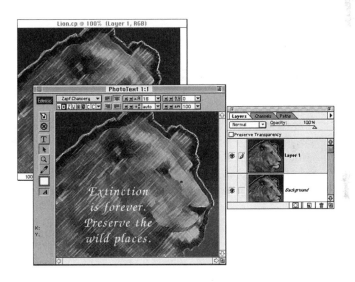

19

You can set width and tracking for your type, adjust leading, and set anti-aliased, justified, flush left or right, or centered type at the click of a mouse, just as in any other good graphics program. Text handling is Photoshop's only deficiency, and PhotoText definitely fills in the gap. Even better, it's easy to use.

1. Prepare your background first. Remember that a busy picture makes type harder to read. Fade it down or reduce it to two colors as we've done here.

2. Open the PhotoText window. Choose a font and size and click the T icon to place a text block. Position the cursor where you want to start typing and set your type. Drag the handles on the text block to make it larger, if necessary. Type is being set in a new layer, so you needn't worry about covering background elements.

3. Use the arrow icon or just press and hold the Option key to bring back the pointer tool. This enables you to move your text around onscreen if you decide to reposition it. Adjust the leading and tracking in the windows above the preview screen. Change the color with the eyedropper and color picker window.

4. If you're using larger fonts (over 14 point) and want to apply anti-aliasing to prevent jaggies, click the anti-alias button under the color picker.

5. When your page is as you want it, click the arrow icon (top button) to save it or the X button to cancel. Closing the window also cancels the type.

You can change type attributes on individual characters by selecting them with the type tool, or on the entire text block by selecting it. Because the type is set on a new layer, you can easily apply Photoshop's Type Mask tool to turn it into a selection and use it for special effects. Headlines set in this way, because they can be properly kerned and letter-spaced, look better than those done directly in Photoshop.

Sucking Fish Filters

The Sucking Fish filters are freeware ("mailware," actually—the author wants email), but they have one of the most carefully thought out and complicated interfaces you're likely to see. Figure 19.13 shows one of the set, the Frame Curtain filter, which places a beveled edge around your picture. You can vary the bevel type and depth and design your own custom frames. Figure 19.14 shows one way to use it. This would be very nice for a web page displaying your best work.

Figure 19.13

A frame-up?

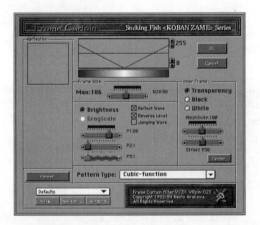

19

Figure 19.14
Framed art.

Summary

In this hour we checked out some of the cool third-party filters you can use with Photoshop. The most versatile and complete package is MetaTools Kai's Power Tools (KPT 3.0), although it's probably not the easiest to use. Alien Skin's Eye Candy filter set includes a great many really odd filters, such as Fur and Fire, as well as very simple-to-apply drop shadow and glow filters. Intellihance PhotoTools, another set of plug-ins, is a little less weird than the others, and the set includes an excellent TextTool that's far easier to use than Photoshop's own, and is also much more versatile. I strongly recommend this one.

Q&A

Q Is there a way to design your own Photoshop filters?

A The CD-ROM includes a plug-in called Filter Factory, which supposedly lets you do so. It's a fairly complicated procedure, and the documentation is lacking. Probably the best (easiest) way to get custom effects is to use KPT Convolver, either alone or in combination with other filters.

19

Hour **20**

Compositing

You may know compositing by another name. You may call it "combining" or making a collage or a photo-montage. Whatever the name, the goal is the same: to make one picture from pieces of other ones. Photoshop is the ideal program for this kind of work for several reasons:

- ☐ It has the tools to assemble pieces of different pictures.
- ☐ It gives you the capability to work in layers.
- ☐ Its filters enable you to blend pictures and add shadows and reflections more easily and effectively than any other graphics program could.

You can use the techniques described here, along with the ones you've already learned, to produce all sorts of surrealistic images, and for many users, this is what Photoshop is all about. For others, myself included, compositing is a way of making up for deficiencies in the original picture.

Sources for Images

Pictures are everywhere. You can download thousands of images from the web, or you can buy CDs full of photographs and line art. In addition, you can either scan conventional photos or import from a digital camera into Photoshop.

When you start thinking about combining images, you'll probably realize there are some pictures more suitable than others for this kind of use. You could even classify some as backgrounds, others as objects, and some as the raw materials from which to create special effects. As you browse through your own pictures and look at collections of *stock photos*, some images will jump out at you and you'll begin to see possible combinations.

NEW TERM   Stock photos are pictures that are made available to you, either royalty free or for payment (usually the latter), to do with as you see fit. You can use stock photos in your reports, ads—practically any way you want, as long as you're not reselling them as is or using them in any way that's libelous, defamatory, pornographic, or otherwise illegal. Be sure you read and understand the licensing policies before you use stock photos.

Extensis PhotoDisc is typical of stock photo collections. The PhotoDisc collection includes over 50,000 pictures of everything you can imagine. A few samples are included on the PhotoTools and Fetch CDs. You can purchase the Extensis PhotoDisc from your usual software sources or from Extensis at http://www.extensis.com. Figure 20.1 shows a page from their catalog. You can use these kinds of images in combination with your own. If you need something basic, such as a slab of concrete to use as a background, it is faster, cheaper, and just as effective to use one from stock. Let's start compositing with a couple of images from the Extensis stock catalog.

Figure 20.1

Stock photos.

Of course, as you wander around town with your digital camera in your pocket, you can start your own stock collection. In fact, it's one of the ways you can make money with your pictures, allowing you to invest the profits in more software and higher resolution cameras.

TIME SAVER

> If you are interested in learning more about digital photography, look for *Teach Yourself Digital Photography in 14 Days*, from Hayden Books. It's a good one—I wrote it.

Making One Picture from Two

Looking through the catalog of stock photos, I noticed a picture of a light bulb and another of a rose. Combining them could give us an interesting image. First, open the light bulb in Photoshop, because it will be the main image (see Figure 20.2).

Figure 20.2
And there was light.

Next, open the rose picture. Because it's horizontal and the other one is vertical, the first steps will be to rotate it and crop it. Figure 20.3 shows the rose after this step.

The photo is still not what's wanted here. We want it to stand up straight. Select it with the rectangular Marquee tool and free rotate it until the flower is vertical. Check out the action in Figure 20.4. Now it's oriented correctly.

20

Figure 20.3

Cropped and rotated.

Figure 20.4

Standing tall.

There are several ways to get rid of the background; the easiest is to select the rose and copy it, leaving everything else behind. After doing this, jump back to the light bulb picture, and make a new layer. When you paste the rose into the new layer, it the screen should look like Figure 20.5.

20

Figure 20.5

I moved it over the bulb.

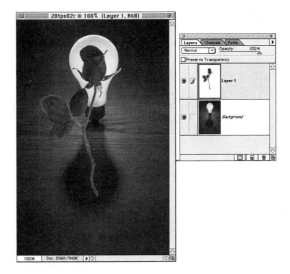

Now, we're about halfway there. The rose is just a little large, so we'll scale it down until it fits inside the bulb. Layer➡Transform➡Scale puts a scaling box over the flower, so I can resize it to fit properly inside the bulb. While I'm at it, I'll use the Eraser and trim the stem to fit. Figure 20.6 shows the results of this step. Because the rose is on a separate layer, I don't have to worry about damaging the background.

Figure 20.6

Trimmed to fit.

It looks almost right, but the rose appears to be on top of the light bulb instead of in it. Reducing the opacity of the new layer to 70% gives the flower the same sort of milkiness as the light bulb.

As a final touch, deselect the rose layer for a moment, and select the light bulb. Applying the Eye Candy Glow filter to the bulb, as shown in Figure 20.7 turns on the light. At the same time, we can add a little pink to the glow, to suggest that the rose, rather than just the bulb, is glowing. Figure 20.8 shows the final picture.

Figure 20.7

The Glow filter adds some light.

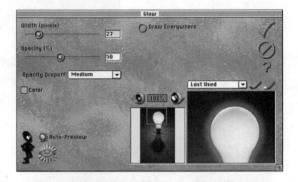

Figure 20.8

A rosy glow, perhaps?

20

Controlling Transparency in Overlaid Images

It's simple to paste one opaque image over another one. You just do it. Transparent images are harder to work with, though Photoshop makes it a little bit easier by giving you transparency control. When you're creating a multi-layered picture, as in Figure 20.7, you have two ways to control the way the layers blend. One is the Opacity slider. You can set any amount of opacity, from 100% all the way down to zero, at which point whatever is on the layer has become transparent and completely disappeared. You can also control the effect by using the Blending Modes menu. By applying different modes to different layers, you can control the way each layer overlies the others.

Realistic Composites

Creating an image that's not meant to be completely realistic is relatively easy; faking realism is a lot harder. The main things to consider in making composites are:

- ☐ Keep your backgrounds simple.
- ☐ Isolate the elements on different layers for easier editing.
- ☐ Make sure the pieces you combine are in the proper scale for each other.
- ☐ When you're done, merge the layers for a smaller file.

CAUTION

Remember that adding shadows, reflections, or other special effects can make a big difference in the end result. Watch out for perspective, too. If it's wrong, you'll know it, although you may not know exactly why.

The series of pictures that follows shows a problem that I encountered with perspective and how I solved it.

Figure 20.9 is a photo I shot of an old windmill on Cape Cod. It was an overcast day, in the middle of a hot summer. The sky is gray, and the grass is more brown than green. As for the flowers along the fence…they're best forgotten. But the windmill is interesting. What can I do to improve this picture?

On that same trip, I found a pretty cottage with a rose-covered fence (see Figure 20.10). Perhaps the fence from that picture could replace the boring one? It looks as if it might work, but first we'll have to get rid of everything that's not part of the fence.

20

Figure 20.9

Not very exciting…

Figure 20.10

Can we make this fence fit?

Selecting with the Polygon Lasso tool and deleting removes the sidewalk and everything below it. Cropping and then using a combination of the Magic Wand and Eraser tools gets rid of the rest, leaving nothing but fence. Figure 20.11 shows just the fence.

20

Figure 20.11

Fence minus everything else.

I'll make a new layer on the windmill picture and copy the fence into it. Then I need to select and remove the white background that imported along with it, but that's a matter of two clicks with the Magic Wand and one click of the Delete key. With the fence moved into position, I see one minor problem. I stood to the left of the fence and to the right of the windmill (see Figure 20.12).

Figure 20.12

Oops. The perspective is wrong.

Flipping the fence is easy. I just select Layer➡Transform➡Flip horizontal, and the fence reverses. Now it looks better. Applying some extra roses with the Rubber Stamp helps fill in some gaps, and adding clouds to the (selected) sky completes the effect. After some experimenting, I decided to use Darken Only as the Blending mode when I brought in the sky, so it didn't overpower the delicate lines on the windmill blades. As a final step, I'll merge the layers. Figure 20.13 shows the final photo—much improved from the original.

Replacing a Background

Grandpa wanted an up-to-date picture of his two grandsons, but the boys are both away at college most of the year. I had a digital snapshot I took on a rare occasion when they were both together, but it was one that I'd shot to test a new camera. They were acting silly, and the background was really awful. It seemed as if this one was beyond help, but I never underestimate Photoshop.

Figure 20.14 shows the original picture. Pretty awful—but because the background was so complicated, the Magic Wand won't do much good. I could select and delete it a piece at a

20

time with the rectangular Marquee tool and Lasso, but that would take quite a while. Instead, I started with the Polygon Lasso and worked around their heads and shoulders, carefully drawing a line around the two boys. I then circled it around the top of the screen so that I'd selected everything behind their heads (see Figure 20.15). What I wasn't able to select and delete I erased. When I had both boys selected with no background, I cut them out and pasted them into a new page. It's shown below in Figure 20.16. But they don't look right without anything behind them.

Figure 20.13
All it needed was a new fence and some enhanced color.

Figure 20.14.
Complete with bunny ears...

20

Figure 20.15

Deleting the background.

Figure 20.16

Plain vanilla boys.

20

To make it easier to blend them into a background, I selected the white space behind them, and chose Select➡Inverse, to select just the boys. Then I applied Select➡Feather and feathered the edges by 4 pixels.

Because they've never been to San Francisco, I decided to give them a free trip. I found a picture that made a nice background and simply pasted them on a layer in front of it. Then I used the Smudge tool to gently blur some hard edges. I used the Despeckle filter to smooth out skin tones that were uneven, and Figure 20.17 shows the final result. Grampa will be delighted, and I didn't have to pay for plane tickets.

Figure 20.17

Two dudes, California dreaming.

Combining pictures isn't difficult. You simply need to prepare them by removing unwanted backgrounds or other bits, and then assemble them in layers. Don't forget to merge the layers when you're sure that you're done working on the picture. Otherwise, your files, if they have several layers, can be quite large.

"Composites" from Nowhere

You've seen in some of the earlier hours that Photoshop can create art "from scratch," as well as edit and alter existing photos. As a final attempt at compositing, let's see what we can make out of nothing.

I'll start with a new page and apply a gradient as a background. Gradients can be either linear or radial and can have as many transparent or opaque colors as you want. To create a gradient, follow these steps:

1. Click the Gradient tool, and double-click to open its Options palette, which is shown in Figure 20.18.

Figure 20.18

The Gradient Tool Options palette.

20

2. Use the Type menu to choose radial or linear blend. I want to use a linear blend, which will apply the colors in a straight line from one point to another. Check Dither to create a smoother blend.

3. Choose a color combination from the pop-up menu. The preview bar at the bottom of the window shows the currently selected gradient. If it's not precisely what you want, that's okay.

4. Click the Edit button to open the Gradient Editor, shown in Figure 20.19.

Figure 20.19

The Gradient Editor.

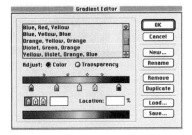

5. Select the Color button to adjust the colors in the gradient.

6. Click the left square beneath the gradient bar to change the starting color. The triangle above it will turn black, showing that you're editing that part of the gradient. To change the color, click the color swatch and choose a color from the color picker, or click either the Foreground or Background selection boxes (marked F and B, respectively) to pick either of those colors. Or, hold the cursor over a color on the gradient to sample, and when it becomes an eyedropper, click it.

7. Click the right square and follow the procedures in Step 6 to change the ending color of the gradient.

8. Drag the diamond(s) above the gradient left or right to adjust the midpoint, or blend points if there are more than two colors.

9. Click an additional color selection box and drag it to the gradient to add another color. Choose F or B, or the empty box to add another color. Clicking on it will open the color picker so you can choose the color.

10. Click OK when you are satisfied with the colors on your gradient.

11. Use the cross-hair cursor, which will automatically appear to draw a line onscreen where the gradient should be applied.

TIME SAVER

If you want to start from scratch, don't bother to select an existing gradient. Just click Edit to open the Editor. Then, click New and give your new gradient a name. Follow the previous steps to define its colors.

In Figure 20.20, I have drawn the line from top to bottom to fill the screen with my gradient. It's starting to look like a sunset, which is what I had in mind, but it needs a sun. I'll use Eye

---

Candy's Star filter to create one. Figure 20.21 shows the Star designer box, and Figure 20.22 shows the star applied.

Figure 20.20
The gradient applied.

Figure 20.21
Eye Candy Star filter.

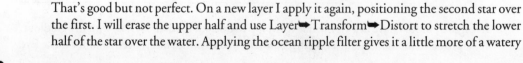

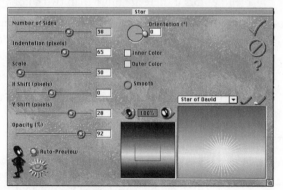

20

That's good but not perfect. On a new layer I apply it again, positioning the second star over the first. I will erase the upper half and use Layer➡Transform➡Distort to stretch the lower half of the star over the water. Applying the ocean ripple filter gives it a little more of a watery quality. A few evening stars and comet Hale-Bopp (applied with the paintbrush) add to the tranquillity.

Figure 20.22

Adding a sun. (Well, okay, it's a star, but so is the sun.)

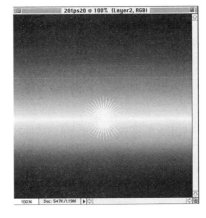

As a final touch, I drew in a sailboat, copied it on a separate layer, and flipped it vertically. After again applying the ripple filter to it, I faded the reflection. Figure 20.23 shows the final picture.

Figure 20.23

Sunset sail.

20

Summary

Composites, montages—whatever you call them, they're simply combinations of two or more images, carefully merged. Use your own pictures, stock photos from collections, or create images by combining techniques and filters. It's fun, and it's effective. It's one of the things Photoshop does exceptionally well. Be sure to spend some time playing with compositing.

Q&A

Q Can I apply a filter to a gradient?

A Certainly. It's easiest if the gradient is on a separate layer. Just make the gradient the active layer and apply any filter or combination you like. The results often make an interesting background for other pictures, too. Start by trying the texture filters and some of the brush stroke ones. These are generally successful.

20

Hour 21

Photo Repair—Black and White

Fixing damaged or "just plain lousy" pictures is the number one reason why most people buy Photoshop. It can really work miracles on old, torn, faded photographs and it can also make up for most, if not all, of the flaws in your snapshots. You can use Photoshop to recompose a picture that's off-center, tilted, or has too much empty space.

You can edit out the power lines and trash cans that spoil the landscape. You can even remove unwanted former spouses, or that awful boyfriend your daughter finally dumped, from family portraits. It's much easier to erase them from the pictures than to get rid of them in real life.

Easy Fixes

Let's start by looking at some of the things you can do to fix up an old picture that may have faded, yellowed, or been torn or damaged. First, we'll consider a couple of old wedding pictures that need a little bit of adjusting and touching up. We'll run (literally) through the steps involved in fixing them and the tools you'll need to know how to use. (Remember, you can always flip to the front of the book to refresh your memory about these tools, too.) Finally, we'll take an extremely damaged picture and work through it step-by-step, until it looks like new again.

Adjusting for Age

Some pictures don't need very much work. The photo in Figure 21.1 was taken in 1900 but has been kept in an album away from sunlight for most of the past 97 years. It's turned a little yellow, but it is remarkably well-preserved.

Figure 21.1
This needs only minor touch-ups.

21

To fix this picture, first crop the borders to remove any unnecessary edges. Then, set the mode to Grayscale, which will remove any color information that the scan picked up. That immediately eliminates the yellow and brown tones. Next, use Curves (Image➡Adjust➡Curves) to tweak the contrast a little. By using Curves, we can lighten the light tones without affecting the darks. In Figure 21.2, the slight curve in the window enables you to see just how subtle this adjustment is. Figure 21.3 shows a magnified before and after view, so you can see how the contrast has improved.

Figure 21.2

A slight curve adjustment.

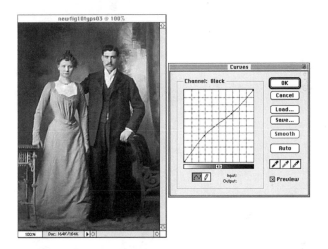

Figure 21.3

The contrast was good before (before: upper left), now it's better (after: lower right).

A couple of spots in the picture could use some minor enhancement. We'll apply the Burn tool to darken some areas where the contrast could be a little better. By applying the Burn tool to only the shadows and with a low percentage setting, we can darken the gentleman's fingers without darkening his whole hand. Similarly, by applying it to midtones, we can separate the lady's jawline from her high whalebone collar. Figure 21.4 shows the final result.

Figure 21.4
Studio portraits, even of this age, generally come out well.

JUST A MINUTE

Many Photoshop users make a habit of applying the Dust & Scratches filter (Filters➡Noise➡Dust & Scratches) to every scanned photo. This is often a mistake, because although it does make dust particles less

21

obvious, it also softens the focus of the picture. If you decide to try it, evaluate the results carefully, using the Preview checkbox to toggle back and forth, turning the filter preview on and off until you're certain that it's an improvement.

A second wedding picture, this one only 50 years old, is in much worse shape. It is both yellowed and faded, and it looks as if somebody tried to do some retouching on it with a pencil, making matters worse. The untouched photo is shown in Figure 21.5.

Figure 21.5

This one needs more serious work.

21

Again, start by cropping, and then convert the photo to Grayscale to get rid of the yellow tones. The contrast ratio in this picture isn't as good as in the previous one, so the next step is to attempt to improve it. The Levels window shows the histogram for this picture, which tells us that the whites are too dark and the darks not dark enough (see Figure 21.6). Resetting the black and white points helps a lot. Resetting the midpoint to the center of the peak in the histogram helps even more. The best way to learn to make these adjustments is to work on a copy of a "bad" picture, and simply experiment with the settings until you see the picture looking the way you want it to. Notice what happens when you move the sliders to the right or left.

Figure 21.6
Changing the Levels adjusts the contrast.

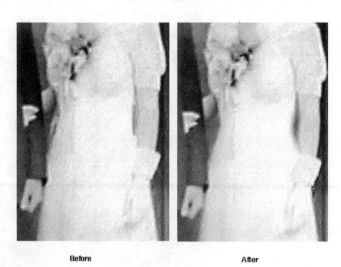

Before   After

Correcting Scratches and Problem Areas

Sometimes you need to paint over part of the image, either to fill in scratches or to remove unwanted lines, spots, or in-laws. Use the Eyedropper tool to select a color to paint with. Simply click the Eyedropper on any color (or in this case, shade of gray) in the image that you want to replicate, and that color becomes the foreground color, ready to apply with the Paintbrush, Airbrush, or whatever painting tool you choose. Double-clicking the Eyedropper opens its options window (see Figure 21.7). A pop-up menu gives you the choice of a single pixel color sample or taking an average color from either a 3×3 or 5×5 pixel sample.

In the previous photo, someone, probably the bride, tried to shave a few pounds off her waistline the easy way, by drawing on the photo. You can see it better in the magnified view in Figure 21.8. With the Eyedropper, Brush and Smudge tools, we'll repair the damage and, at the same time, give her the silhouette she hoped for. We need to pick up the appropriate background gray from elsewhere in the picture, paint it in, and smudge it a little bit so it blends. At the same time, we'll darken the edge of her glove, just a little, so it doesn't blend into her dress quite so much.

21

Figure 21.7

The Eyedropper is selected from Photoshop's Toolbox.

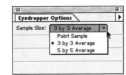

Figure 21.8

You can see the changes from "Before" to "After".

Before   After

Using the Eyedropper tool in a situation like this is much easier than trying to match an existing color or shade of gray on the color wheel. To paint in the background, you need to find another spot in the picture where the color or gray shade is the same one that you'd like to use. Select the Eyedropper and click on it to make that color the foreground color. Then, use your brush to paint in the selected shade. Smudge the edges slightly if necessary to make the new paint blend in.

Taking a closer look at the couple's faces, we can see white streaks, which are apparently an artifact from the scan, because they aren't on the original. Again, figure 21.9 shows the close-up view, before and after retouching. Because the area to work on was so small, we used a single pixel brush as a Smudge tool, and set it for only 20% pressure to not overdo the smudges. When you are working on corrections this small, it's much easier to apply them gradually and let the effect build up rather than trying to do it all in one pass.

21

Figure 21.9
We also darkened the groom's hair, which the photo had made lighter than it was.

Before

After

Cloning with the Rubber Stamp

The Rubber stamp tool is perfect when you need to copy small pieces of the picture and paste them elsewhere. Technically, it's a cloning brush. It samples from a chosen point in the image and duplicates it, exactly as if you'd made a rubber stamp of the selection. Figure 21.10 shows the Rubber Stamp tool and its options window. To select a point to clone from, press (Option)[Alt] while clicking the mouse on the spot you want to copy. Release the key, and start stamping by moving the mouse to the new spot and clicking. You can stamp as many times as you need to.

Figure 21.10
The Rubber Stamp tool's icon looks just like a rubber stamp.

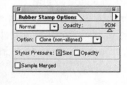

21

Because the Rubber Stamp tool functions like a brush, you can apply all of the brush modes, such as Dissolve, Multiply, and so on. The size and shape of the Rubber Stamp area will be the same as the brush size and shape you have selected. You can also apply the same opacity settings that you would to any brush. Feel free to flip back to Hour 7 to review these tools and settings in greater detail.

The Rubber Stamp Options window lets you select among several ways for the stamp to operate:

- ☐ **Clone (aligned):** When you select a reference point, the stamp creates a duplicate of the image anywhere you start painting, expanding the duplicated portion of the image as you go. Conceivably, you could reproduce the entire image, if you have enough blank canvas.

- ☐ **Clone (non-aligned):** After you select your reference point and start painting, the duplicate portion of the image expands only while you continue to hold down the mouse button. When you release the mouse button and press it again, you start painting another duplicate image from the same reference point.

- ☐ **Pattern (aligned):** You can define a pattern and stamp it with the Rubber Stamp tool. Use the Rectangular marquee to select a piece of image to use as a pattern, and select Define Pattern from the Edit menu. Now, when you use the Rubber Stamp, the pattern will be tiled over the area as you stamp.

- ☐ **Pattern (non-aligned):** Select a pattern as described previously, but each time you release the mouse button and then press it again, the pattern starts over instead of tiling.

- ☐ **From Snapshot:** Use the Rubber Stamp to apply changes to your image selectively. Make the change, take a snapshot of it, then undo the change, and apply it selectively with the Rubber Stamp. You can take a snapshot of your image by choosing Take Snapshot from the Edit menu.

- ☐ **From Saved:** This works like a magic eraser. Where you stamp, the image reverts to the way it was the last time you saved. It's essentially the opposite of the previous process. Instead of selectively applying the changes, you're selectively undoing them.

- ☐ **Impressionist:** This is basically useless. This stamp applies the last saved version of the image in a smudged, spotty, uneven pattern.

TIME SAVER

When you use the Rubber Stamp tool to retouch, always choose a soft-edged brush in a size only slightly larger than the scratch or blemish you're hiding. Retouching is generally easier if you enlarge the image first.

21

For this next photo, we'll need the Rubber Stamp tool and probably all of the tricks in the book. As you can see in Figure 21.11, this picture has been folded, ripped, spilled on, and generally beaten up. We'll go through this one step by step, so you can see exactly what happens at each stage.

Figure 21.11

When it's the only picture of her, you try hard to salvage it.

Cleaning Up a Picture, Step by Step

To make this picture, or any other, look like new:

1. Crop the image to remove the border and any unnecessary parts of the image (anything you remove doesn't have to be retouched.) Select the Cropping tool from the Toolbox. (It pops out from the Marquee tool when you hold down the mouse button.) Drag it across the picture, holding the mouse button down. Use the handles on the Cropping window to fine-tune the selection, then double-click inside the window to crop the image.

2. Set the mode to Grayscale (Image➡Mode➡Grayscale) to remove the colored stains.

3. Open the Histogram window (Image➡Histogram). Look at the Histogram to see what needs to be done to equalize the contrast (see Figure 21.12). In this case, the white and dark points need to be reset and the middle point shifted lighter. To make these changes, we'll need to adjust the Levels.

21

Figure 21.12

The histogram shows a preponderance of darks.

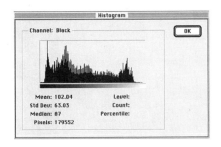

4. Open the Levels window (Image➟Adjust➟Levels) and adjust the levels by dragging the dark point to the right until it's under the beginning of the dark peak of the Histogram. Drag the white point to the left until it's under the beginning of the white peak. Figure 21.13 shows our adjustments.

Figure 21.13

Adjusting the levels improves the contrast.

5. Now, we'll try out the Dust & Scratches filter. (Filters➟Noise➟Dust & Scratches) In this case, it seems that the good it does outweighs the slight fuzziness it adds. (See Figure 21.14 to see the filter applied.) Click OK to apply the filter.

21

Figure 21.14

Removing dust can also remove detail.

6. The filter took care of some of the dust, but left most of the scratches. Use the Rubber Stamp tool to cover them. Select the tool, and open the Brushes and Options windows (Window➡Show Brushes and Window➡Show Options). Choose a small brush and set the Opacity to 90%. Choose Clone non-aligned, pick the dark tone adjacent to the scratch, and start stamping it out. Remember, to set a spot to use as a stamp, press (Option)[Alt] while you click the mouse on the spot you want to copy. Figure 21.15 shows the partially treated photo. Remember to change your stamp selection as the areas the scratch runs through change value.

Figure 21.15

Help stamp out scratched photos!

7. The best way to remove the scratches in the little girl's hair is to use a Paintbrush and repaint the hair, rather than trying to stamp it. To make the task easier, enlarge the picture. Click the Zoom tool at the bottom of the Toolbox to enlarge the picture.

8. Select the Eyedropper tool and click the medium dark gray on the right side of her bangs. Choose a small Paintbrush and paint over the scratches, changing shades of gray with the Eyedropper as you need to. Figure 21.16 shows before and after views of this step.

21

Figure 21.16

Be careful not to apply paint too evenly.

Before   After

9. At the same time, you can use the Smudge tool to remove the dark shadows under her eyes. Select the Smudge tool and a small Paintbrush. Then set the pressure option to about 40% and smudge gently, as if you were using a fingertip to wipe away the spots. You can also use the Smudge tool to make the hair blend in better. Stroke it gently with short strokes.

10. Next, apply the Dodge and Burn tools as needed to bring out details. Dodging lightens the image and burning darkens it. Sponging increases or decreases the saturation of colors. Figure 21.17 shows these useful tools. (See Hour 9 for more details on using them.) Select the Dodge tool and set its exposure to 25%, so the effect will be gradual.

Figure 21.17

The Dodge tool looks like a lollipop, the Burn tool like a hand, and the Sponge tool like a sponge.

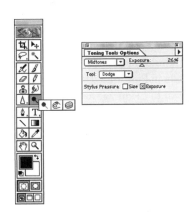

11. We can dodge her shoes so they aren't lost in the grass and burn a little on the top of her head to even out the hair tones. The effect will build if you release the mouse button and then click it, and go over the same area again. Be careful not to overdo it. Burning in the background behind her head gets rid of the light patch. Figure 21.18 shows the final version.

21

Figure 21.18
Compare this to the
picture we started with.

Applying Tints

It was common in the early days of photography for pictures to be brown, blue, or silver instead of plain black and white. Sepia toning, which gave a warm reddish brown color, is the most common, and one we tend to associate with most "old time" photos.

If you want to restore the sepia tone to a picture you've been working on, Photoshop gives you several ways to accomplish this. Perhaps the easiest is to reset the mode to CMYK or RGB, depending on whether the finished photo will be viewed in print or onscreen, and use the Hue/Saturation window (Image➡Adjust➡Hue) to add color. After you open the window, as shown in Figure 21.19, check the Colorize box, as well as the Preview box. Then move the sliders until the image looks the way you want it to. Click OK when you're satisfied with the color.

Duotones

A somewhat richer tone can be achieved by using Duotone mode, which combines the grayscale image with a colored ink. Duotones are often used to extend the gray range of a photograph, because a typical printing press is capable of reproducing only about 50 shades of gray, whereas Photoshop can generate 256. To create a duotone, start with a grayscale image. Within Duotone mode, you also have the option of adding additional colors, to make a tritone or quadtone. Although duotones are usually composed of black and a single color, as in Figure 21.20, there's no good reason why you can't use two colors instead, especially if the end result is to be displayed on a web page or as part of a desktop presentation, rather than in printed form.

21

Figure 21.19

This old paddle wheel steamer was digitally photographed in April, 1997.

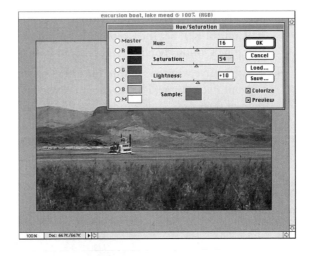

Figure 21.20

To create a tritone, add another color.

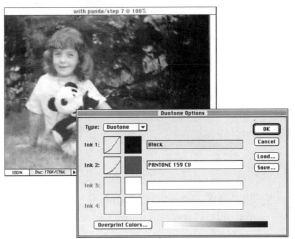

Because it has a nice range of grays, the photo of the little girl and panda is a good candidate for conversion to a duotone. To make a duotone from a grayscale image, follow these steps:

1. Open the Duotone Options window (Image➧Mode➧Duotone).

2. Select Duotone from the Type pop-up menu, if it's not already selected (see Figure 21.20). This menu is in the upper-left corner of the dialog box.

3. Choose colors for your duotone by clicking the color swatches. Choose Black or a dark color for Ink 1, and a lighter color for Ink 2. You must have selected the Photoshop color picker rather than the system color picker in order to access the Custom colors (PANTONE process colors). If you need to switch to the Photoshop color picker, close this window temporarily by clicking Cancel, and

21

open the General Preferences window (File➡Preferences➡General or (Command-K)[Control-K]). Set the Color Picker to Photoshop and click OK. Reopen the Duotone Options window and proceed from Step 2.

4. Use the curve windows within the Duotone Options window to adjust the curves for your two colors. (They're the small windows with diagonal lines, just to the right of the words "Ink 1" and "Ink 2".) If you click the small window, it expands to a full size curve grid, which works just like the regular one (see Figure 21.21). Click to set points and drag to adjust the curve. You can't see the effect on the image, but you can see it on the strip of tone in the Duotone window.

Figure 21.21

Here we're adjusting the curve for ink 2.

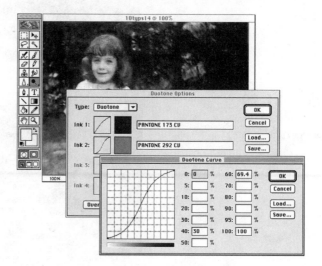

5. Click OK to apply the Duotone to the image. Unfortunately, there's no preview available. If you're not satisfied with the result, Undo it and try again.

JUST A MINUTE

> Using blue as the color with black gives you an image that replicates an old, black-and-white television set. Using a light to medium brown with black gives a pretty good imitation sepia, as does a combination of red and green.

"Hand-Colored" Photos

Years ago, before color film was readily available, it was common to see hand-tinted photos. These had been painstakingly overpainted with thinned out watercolors to add a pale suggestion of color to the picture. The Photoshop Paintbrush and Airbrush are well-suited for re-creating the look of a hand-colored photograph. You can even do the whole Ted Turner routine and colorize stills from your favorite Marx Brothers movie or Bogart classic. (You can find lots of movie stills and movie star pictures on the web that you can use for practice.)

After you have cleaned up the image that you want to hand-tint, change the mode back to color, either RGB or CMYK, as you did previously for the duotone. Double-click the Paintbrush tool to show the Paintbrush Options, if this window isn't already open. Set the Blending mode to Color and the Opacity to somewhere between 15–20%. Remember to keep the mouse button down as you paint, because releasing it and clicking it again will add a second 20% of color over the image.

If you have large, uncomplicated areas to tint, use one of the selection tools, such as the Lasso or the Magic Wand, to select the area. Select a foreground color, and choose Fill from the Edit menu, as shown in Figure 21.22.

Figure 21.22

Use Fill for large areas. It's faster and smoother than painting.

When the Fill window opens, set the Opacity to about 25% and choose Color from the Blending mode options. Set Foreground color on the Use: pop-up menu. Click OK to fill all of the selected areas with your chosen color at that opacity. If it's not enough, either re-open the fill window and apply it again, or Undo it and set a higher percentage. If it's too much, Undo and set a lower percentage.

Summary

We have been looking at ways to repair photographs that need help. When you have old, cracked, torn, or faded pictures, you can use a variety of Photoshop tools to cover up the imperfections and restore the image. The Eyedropper tool enables you to select a color or gray tone and apply it with any of your painting tools. The Rubber Stamp clones a selected piece of the picture and places it wherever you want it, as much or as little as needed to cover a crack, fill in an empty space, or cover objects you want to hide.

21

Tinting old photos can be managed in any of several ways. Toning may be applied by colorizing, or by turning the picture into a duotone, tritone or quadtone. Hand coloring can give you a different "old" picture look.

Q&A

Q How can I remove my ex-husband from a group shot of the family?

A It depends on where he is in the group and what's behind him. If you can drag background to cover him, that might work. Otherwise, perhaps you can find some other face of the right size and colors to replace him. (Robert Redford or Brad Pitt, perhaps?) Adjust the size and position of the new face on a separate layer. Blur the face you want to hide, and use the Opacity slider to bring in the replacement. If you leave it at about 80%, it should merge right in.

21

Hour **22**

Photo Repair—Color

In Hour 21, we worked on black-and-white pictures that needed help. This hour, we do the same with color. You can adjust the colors to fix a picture that's faded with age, or has too much red, green, or some other color in it. You can compensate for slight to moderate under- or overexposure, but you can't put back an image that's just not there, unless you paint it in.

You can take the red out of your daughter's eyes, or the unearthly green out of the cat's eyes. Does your teenager wonder how she'd look with orange or green hair or a half-shaved head? Try it onscreen first. Maybe she'll settle for a second set of earrings.

Color Retouching

So far, all the pictures we've worked on were old, black-and-white photos. This doesn't mean that you can only retouch in grayscale. You can use the same tools and tricks in color, with the exception of converting your pictures to grayscale to get rid of unwanted stains and yellowing. Obviously, if you convert a color picture to grays, you lose all of the color. Instead, you must apply the curves and color balance adjustments to change the overall coloring of the image.

Figure 22.1 is a digital photo taken on a snowy day. Glare on the snow made the white look pink in places. (I know, it's hard to see this in black and white. Use your imagination.) Using the Curves window, as shown in Figure 22.2, we can adjust the Red channel to remove most of the pink. Rather than trying to remove all of it, which would turn the image too blue, it's better to compromise and leave a faint warmth. To adjust a single color with the curves window:

1. With the image open, open the Curves window (Image➡Adjust➡Curves).

2. Choose the color closest to, or the complement to the color that needs adjusting, from the Channels palette menu. Choose Red, Green, or Blue if those colors need lessening. If there's too much Yellow, add Blue. If there's too much Magenta, add Green. If there's too much Cyan, add Red.

Figure 22.1

The snow on the tree looked pink.

3. Drag the curve up to increase the amount of the color. Drag it down to decrease the amount, by adding the complement. Watch the preview as you drag. Click OK when the colors look right.

Figure 22.2

Adjusting the Red channel separately enables us to get the red out.

The power lines at the top of the picture can easily be removed either with the Rubber Stamp tool or by Lassoing a piece of sky and placing it over the wires. This is a simple way to fix large, plain areas. You can also use it to hide something such as a trash can, by dragging shrubbery over it.

To use the Lasso for this purpose:

1. Select the Lasso tool from the Toolbox. Open the Feather dialog box (Select➡Feather) and set the Feather radius to somewhere between 3 and 6 pixels. This will help the copied sky blend in.

2. Select a piece of sky the same color as the sky behind the wires by circling it with the Lasso.

3. With the Dotted Line marquee flashing, choose the Move tool, and press (Option)[Alt] as you drag the selection. (See a close view of this in Figure 22.3.)

4. Repeat as needed, selecting different pieces of sky as the color behind the wires changes. You can also use this trick to hide any other parts of the picture that you don't want, like the small gray thing in the lower-right corner.

5. Press (Command-D)[Control-D] when you're finished dragging and copying to deselect the selection. Figure 22.4 shows the cleaned-up picture.

Figure 22.3

Be sure to cover all of the wires.

Figure 22.4

The finished picture minus wires and other unidentified clutter.

Fixing Red Eye

You've seen red eye. It's not a problem in black-and-white photos that you colorize, but it's often a problem in color pictures of people and animals taken with a flash camera. Basically, what happens is that the flash reflects off the blood vessels at the back of the eye and puts an eerie red glow into the pupils of anyone looking straight at the flash. Cats, by the way, can also display a similar phenomenon called "green eye," caused by the flash reflecting off taurine crystals in the back of the eye. You can avoid this if you make sure your portrait subject, human or otherwise, isn't looking directly at the flash, and by making sure there's plenty of light in the room so the subject's pupils have contracted as small as possible.

Figure 22.5 shows a portrait of a cat suffering from a combination of red and green eye. This one was shot in a dark room and the flash caught the cat staring wide-eyed. If we correct the off-color eyes, it will be a nice picture.

Figure 22.5

Even printed in black-and-white the eyes look wrong.

The correction is actually quite easy. Here's how to do it:

1. Open the image and zoom in on the eyes, by clicking the Zoom tool.

2. Use the Magic Wand to select the parts that need to be corrected (see Figure 22.6).

3. Choose the Paint Bucket tool. Set the Foreground color to black. Double-click the tool icon to open the Paint Bucket Options palette and set the Paint mode to Darken with an Opacity of about 80%. This setting will darken the eye while maintaining the detail.

Figure 22.6

The cat's eye selected at 200% magnification.

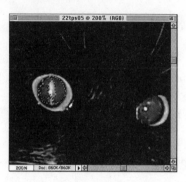

4. Pour the paint carefully into the pupils of the eyes, making sure not to pour it into any white or colored highlights in the pupil. You may need to click different selected parts of the pupil in order to cover all of it. If you accidentally fill one of the highlights, undo. If it's too late for that, or if you want to accent the highlights more, use a single pixel pencil (select the smallest possible brush size) and touch up as needed.

5. Press (Command-D)[Control-D] to deselect the eyes so that you can evaluate the effect of the change. Figure 22.7 shows the finished cat.

Figure 22.7

The highlights in the pupils are called catchlights.

22

22

The semi-opaque black that we poured in effectively darkened the pupils without losing detail. You can use this technique any time you have a small area in a picture that needs to have the color changed drastically. Be careful not to select any part of the image that you *don't* want to change.

COFFEE BREAK

How Much Change Is Okay?

Editing a picture to improve the composition is entirely reasonable, if it's a picture for your own use. But it was precisely that action which got the esteemed *National Geographic* magazine in trouble some years ago. They were doing a piece on Egypt and sent a photographer to take pictures of the pyramids. The art director studied the pictures and decided the composition would be better if he moved one of the pyramids closer to the next. As soon as the issue was published, astute readers began calling and writing to the magazine to complain. An apology appeared in the following issue, but simply knowing that the manipulation was possible waved a red flag for many people both inside and outside the publishing industry. The question has been debated ever since. How much change is okay? How much is too much?

It's clear that you can't always believe what you see. The supermarket tabloids frequently feature pictures that stretch the bounds of believability. Remember the one of the President shaking hands with the "space alien"? Or "Bigfoot" carrying off the scantily clad woman. (Why was she dressed like that in the snow, anyway?) On the other hand, if a model is having a bad hair day or her face breaks out, retouching is required and expected. Where do you draw the line? The answer depends on how the picture is to be used. Reputable newspapers and magazines tend to have strict guidelines about what they'll allow for photo manipulation. The general rule seems to be that if a change affects the *content* of the photo rather than its appearance, you can't do it. You can lighten a too-dark picture of a politician, but you can't change the soda can in his hand into a beer can (or vice versa).

"Editing" a Picture

There are times when you have to remove more than a scratch or a small imperfection from a photo. Sometimes you have to take out larger objects in order to save a potentially good picture. Figure 22.8 shows just such a photo, snapped from a moving car as the sun came out from a crack in the clouds just in time to produce a marvelous sunset.

Figure 22.8

Many things in here need to come out.

Because it was basically a "grab shot," however, there was no time to compose, no time to even stop the car. A fast shutter stopped the motion, and we can clean up the rest of the problems.

1. First, let's crop the picture to improve the composition. Select the Crop tool from the Toolbox and drag a rectangle that includes everything but the bottom of the picture (see Figure 22.9). Double-click inside the rectangle or choose Image➡Crop to remove the non-selected part. Taking out some of the road at the bottom of the frame lowers the horizon, making the sky more important, and that's really what the picture is about.

Figure 22.9

The sky, not the road, is what's important.

22

22

2. The next step will be to get rid of those cars. The easiest way to do that is to darken the road so they're just about to disappear. Then we can just blend them out. Using the Magic Wand, I can select the dark part of the road. Figure 22.10 shows this step.

Figure 22.10

Click the road with the Magic Wand to select it.

3. Go to the Layer menu and select Layer➡New➡Adjustment Layer. Choosing Brightness/Contrast from the "type" pop-up menu will open the Brightness/Contrast Layer adjustment window. Adjustment layers enable you to apply corrections to the whole picture or selected parts, but in a way that allows you to change your mind.

4. Move the sliders in the Brightness/Contrast Adjustment window to lower the brightness and contrast in the image. You can set both to –48. Doing so enables us to darken the road without darkening the entire picture. Figure 22.11 shows this step.

Figure 22.11

After you get past –50, there's not much difference.

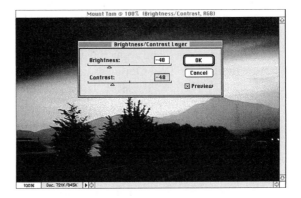

5. Open the Layers palette (Window➡Show Layers). Click the Background layer to select it. Because we've been working with the adjustment layer, it has been automatically selected.

6. To get rid of the cars for good, we can pick up a piece of road and drag it over them using the Lasso and Move tools. Use the Lasso tool to circle a piece of dark road about the same size and shape as the car you're going to cover. Click the Move tool. (It's the pointer with crosshairs at the top-right corner of the Toolbox.) Hold down the (Option)[Alt] key and drag the selection to cover the car. Keep the (Option)[Alt] key pressed to copy the selection instead of just moving it.

7. After you have covered the cars on the right, drag some more black with the Lasso and Move tools, as done previously, to cover the white lines in the road (see Figure 22.12).

Figure 22.12

Use (Option)[Alt] to make the Move tool copy as you drag.

8. We should also merge the layers at this point, so we'll be able to paint over the car. To merge the visible layers, select Merge Visible from the Layers menu, or from the pop-out menu in the Layers palette, or type (Shift-Command-E)[Shift-Control-E].

9. Using the Eyedropper tool, we'll select some color from the water that shows between the trees, and apply it with a small paintbrush and 100% Opacity (set on the Eyedropper Tool Options palette menu) and paint in some more water on top of the car. Then, we'll select a darker tone to match the shoreline and paint it in. Figure 22.13 shows this step.

10. The next step is to get rid of the radio tower, or whatever that structure is that's sticking up in front of the mountain. Because it's barely visible, the Smudge tool is all we need to rub it out. Select the Smudge tool, and a small soft-edged brush. Set the pressure to no more than 40% in the Options palette. Smudge the tower into the mountain, with short strokes, until you can't see it anymore.

22

Figure 22.13
*Use a small paintbrush
for this detailed work.*

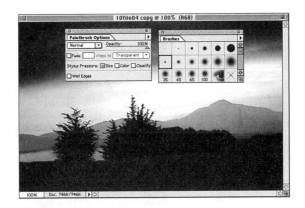

22

11. As a final "fix" we can go back to the Curves adjustment (Image➡Adjust➡
    Curves), darken the sky a little more, and add more red by adjusting the Red
    channel to make the sky even more dramatic (see Figure 22.14). I wish you could
    see this one in color.

Figure 22.14
*Boosting the red level will
make the sunset more
remarkable.*

Putting Back What Was Never There

I don't know which of my kids decided to crop my picture of a tiger washing up after lunch.
He obviously didn't know Photoshop because he trimmed the picture down to size by ripping
off the edges. I still like the photo, and I think there's enough background left that I can restore
it. Figure 22.15 shows the raw scan.

Figure 22.15

Poor tiger...

1. Crop the picture down enough to lose the extra space (see Figure 22.16).
2. Copy pieces of ground to fill in the holes.

Figure 22.16

Cropping removes many of the gaps, but leaves some.

Instead of just dragging and copying the background, cut and paste to as many new layers as needed and vary the opacity so the background doesn't all look the same.

3. After filling the gaps, apply the Unsharp mask filter to improve the focus a little. (Some of the detail was lost in the scan.) See the results in Figure 22.17.

Figure 22.17
The final image.

22

Summary

Color repair isn't much different from black-and-white photo repair, except that you need to be a little more aware of the colors and color blending modes. Off-color photos are fixed with Photoshop's regular color adjustment tools. Retouching to get rid of obvious flaws and red eye is best accomplished with the Paint Brush and Eyedropper, and with the image enlarged so you can see what you're doing. Use Layers to protect your original while you're working, and merge the changes when you are satisfied with the results.

Q&A

Q **If the picture I need to repair doesn't have enough background to copy, or doesn't have a good background, what should I do?**

A Remember that Photoshop enables you to have more than one file open at a time. You can "borrow" from another picture, and copy the selection onto a new layer of the picture that needs fixing. Shrink it or enlarge it so the texture is in scale with the rest of the scene, and then copy and paste it as needed.

Hour 23

Printing

We're almost done. You've created some wonderful Photoshop art, and you'd like to hang it in the walls and send copies to your friends. (You'd probably also like to add these masterpieces to your web page, but you'll learn that in Hour 24.) Even in this brave new world of the Internet, CD-ROM, and other electronic media, printing isn't going away, and it never will. Getting your image to output correctly is as important as any other step in the process of image creation, and that's why it deserves its own chapter.

Printing should be easy, right? Click the Print button and watch your image emerge on paper. Unfortunately, getting Photoshop images to print well can involve quite a few variables and decisions. In this chapter we look at what those are, from choosing a printer through setting up inks, separations, halftones, and other issues.

Be warned. Some of this stuff gets into deep detail and gets technical, and some of it's irrelevant if you only print to one kind of printer. Feel free to ignore the sections that don't relate to the kind(s) of printing you do. If *none* of it makes sense, stick with the default settings. Your pages will be, at the least, adequately printed.

Choosing a Printer

You know this already: There are lots of printers out there, and lots of printing technologies. How you print obviously depends a lot on what printer you're using. In fact, the printer you use can and should influence how you work in Photoshop and how you prepare your image because you'll want to create a final image that will best print from your particular printer.

An entire book could be written about all the varieties of printers. In this section, we'll make do with a snapshot of what's available: inkjet printers, laser printers, dye-sublimation printers, thermal wax printers, and imagesetters.

Inkjet Printers

At the most inexpensive end of the spectrum are inkjet printers, almost all of which can deliver acceptable-quality color printing (depending on your definition of "acceptable," of course). Examples of inkjets (sometimes also called "bubble jets") include Apple's StyleWriter printers, HP's Deskjet, and Epson's Stylus printers.

Inkjet printers are not necessarily PostScript-compatible, which means some of them can't print *PostScript* information that might be in your documents. But for most Photoshop images, this isn't a problem.

 PostScript is a page-description language that enables any two devices (computer and compatible printer) to describe and reproduce exactly the same page.

Quality of output varies tremendously on an inkjet printer, from fair to excellent, depending on how much you want to spend. High-end inkjets such as the Iris can cost tens of thousands of dollars, but can be perfect for graphics professionals. Less expensive inkjet printers, in the $300-600 range, are still very good for most color printing work, and many professional artists use them to print proofs before sending the files out for high resolution color prints.

Laser Printers

The laser printer is the professional standard and a good balance of price, quality, and speed. Laser printers abound from well-known companies such as Apple and Hewlett-Packard.

Most laser printers output 300–600 dpi (or even higher) and are particularly good with halftone and grayscale images. Some can subtly alter the size of the printed dots, thus improving quality. Speed is generally better than that of inkjet printers, though they tend to be more expensive. Color laser printers are still on the expensive side, but deliver beautiful, crisp images. You would probably want to look into color laser printing if you were equipping a graphics studio or advertising agency.

23

Dye-Sublimation Printers

Dye-sub printers are expensive photographic-quality printers, but you get what you pay for. Image quality is superb. These printers use special ribbons and paper, however. You can't use ordinary paper with them, and the specially coated paper is expensive.

You probably can't afford one of these, but many service bureaus have one, so you can always output there if you want to. These are the printers that professional photographers and magazine publishers rely on for the high quality ads, cover art, and editorial photos.

Thermal Wax Printers

Thermal wax printers also provide excellent quality color output, but at prices comparable to laser printers. More and more wax printers are now supporting common paper stocks, and not just special paper. So as you can imagine, these printers are becoming increasingly popular.

Because of the materials they use, thermal wax printers are especially useful for producing transparencies.

Imagesetters

Imagesetters are printers used for medium- or large-scale commercial printing jobs. These large, expensive machines burn the image onto photographic film or paper. That film is then developed and used to make printing plates that are used for the actual printing. We're talking high resolution here: 1,200–2,400 dpi, or even better.

Imagesetters don't print in color per se. Instead, you have to create a separate image for each color you want printed. These are called separations, and we'll talk more about them later.

Preparing the Image

Here's the best strategy if you know you'll want to print your final Photoshop image: Keep the printer in mind throughout the entire process! Different printers output differently, so knowing your printer allows you to adjust your image for its particular behaviors, thus guaranteeing the best possible image on the final printed page. This is particularly true for full-color images.

With that in mind, always configure Photoshop to the printer you'll be using, and do this before even considering printing anything important! This configuration involves three different areas: setting up printing inks, separations, and separation tables.

Printing Inks

Choose File➡Color Settings➡Printing Inks Setup to open the dialog box used to control the conversion tables Photoshop uses to define color settings (see Figure 23.1). The primary use of this dialog box is to reconfigure Photoshop's color settings so that they match a printout from a new printer or press. This way you're sure that future print jobs will be what you expect based on what you see on your monitor.

Figure 23.1

The Printing Inks Setup dialog box.

You won't have to mess with these settings much, if at all. Photoshop's default settings work well for most mid- to high-end printers, so feel free to skip this section if you don't need it.

For the ever-curious, however, here are the options in the dialog box:

☐ The Ink Colors pull-down menu is for choosing your printer (or paper type). You should select the option that most closely matches what you're using so that the colors will also closely match what appears onscreen. There are a lot of choices, and even the opportunity to create a custom choice. If these don't look familiar to you, then chances are you don't have to worry about them.

The default is SWOP (Coated), which is the U.S. industry standard for color separation printing.

By the way, *Coated* refers to glossy paper (as in most magazines), and *Uncoated* refers to regular paper, like the page these words are printed on. *Newsprint* refers to, you guessed it, newspaper.

☐ The Dot Gain option relates to the fact that for different kinds of paper, the ink used soaks into the paper and spreads outward differently. Some papers have a higher dot gain because the ink is absorbed more readily and tends to spread out into thicker dots when printing.

You can easily adjust how Photoshop compensates for dot gain. Lower values for this setting mean the printed dots will be smaller; thus creating a lighter image. Higher values mean larger dots and darker images.

23

☐ The four Gray Balance settings are used to help Photoshop compensate for printers that lean too much toward one or a few colors. If your printer prints too little blue, for example, you can increase the cyan (C) setting to compensate. The range is from 0.5 to 2.0.

☐ The final option, Use Dot Gain for Grayscale Images, tells Photoshop to use these settings for grayscale images as well as for color images. By default, Photoshop normally uses these settings only for color images.

TIME SAVER

> Remember that you can also save and load various settings you create through the Save and Load buttons.

Separations

To open the Separation Setup dialog box, choose File➡Color Settings➡Separation Setup (see Figure 23.2). Here you can adjust how Photoshop combines CMYK inks to print colors. Again, in the vast majority of situations, you'll never need to touch these settings. Photoshop's default values are excellent. Only mess around with these settings if your print shop or service bureau tells you to and shows you how.

Figure 23.2

The Separation Setup dialog box.

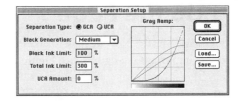

For reference, here are the options in a nutshell:

☐ **Separation Type:** For choosing between GCA (gray component replacement) and UCR (undercolor removal). These are different printing techniques for translating monitor colors (created by light: red, green, and blue) to printed colors (created by ink: cyan, magenta, yellow, and black).

☐ **Black Generation:** For specifying how much the black printing plate is used. The default, Medium, works fine for most images. None means that no black plate is used, and Custom allows you to adjust the curve manually.

☐ **Black Ink Limit:** To define the maximum percentage of black ink used by the printer to create the darkest parts of the image.

☐ **Total Ink Limit:** To define the maximum combined percentage of cyan, magenta, yellow, and black inks that can be used anywhere in the image.

☐ **UCA Amount:** For adding cyan, magenta, and yellow inks to the darker parts of the image. The result is a richer black than what black ink can produce on its own.

Separation Tables

With this dialog box (File➡Color Settings➡Separation Tables), you can easily save your Printing Inks Setup and Separation Setup settings as a separation table that can be loaded back into Photoshop for reuse (see Figure 23.3). Each separation table contains *all* the values found in those two dialog boxes. This feature is perfect for switching among different settings if you have access to multiple printers.

Figure 23.3

The Separation Tables dialog box.

Setting Up the Page

Okay, our image is ready. Now we have to take care of the page setup. Select File➡Page Setup to get to this important dialog box (see Figure 23.4).

Figure 23.4

The standard Mac Page Setup dialog box.

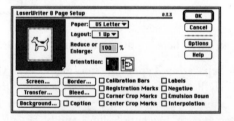

Important: This dialog box can look different depending on what print driver you have selected! Although many Macintosh laser printers use the standard LaserWriter print driver that results in the dialog box you saw in Figure 23.4, for example, other printers ship with their own print drivers. HP Deskjet, for example, ships with a print driver that makes the Page Setup dialog box look like what you see in Figure 23.5. Most of the options are the same; they just appear a bit different. You'll also see additional features offered by individual printers.

23

Figure 23.5

The Page Setup dialog box for my Mac HP Deskjet 855C printer.

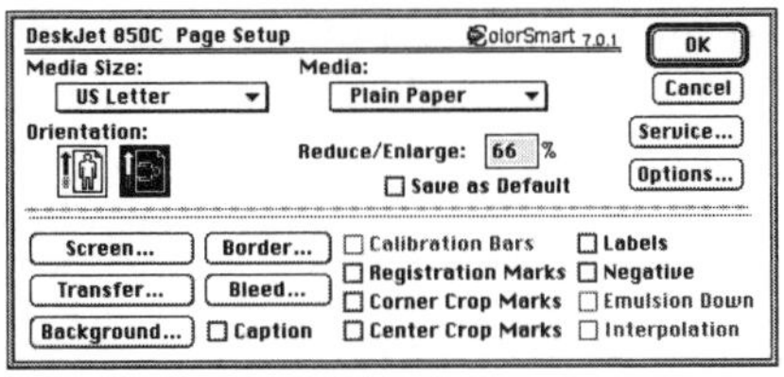

Okay, let's go through all the standard options one by one. I'll only cover the basic and intermediate settings; if you want to play with the other settings, talk with your print shop. (Note that not all options will be available in every situation.)

☐ The name of the printer always appears at the top. Make sure it's correct!

☐ **Properties:** On a Windows machine, you can click this button to access a dialog box that enables you to change things such as paper size and layout, printer resolution, halftone settings, and so on.

☐ **Paper:** Choose the size of the paper you're printing on. On a Mac, if you change the paper, you can see the preview in the upper-left corner change accordingly.

☐ **Source:** On a Windows machine, you might be able to choose the paper tray for the printer to use.

☐ **Layout:** Choose how you want the printed files to be laid out on the printed page.

☐ **Reduce or Enlarge:** Want the image to print smaller or larger? Adjust this percentage appropriately.

JUST A MINUTE

Later, when you actually click the Print button (see the next section), you might run into a problem with files that have large dimensions. If the image dimensions are larger than the dimensions of the page on which you're printing, Photoshop will tell you. You can then choose to either print anyway, resulting in only part of the image printing, or you can cancel and adjust the Reduce or Enlarge value so the whole image fits on the page.

CAUTION

Photoshop always prints images at the center of the page. You can't change this.

☐ **Orientation:** You can print the page with a Portrait orientation (so the page is taller than it is wide) or Landscape orientation (wider than tall).

☐ **Screen:** Press this button to bring up the Halftone Screens dialog box (see Figure 23.6). By default, Use Printer's Default Screens will be checked, and you won't be able to change anything else. Uncheck this option if you want to customize the other halftone options. Most of the time, Photoshop's default settings will work fine.

Figure 23.6

The Halftone Screens dialog box.

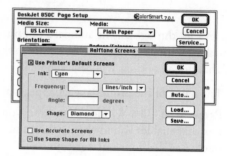

If you need to adjust these settings, here is where to change, for each ink (C, M, Y, and K), the frequency (lines per inch) of the dot grid, the angle of the grid, and the shape of the dot used. If you're printing to a PostScript Level 2 printer, you probably want to check the Use Accurate Screens box.

☐ **Transfer:** Click this button to bring up the Transfer Functions dialog box (see Figure 23.7). Here you can adjust the transfer curve—in other words, change the gray values so they print lighter or darker, depending on your needs. Most printers ship with the capability to calibrate themselves, so it's unlikely you'll need this feature.

Figure 23.7

The Transfer Functions dialog box.

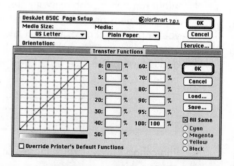

☐ **Background:** Want to print a background color on the page around your image? Click the Background button and you'll be greeted with the standard color picker (see Figure 23.8). Whatever color you pick will be used for printing only and will not alter your actual image file.

23

Figure 23.8

*The Photoshop Color
Picker on a Mac.*

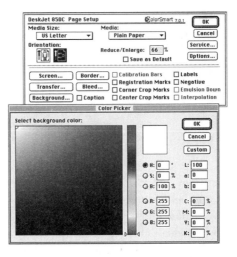

☐ **Border:** Similarly, if you'd like a border around your printed image, press the
Border button. In the resulting dialog box, you can set the width of the printed
border (see Figure 23.9). The border is always black; you can't change the color.
(As with Background, using this feature doesn't affect the actual image file.)

Figure 23.9

The Border dialog box.

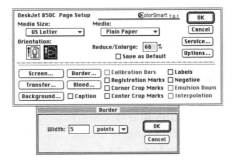

☐ **Bleed:** Bleeding means that part of the image will go right off the edge of the paper
and not get printed at all. There won't be any border or empty space between the
image and the edge of the page. (Note that this feature won't work in every printer.
Some printers are incapable of printing to the edge of a page.)

Clicking the Bleed button results in the appropriate dialog box, where you can
define the bleed area of an image (see Figure 23.10). Higher values move the crop
marks within the boundaries of the image, so that less of the image gets printed.
You can't bleed an image more than an eighth of an inch.

Figure 23.10

The Bleed dialog box.

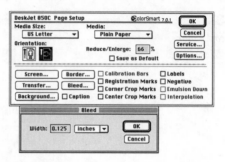

☐ **Caption:** Check this box and on the printed page you'll see whatever text appears in the Caption area of the File Info dialog box for that file. (To get to this dialog box, choose File➡File Info, and make sure Caption is selected on the top pull-down menu.) This can be helpful for providing contact information or copyright details next to your image.

☐ **Calibration Bars:** Check this box and calibration and color bars will be printed next to your image. A calibration bar is a row of 11 gray squares of different values, and a color bar is a row of 11 colors. These bars can help when trying to calibrate to a specific printer, or to see how a specific printer prints. (This option is available only if you're using a PostScript printer.)

☐ **Registration Marks:** Activate this feature and a variety of registration marks will print out around the image. You'll get bull's-eyes (which look like what you'd expect), star targets (two crossed lines within a circle), and precise pinpoint marks (two simple crossed lines), depending on your printer. (We'll actually see some of these marks later in this hour.) These marks can be helpful for aligning color separations.

☐ **Corner Crop Marks:** Corner crop marks appear around each corner of your image, defining where the image should be trimmed. They are simply horizontal and vertical lines.

☐ **Center Crop Marks:** These crop marks are centered and appear along each side of the image, defining the exact center of the image. They look like two crossed lines.

☐ **Labels:** You can have the filename print next to the image with this checkbox. If you are printing color separations, the name of the appropriate color channel is also printed on each color plate.

☐ **Negative:** With this checked, the printer reverses the values of the image. That is, the whites become black and the blacks become white, and everything in between shifts accordingly. You end up with a negative version. This option is useful if you're printing to film for commercial offset printing because these images usually need to be negative.

☐ **Emulsion Down:** Check this setting and your image will print as the horizontal mirror image of the original. Everything gets flipped left-right. Your print shop will tell you if you need to print this way for some reason.

☐ **Interpolation:** Interpolation refers to some printers' capability to resample an image as they print it. That is, any PostScript Level 2 printer can take a low-resolution image and resample it on-the-fly so that the resolution is improved and the printout is of better quality. This is valuable only if you're dealing with low-resolution images.

Before you continue, make sure that whatever you want to print is currently visible onscreen. By default, Photoshop prints all visible layers and channels. If you want to print just certain layers or channels, make them the only ones that are visible, then print.

Printing the Page

Okay, now we're getting around to finally printing the image. I told you there were a lot of printing variables, didn't I?

Let's open the Print dialog box using File➡Print (see Figure 23.11). The first thing to be aware of is that this dialog box will look different depending on what printer you have, what platform you're running on, and what mode the image is in. Let's look at all the fields and options.

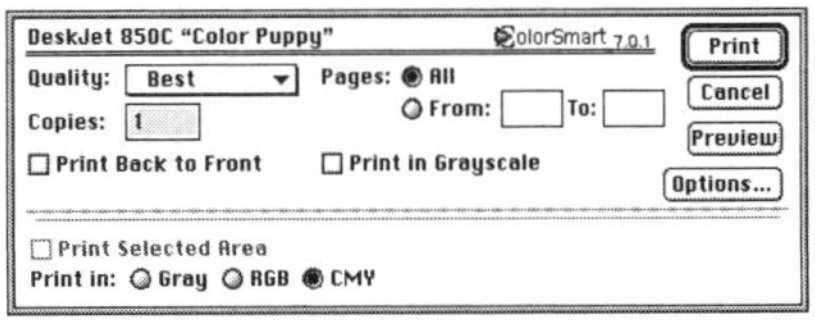

Figure 23.11

The ultimate dialog box: Print.

☐ **Copies:** How many copies of the document do you want printed? Enter a number here.

☐ **Pages:** This area (called Print Range on a Windows machine) specifies range of pages printed. This setting is irrelevant in Photoshop because each document consists of only one "page."

☐ **Paper Source:** Here Mac users can define what paper tray to use.

☐ **Print Quality:** Windows users can often specify a printer resolution here, such as 300 or 600 dpi. Mac users can often specify Best, Normal, or Econofast, or some variation on this theme.

☐ **Destination:** You can print to the printer, obviously, but you can also print to a file. Printing to a file means saving the printed output as a PostScript or EPS file. (This option only works if you have selected a PostScript compatible printer.)

Select File and the Print button will now say Save. Click it and you'll see the Save dialog box, where you can name the file and select what format of file you want (see Figure 23.12). You can also choose an encoding scheme (ASCII is best for PostScript files, and Binary can speed up printing for printers that accept binary data). Level 1 Compatibility means that the file will print on all PostScript printers, whereas Level 2 Only files will work only on PostScript Level 2 printers. Finally, you can specify if you want font information embedded in the file, and for which fonts.

Figure 23.12

Printing to a file.

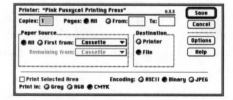

☐ **Print Selected Area:** When this box (simply called Selection for Windows users) is checked and when you have a rectangular area currently selected in your Photoshop image, you can print just that area. This works only with rectangular selections created with the Marquee tool. Also, it doesn't work for feathered selections.

23

☐ **Encoding:** Here you tell Photoshop which encoding method to use when it sends the image data to the printer. ASCII is understood by all PostScript printers, and so is a safe bet. Binary encoding is more compressed and can thus be faster, but doesn't work on all printers. Finally, JPEG encoding is faster yet, but results in some loss of data because JPEG is a lossy compression scheme. JPEG encoding works only with PostScript Level 2 printers.

☐ **Print In:** You can decide here how to print the image: in grayscale, in RGB colors, or in CMYK colors. For some desktop printers, RGB will give better results. (Try both, if you're unsure, and see which looks better to you.)

☐ **Print Separations:** This option appears in place of the Print In option *only* if the image is currently in CMYK or Duotone mode and the composite color channel is active. Check this option, and Photoshop will print each channel as a separate color plate. A CMYK document would print as four separate pages, for example, one for all the cyan data in the image, one for magenta, one for yellow, and one for black.

☐ **Options:** Strangely enough, Options isn't always one of your options. On a non-PostScript printer such as the HP Deskjet series, you'll see the Options button as one of your choices in the Print dialog box. Options enables you to select Intensity, Half-toning, and Color Matching. Leave all three at Auto, unless you're printing a photograph. If you are, choose Photographic, from the Color Matching menu. This will give you the best possible color reproduction.

☐ And now, at long last, when everything's set to your satisfaction, click Print to print!

So, that's how to print from Photoshop. But as you'll probably discover, printing directly from Photoshop doesn't happen as often as you might expect. Most of the time, images created in Photoshop are brought into another application for final placement and output. Most often these are page layout applications such as PageMaker and QuarkXPress. Photoshop images can even be brought into other image-editing applications such as Painter and Illustrator, and can be printed from there.

CAUTION

When printing Photoshop images from other applications, watch the format of your file. Make sure it's compatible with the program you're bringing it into; if it's not, believe me, you'll know! Other than that, any settings related to the image, such as custom colors or halftone screens, will be automatically brought with the image.

Papers

What you print on makes almost as much difference as how you do the printing. You can get various types and weights of paper for all kinds of printers. There are special papers for inkjet, and for laser. If you want your picture to resemble a photograph, consider investing in a pack of "photo weight" glossy paper. It's a much thicker paper, with a glossy surface that really does help make your inkjet or laser printed picture look like something that came out of a real darkroom rather than a digital one.

You can get coated papers for printing color on inkjet printers. These give you photo quality prints with a matte surface, rather than the glossy mentioned earlier. Transparency paper is clear acetate film, specially treated to accept the inks. Use it to make overhead projection slides and overlays.

There are label stocks in all kinds of sizes and shapes, and literally hundreds, if not thousands, of different kinds and weights of paper for both inkjet and laser printers.

Finally, you can buy packs of iron-on transfer paper (for color laser or inkjet printers), which enable you to put your images on T-shirts, aprons, tote bags, or anything else that you can iron on to. Follow the instructions with the paper, and don't forget to flip your image before you print it, so it will transfer reading correctly.

TIME SAVER

I use inexpensive photocopying paper for most of my work. It's fine for printing a quick proof to see how a picture will come out. For work that a client will see, I use a coated paper because the colors are brighter and don't bleed into each other. If I want the picture to look more like a darkroom photo, I will pay the dollar per sheet to print on the special glossy paper.

Summary

Printing Photoshop images isn't difficult; there are just a lot of decisions to make along the way. This hour discussed those choices, from initially preparing an image for printing to setting up the page and finally setting the print options. The wonderful thing about printing is that if you don't get a gorgeous printout the first time, you can simply change settings and try again! Provided you have enough paper and ink, of course.

Q&A

Q What should I know about putting photos on T-shirts or other fabric items?

A Iron-on transfer paper works best with light colored cotton or cotton/polyester blends. Transfer with a household iron on its highest setting, or a professional heat press. Iron the fabric first, and allow it to cool before placing the transfer paper on it. Be sure to put a piece of cardboard under the fabric so the color doesn't bleed through onto the back of the shirt. Press firmly, and plan to iron a large, full page image for 2-3 minutes. Keep the iron moving enough so you don't scorch the fabric. Small images are easier to manage and take less ironing time.

23

Hour 24

Photoshop for the Web

Wow! You are almost finished—this is the last chapter. You've learned enough to work effectively with Photoshop, even if you haven't mastered all of the tricks and time-saving features. The rest will come as you do more work with the program. This final hour is devoted to one of the newest and best uses for Photoshop—putting your work on the World Wide Web.

You've heard about the web, you have probably "surfed" it with your favorite *browser*, such as Internet Explorer or Netscape Navigator, but let's take a moment to review what is really going on out there in cyberspace. Although the web is what you might call a *virtual space,* meaning that it creates the illusion of space and distance, it also exists in a physical space. It is comprised of computers called *servers* that serve files across networks that stretch around the world. The computers can be anything from supercharged SPARC stations to minis and mainframes, or a machine similar to the one sitting on your desktop.

When you type a URL (Uniform Resource Locator) into your browser to access a web site, a message goes out to these remote machines. These machines then send back the files for which you have asked. The files that make up all of the sounds, pictures, and text of the web then have to travel across phone lines. This creates a problem that you have to keep in mind as you create graphics for your web site. Phone lines are slow; there is only so much information that can travel on them at one time. If you are lucky enough to have a T1 (high-speed) connection, you are okay—speed-wise. A 28.8 Kbps (kilobits per second) modem is fairly fast. A 14.4 modem is fairly slow. We used to be satisfied with 2400 bps modems, but those were the pre-web days, when we only used our modems for e-mail and perhaps accessing chats on CompuServe or America Online.

The most popular language used to publish documents on the web is HTML (HyperText Markup Language). HTML isn't really a computer *programming* language, so relax. It is, as its name suggests, a *markup* language: a series of relatively simple *tags* that enable you to specify how text, images, and links to other sites appear in the browser, images, and links to other sites. HTML isn't difficult to learn, but you really don't even need it. There are programs, including desktop publishing programs and word processors that you may already own, that can translate your pages into HTML for you with just a couple of mouse clicks. All you need to do is lay out the page the way you'd like it to look, with your Photoshop pictures pasted in. You do have to make sure they're in a compatible format, though. Because web pages can be viewed on all kinds of computers, the graphics have to be in a format that's common to all.

File Formats and File Size

You need to first learn what type of file format to use for the web. There are two standard choices: GIF (Graphics Interchange Format) and JPEG (Joint Photographic Experts Group). There's also a third, much newer format known as PNG (Portable Network Graphics). It promises to be the best choice of all three, but is not yet widely supported by the major browsers. For the time being, it is enough to know that Photoshop will enable you to save to this format, as soon as other software can read it.

The most important thing to remember, regardless of the file format you decide to use, is that the web has limited bandwidth. This means that if you create an absolutely beautiful image, and, say, it is 2 MB in size, it will take several minutes to download on a 14.4 modem. This is not to say that you *can't* create images with as large a file size as you want. I am just suggesting that few web surfers out there will have the patience to sit and wait while your 2MB image downloads. If you know that your primary audience is surfing from home with slower modems, you might want to keep your web pages well under 30KB apiece.

This is the challenge of web development. There are ways around it, but you will ultimately have to make sacrifices. It's okay though…everybody does it.

TIME SAVER

If you have some big files that you want to publish on the web, don't fret. There are ways around the big file issue. Most surfers won't mind the wait for a big file if they have a warning. Give them a thumbnail version of the image and tell them how big the file is. This way, they can decide for themselves if they want to spend the time waiting for the download. A little courtesy, as in all aspects of life, goes a long way on the web.

24

JPEG (Joint Photographic Experts Group)

Depending on your needs, JPEG could be the best file format for you. It is great for photographs and other continuous tone images. JPEG maintains color information. It does, however, employ a *lossy* compression scheme, which means that you can adjust and reduce the file size—at the expense of the image quality.

To save a file as a JPEG, you need to work in RGB mode within Photoshop. Figure 24.1 shows the JPEG Options box, which opens whenever you elect to save a file as a JPEG. It gives you several choices. In Figure 24.2, I've set the options to give a smaller file, and Figure 24.3 shows the results.

Figure 24.1

The JPEG Options dialog box.

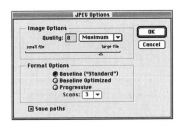

Figure 24.2

Saving a smaller file.

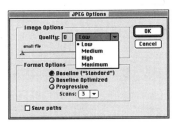

Figure 24.3

Two JPEG files with similar quality but very different file sizes.

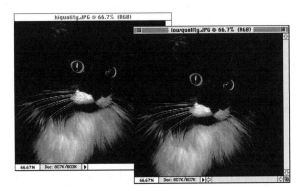

The cat picture on the right is 50KB. The same cat photo on the left is 330KB. This is a staggering difference in file size for a minimal difference in file quality.

Give any image that you plan to take to the web a close look. Use the File➡Save a Copy command so that you don't lose your original image, and try different compressions. If using a heavy compression (one that reduces the file size a great deal) causes degradation to the image quality, save again with less compression to get a better quality image.

Also, notice the section in the JPEG options dialog box that prompts you for format options.

☐ **Baseline (Standard):** This is the standard option.

☐ **Baseline (Optimized):** This option optimizes the colors in the file. When I tested to see if Optimized created a larger file, I was surprised to see that the Optimized file was actually smaller than the Baseline Standard file.

☐ **Progressive:** For web work, this is your best bet. Progressive means that your file will be loaded into a web browser faster and then refined by subsequent passes, or *scans*, as more file information is downloaded. Notice the drop-down menu that becomes active when you select this option (see Figure 24.4). This enables you to specify how many scans you will permit before the image is finished downloading to a user's browser. Three scans is a good choice, but if your file is fairly large, go with 4 or 5.

Figure 24.4

Setting the number of progressive scans.

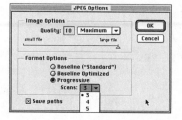

JUST A MINUTE

> Always keep your web browser open when you are creating web graphics. This enables you to take a look at them to determine their quality.
>
> Also, don't be fooled by how quickly File➡Open File in your browser opens one of your files. These files are on your hard drive, or *local*. When a person has to go out on the web to get your pages, the process is slowed down incredibly.

GIF (Graphics Interchange Format)

GIFs are your other (current) option for web file formats. GIFs enable you to save files with transparent backgrounds, which is useful when you are creating buttons and other round graphics. Photoshop does not enable you to have anything but a square or rectangular canvas. Thus, if you don't save your button as a transparent GIF, you will end up with a white square of canvas around the image.

24

JUST A MINUTE

A good way to select which file format is right for you is to visit web sites that have graphics similar to what you want to publish. To find out what kind of file format an image is, simply click the image. On a Macintosh, click the image and hold until a dialog box appears. On a Windows machine, click the image with the right mouse button.

In the dialog box, choose to save the image. When you are prompted for where you want to save the image, note the file extension—.jpg for JPEG or .gif for GIF. Click OK to save the file or click Cancel if you were just looking.

Backgrounds, Buttons, and Bouncing GIFs

24

I admit that I have mixed feelings about backgrounds on web pages. These can really add personality to a web site, but they also can make reading the text of your site really difficult and frustrating. To quote web designer David Siegel, "Gift wrap makes poor stationery." That said, however, if you use backgrounds with discretion, they can add to a site's presence and look. Fancy buttons are commonplace on web pages, and you'll even see GIF animations: Dogs wagging their tails endlessly, cats catching mice, balls bouncing...it's enough to make you dizzy. Photoshop can supply the graphic elements for any of these goodies.

Creating backgrounds, buttons, and animated GIFs, however, is beyond the scope of this book. If you want to get serious about web page design and using HTML, run back to your local bookstore or computer store and look for Hayden's *Photoshop Web Magic* and *HTML Web Magic.* They are great sources for these tricks and techniques.

If you want to stay casual about web design, but still end up with good looking pages, use one of the graphic web layout packages that enables you paste up the pages as you want to see them. Some even come with buttons and other goodies you can apply to your page, and instructions on how to put your own graphics onto their buttons. Nothing could be easier. After you're done playing, the application makes the conversion to HTML for you, in the background, and gives you files ready to upload to your web page provider.

Preparing Text for the Web

HTML web standards include a handful of different type sizes and fonts, some for headings, some for text, and some for "emphasis." Uh huh. "Bo-ring," to quote the kids. You're not necessarily limited to what HTML has to offer. If you want an elaborate title for your page, create it in Photoshop, using filled letters, filters, drop shadows, glows, or whatever other special effects you like. Crop it tight, and save it as either a GIF or JPEG. Figure 24.5 shows one that I created for my husband's page. Compressed, the file is only 17K.

Figure 24.5
Saved as a GIF.

You have the option of converting your file to JPEG or to GIF. One good thing about text is that it usually, but of course not always, is applied to a white background. If this is the case with your web site, there is no need to go through the trouble of exporting a GIF89a file. Just make sure that your background is white and save it as a plain GIF file.

TIME SAVER

> There's one rule of thumb that professional web page designers apply to choosing formats. For line art, or anything with a limited palette (less than 255 colors), choose GIF. For photos or art in full color, choose JPEG.

When designing images for the web and writing the HTML code, save yourself work as often as possible because new problems and new challenges will always appear—usually when you least expect it, and when you're absolutely sure that you've got it right, but it refuses to work.

Take heart. You are by no means alone. A sign of the Photoshop pro is realizing that there are about 10 ways to accomplish any one given task. Keep experimenting and never give up.

Making Pages Load Faster

The bottom line is, you can't. The page will load as fast as the server can send it and the recipient can receive it. Those are both factors beyond your control. What you can do, though, is to make sure that your page is arranged so there's something to see while the graphic loads. Bring up a Welcome… headline first, then add the background. If there's a graphic that will take some time to load, bring up a block of text before it. The load time for the picture will seem much shorter if the person waiting has something else to read, or think about. Keep your images small, or put up a thumbnail and link the full size picture to it, so visitors have the option of waiting to see the big picture. Remember that some people use text-based web browsers and don't see images at all. If the content of your picture is important, put a text description of it on the page too. (This also helps make your web site handicapped-accessible, which is a nice thing to do for the estimated two million visually impaired web users.)

24

Summary

In this final hour, we looked at putting your work on the web. We examined what file formats the web uses, and how you might best choose the right formats for your own work.

So, what comes next? You've finished your 24th hour and you know a lot more about Photoshop than you did when you began. That doesn't mean you know it all, but you now have the tools—your imagination, creativity, and a basic understanding of Photoshop. There is still plenty out there to learn and experiment with.

Above all else, have fun!

Q&A

Q Can I mix the kinds of images I use on the web page...some GIFs and some JPEGs or PNGs?

A Yes, there's no reason not to. Use whatever will give you the best picture in the smallest file size.

Q What's the trick for using a picture as a page background?

A The most important trick is to keep the picture quite small and apply it as a tiled background. Keep the edges blurry so they'll blend smoothly. Save it as a GIF with the name "background." Your web page creator should be able to insert it automatically, but if not, use the HTML tag `<body background= "background.gif">`.

24

INDEX

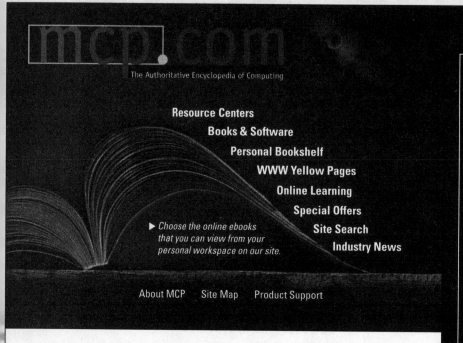